Approaches to Teaching Stowe's *Uncle Tom's Cabin*

Approaches to Teaching
World Literature

Joseph Gibaldi, series editor

For a complete listing of titles,
see the last pages of this book.

Approaches to Teaching Stowe's *Uncle Tom's Cabin*

Edited by

Elizabeth Ammons

and

Susan Belasco

The Modern Language Association of America
New York   2000

For information about obtaining permission to reprint material from
MLA book publications, send your request by mail (see address below),
e-mail (permissions@mla.org), or fax (212 477-9863).

Library of Congress Cataloging-in-Publication Data

Approaches to teaching Stowe's Uncle Tom's Cabin / edited by Elizabeth Ammons
and Susan Belasco.
p. cm. — (Approaches to teaching world literature ; 66)
Includes bibliographical references and index.
ISBN 0-87352-755-0 — ISBN 0-87352-756-9 (paper)
1. Stowe, Harriet Beecher, 1811–1896. Uncle Tom's cabin. 2. Stowe, Harriet Beecher,
1811–1896—Study and teaching. 3. Didactic fiction, American—History and criticism.
4. Southern States—In literature. 5. Plantation life in literature. 6. Afro-Americans in
literature. 7. Slavery in literature. I. Ammons, Elizabeth. II. Belasco, Susan, 1950–
III. Series.
PS2954.U6 A66 2000
813'.3—dc21   99-089158

ISSN 1059-1133

Cover illustration for the paperback edition: *Firewood* #55, by Jacob Lawrence.
National Museum of American Art, Smithsonian Institution,
Transfer from the US Information Agency.
In Paul C. Gutjahr's essay, figures 1, 2, 3, and 5 are reproduced courtesy of Special
Collections Department, University of Iowa Libraries, Iowa City. Figure 4 is © 1928
by Universal City Studios, Inc.; courtesy of Universal Studios Publishing Rights;
all rights reserved. Figure 6 is reproduced with permission of Easton Press. • "The Problem
of Sentimental Possession," by Gillian Brown, is a shortened version of chapter 2
in her book *Domestic Individualism: Imagining Self in Nineteenth-Century America*;
© 1991 by The Regents of the University of California; used with permission
of the University of California Press.

Set in Caledonia and Bodoni. Printed on recycled paper

Published by The Modern Language Association of America
10 Astor Place, New York, New York 10003-6981

CONTENTS

PREFACE TO THE SERIES

In *The Art of Teaching* Gilbert Highet wrote, "Bad teaching wastes a great deal of effort, and spoils many lives which might have been full of energy and happiness." All too many teachers have failed in their work, Highet argued, simply "because they have not thought about it." We hope that the Approaches to Teaching World Literature series, sponsored by the Modern Language Association's Publications Committee, will not only improve the craft—as well as the art—of teaching but also encourage serious and continuing discussion of the aims and methods of teaching literature.

The principal objective of the series is to collect within each volume different points of view on teaching a specific literary work, a literary tradition, or a writer widely taught at the undergraduate level. The preparation of each volume begins with a wide-ranging survey of instructors, thus enabling us to include in the volume the philosophies and approaches, thoughts and methods of scores of experienced teachers. The result is a sourcebook of material, information, and ideas on teaching the subject of the volume to undergraduates.

The series is intended to serve nonspecialists as well as specialists, inexperienced as well as experienced teachers, graduate students who wish to learn effective ways of teaching as well as senior professors who wish to compare their own approaches with the approaches of colleagues in other schools. Of course, no volume in the series can ever substitute for erudition, intelligence, creativity, and sensitivity in teaching. We hope merely that each book will point readers in useful directions; at most each will offer only a first step in the long journey to successful teaching.

Joseph Gibaldi
Series Editor

PREFACE TO THE VOLUME

We are grateful to several people and institutions for their assistance at various stages in the preparation of this volume. We are especially appreciative of the many scholars and teachers who responded with helpful information to our original survey about current practices in teaching *Uncle Tom's Cabin*. All of us who teach and write about Harriet Beecher Stowe are guided by the indispensable biographical work of Joan Hedrick, who provided valuable encouragement at a crucial stage in this project. We are also grateful to the library staffs of Tufts University, the University of Tulsa, and Colgate University for their assistance in obtaining materials and helping with reference questions. At several stages in the development of this volume, we were helped enormously by the insights of the anonymous readers, the Publications Committee, and Sonia Kane, all of the Modern Language Association. Elizabeth Ammons would like to thank Valery Rohy, her graduate student assistant at Tufts University, and both of us are indebted to Allen Culpepper, Susan Belasco's graduate student assistant at the University of Tulsa. Finally, we offer a special thank you to Linck Johnson for his encouragement, advice, and strong support.

Introduction: Stowe's Challenge to Teachers

In the classroom *Uncle Tom's Cabin* can generate intense, and quite various, responses. Some students love the novel, others hate it, and sometimes the same students experience both reactions. Rarely does the novel elicit indifference. Thus the challenge of teaching the book often has to do with mediating differences of opinion or with encouraging students to say what they think and feel when they fear that their responses—positive or negative—may be unpopular. In many classes, the task is also one of urging a more historically informed view of Harriet Beecher Stowe's novel.

These challenges are relatively recent. Even though a 1990 MLA survey indicates that *Uncle Tom's Cabin* is now the most frequently named addition to nineteenth-century American literature courses, it rarely showed up on a syllabus until the last decade or two. Before the women's movement of the late 1960s and the emergence of feminist criticism in the 1970s, women writers received little attention. Similarly, popular works, unless written by Fitzgerald or Hemingway, did not qualify for the college classroom; and sentimental fiction—fiction that actually sought to make the reader cry—fell beneath contempt. And before the civil rights movement of the 1960s, literature that focused directly on the issue of race, other than a few texts such as *Huckleberry Finn*, titles by Faulkner, and perhaps Ellison's *Invisible Man*, did not warrant serious study.

Although there have been significant changes, each of these issues remains, to one degree or another, for the teacher of *Uncle Tom's Cabin*. While studying texts by women—or at least white women—has become common, debate has by no means ended. Which women writers should we teach? How many do we include? What male writers will we supplant? Nor have we settled the question of whether to incorporate popular or nonelite works into the serious literature classroom. Many contemporary critical approaches, including feminist, historicist, and deconstructionist criticism, race studies, cultural studies, and reader-response theories, advocate teaching popular culture texts. Nevertheless the legacy of New Criticism persists in the question regularly put to Stowe's novel: Is it "good" literature? Since popularity by definition means accessibility, anyone can read this book. Consequently, how worthy of study (difficult, erudite) can it be? Likewise, the novel's sentimentality, its active participation in an aesthetic of empathy, continues to open it up to criticism. Given the fact that education in the modern west prides itself on appealing to highly trained disembodied reason, how do we deal with *Uncle Tom's Cabin's* overt reliance on rhetorical strategies designed to involve readers emotionally, even physically, as well as intellectually? As a sentimental text, the book raises complex questions about literature and the political power of embodied human emotions and also threatens certain key academic assumptions about how "great" art should operate—namely, subtly, indirectly, arcanely.

But even more challenging in the classroom than Stowe's gender, *Uncle Tom's Cabin*'s commercial success, or the book's aesthetic is the topic of race. From the time of the book's initial publication, controversy has surrounded Stowe's representation of black people. The novel condemns slavery yet reproduces racial stereotypes with such fervor that characters such as Uncle Tom and Topsy have passed permanently into the culture, becoming repositories for each subsequent era's variations on basic racist themes. *Uncle Tom's Cabin* presents blacks as ignorant, docile or devilish (Tom, Topsy), and childish. Moreover, the farther away a black character moves from those stereotypes in Stowe's novel, the whiter he or she is in ancestry. Because the issue is so central and dominant, this volume includes a number of essays addressing *Uncle Tom's Cabin*'s racism, such as Stephen Railton's speculation on white readers' investment in the novel, Gillian Brown's concentration on the link between sentimentalism and racism, Elizabeth Ammons's discussion of African colonization, and Kimberly Hébert's analysis of Topsy's continuing legacy in Shirley Temple movies.

On the subject of race, Stowe's novel presents considerable challenges for teachers. It is important to historicize race theories and attitudes so that students do not simply judge Stowe by the values of our own day. At the same time, we need to create this historical context without denying or excusing the racism of the novel in its own time, when Stowe's views, though enlightened compared with the views of many white people, attracted some criticism. Further, it is important to ask several questions: Are there ways in which we *should* judge *Uncle Tom's Cabin* by standards we now apply? In the light of the book's continuing influence and the fact that we are reading it now, why would we believe it important or even possible to separate the book from current race issues? That is, what kind of an academic sleight of hand allows us to make a text part of the present—we ask students to read it today—yet say it must not be judged by and connected to the values that operate now? Feminists ask students to judge sexist portraits of women in literature of the past; postcolonialists tell classes to connect past and present when reading texts published in earlier eras. Perhaps one of the central and most worthwhile challenges in teaching *Uncle Tom's Cabin* lies in finding ways to discuss the book's racism not simply as a historical phenomenon, important as that is, but also as a force operating in and intersecting with issues in our own world.

In our survey of teachers of *Uncle Tom's Cabin*, respondents underline race as the topic of most, though not exclusive, concern in teaching the novel. It is engaging and "easy" to teach, many report, because of its emotional power, Stowe's humor, the vitality of the plot, students' experience of being assigned a book they have heard of but have not read, and the novel's depiction of slavery, which many students find shocking and eye-opening since their education has not previously focused on the subject. But topping the list of difficulties in the classroom is the novel's treatment of race. Many students express confusion about how Stowe could be against slavery yet racist, and teachers report that there are often significant differences between black students' responses to the book and the responses of students who are not black. Also posing problems, though more easily dealt with, are the novel's length, its abundance of description, Stowe's use of dialect, her direct authorial intrusions, the characterization of Eva, and the baldness of the book's melodrama. Other teachers note the challenges presented by students' lack of historical knowledge about nineteenth-century events and ideas, especially domestic ideology, religious beliefs, slavery as an institution, and the struggle for abolition.

The essays in this volume attempt to address these issues, almost always with the emphasis falling on how to create successful strategies in the classroom. Our survey of teachers shows that *Uncle Tom's Cabin* gets taught in many different courses. It appears in classes on the American novel, American sentimentalism, the nineteenth-century novel, women writers, the American Renaissance, American masterpieces, and American Romanticism, as well as in surveys of American literature, classes in American studies, and various special topics courses such as Outcasts, Rebels, and Dissidents in the English and American Novel, Mothering America, and Race Issues in American Fiction. The context in which the novel is taught also varies from course to course. It is frequently paired with other sentimental or domestic novels such as Susan Warner's *The Wide, Wide World*, with well-known novels of the American Renaissance such as Nathaniel Hawthorne's *The Scarlet Letter* or Herman Melville's *Moby-Dick*, or with other novels of the 1850s about race relations such as William Wells Brown's *Clotel* or Harriet Wilson's *Our Nig*. A standard classroom connection brings together *Uncle Tom's Cabin* and one or more slave narratives, such as Frederick Douglass's *Narrative* or Harriet Jacobs's *Incidents in the Life of a Slave Girl*. Teachers also pair the novel with other abolitionist literature, such as Henry David Thoreau's *Resistance to Civil Government* or Douglass's famous essay "What to the Slave Is the Fourth of July?" Reading *Uncle Tom's Cabin* next to essays by Ralph Waldo Emerson or alongside Thoreau's *Walden* often sets up provocative contrasts.

If *Uncle Tom's Cabin* presents challenges in the classroom, it can also yield extraordinary rewards. Except for the Bible, Stowe's novel outsold every other book in print until early in the twentieth century. As a window on popular culture and taste in nineteenth-century America, *Uncle Tom's Cabin* is hard to surpass. Its celebration of domestic values, validation of emotional knowledge, and belief in separate gender roles acquaint students with basic principles of mainstream midcentury social feminism. Its antislavery arguments, romantic racialism, enthusiasm for African colonization, and racist stereotypes reveal how complex and contradictory many white people's views on race were. Its exploitation of sentimental, melodramatic narrative strategies expands and complicates many students' understanding of the "great" American novel and the literary tradition of the United States. Its overt religious exhortations and critique remind us of how important Protestant Christianity was, or was believed to be, as a political force in the United States 150 years ago. And, not least of all, the

power of Stowe's storytelling, the way in which *Uncle Tom's Cabin* still capti-
vates many readers, raises basic questions about the function of story, the
responsibilities of storytellers, the way readers' responses depend on who they
are, and the purpose and value of coming together in classrooms to talk about
literature.

Above all, *Uncle Tom's Cabin* continues to raise important, controversial
questions. How do we deal with Stowe's racism? Is the novel "good" art—and
what do we mean by that question? Is there anything to learn from its representation of gender? Why has this book not been much taught? Should it continue to be read and taught? Is it enlightening or pernicious? *Uncle Tom's
Cabin* can and should provoke real debate in the classroom, which of course
means—no matter what else we might say about Stowe's famous novel—that it
remains a vital text.

Part One

MATERIALS

Classroom Texts

Uncle Tom's Cabin was first published as a serialized novel that appeared in the *National Era* from 2 June 1851 through 1 April 1852. The *National Era* is available on microfilm in some libraries. The entire run of the *Era* was reprinted in 1969 by the Negro Universities Press in full-size volumes, which enable students and teachers to read the novel easily in its original form. There is, however, no book-length edition of the novel that reflects its original serial publication form. John P. Jewett and Company published *Uncle Tom's Cabin* in two volumes in March 1852; this edition can be found on the open stacks of many university and public libraries. Modern editions are based on reprintings of the 1852 book; for an account of the differences between the serial and the novel, see E. Bruce Kirkham's *The Building of* Uncle Tom's Cabin. Because of its length, the full text of *Uncle Tom's Cabin* is not published in any of the current, widely used anthologies. While *The Norton Anthology of American Literature* (Baym et al.) includes the texts of both *The Scarlet Letter* and *Walden*, the representation of *Uncle Tom's Cabin* is limited to chapter 7, "The Mother's Struggle." *The Heath Anthology of American Literature* (Lauter et al.) is more generous, with the editors providing eight chapters of the novel in the first volume. But none of the respondents to our survey of teachers indicated that they use such abridged texts for teaching the novel; in general these short excerpts are suitable only for brief comparisons with other works included in the anthologies. With several inexpensive paperbacks of the novel in print and readily available, teachers can easily use the full text of *Uncle Tom's Cabin* in a course.

At this writing, there are at least a dozen available paperback editions of *Uncle Tom's Cabin*, including a large-type edition. The most recent is the Norton Critical Edition of *Uncle Tom's Cabin* (ed. Ammons), which includes the full text of the novel and annotations by the editor, a chronology of Stowe's life, a select bibliography, relevant background materials such as illustrations for the novel and excerpts from *Life of Josiah Henson* and *Incidents in the Life of a Slave Girl*, and a spectrum of both nineteenth- and twentieth-century criticism. Respondents also mentioned the Penguin edition (ed. Douglas), as well as editions published by Bantam, Signet–New American Library, and Everyman's Library (ed. Bigsby). All these editions have helpful introductions or afterwords.

Older and out-of-print editions are useful for their introductions, especially those edited by Kenneth Lynn (considered the standard edition) and Raymond Weaver; the latter is especially interesting for its sixteen lithographs by Miguel Covarrubias. *Uncle Tom's Cabin* is also available in a Library of America volume with two of Stowe's other novels, *The Minister's Wooing* and *Oldtown Folks*. There is no modern edition of Stowe's complete works.

Biographical Works

The standard biography of Harriet Beecher Stowe is Joan D. Hedrick's *Harriet Beecher Stowe: A Life* (1994), which is the indispensable source for authoritative details of Stowe's life and times. Based on hundreds of unpublished personal letters and papers as well as historical, social, and literary sources, Hedrick's biography is the place for students and teachers alike to begin a study of Stowe. It provides a wealth of information about the literary and intellectual milieu of the nineteenth century and focuses on Stowe's career as a writer. This biography easily displaces the only other modern effort at a definitive biography, Forrest Wilson's *Crusader in Crinoline: The Life of Harriet Beecher Stowe* (1941). Although the book was groundbreaking for its time, Wilson mainly concentrates on the details of Stowe's life and her relationships with family members and friends; there is little in his biography about the social and intellectual climate of mid-nineteenth-century America, nor is there much discussion about what the publication of *Uncle Tom's Cabin* contributed to the debates about slavery. Although some of Stowe's letters are published in various biographies and critical studies, no complete edition of her correspondence exists. For the first-time teacher of *Uncle Tom's Cabin* or for those wanting a brief introduction to Stowe's life and works, the best short biography is John R. Adams, *Harriet Beecher Stowe*. Although Thomas F. Gossett's Uncle Tom's Cabin *and American Culture* is not merely a biography, the early chapters provide a succinct account of Stowe's life.

Because Stowe was a member of a famous nineteenth-century family, other useful sources of information for teachers and students include Barbara M. Cross, *The Autobiography of Lyman Beecher*; Clifford E. Clark, Jr., *Henry Ward Beecher: Spokesman for a Middle-Class America*; Kathryn Kish Sklar, *Catharine Beecher: A Study in American Domesticity*; and Milton Rugoff, *The Beechers: An American Family in the Nineteenth Century*. Contemporaries also wrote biographies of Stowe, including family members and friends. Her son Charles published *Life of Harriet Beecher Stowe, Compiled from Her Letters and Journals*, which is based on the contributions of many of her friends and acquaintances who provided letters and papers. Stowe's closest friend, Annie Fields, published *Life and Letters of Harriet Beecher Stowe* in 1897, a year after Stowe's death. In 1911 Charles Stowe published another biography of his mother, this time with Stowe's grandson Lyman Beecher Stowe, entitled *Harriet Beecher Stowe: The Story of Her Life*.

For additional materials on Stowe, teachers and students should consult the bibliographies in Hedrick's biography and The Norton Critical Edition of *Uncle Tom's Cabin* (ed. Ammons). Jean W. Ashton's *Harriet Beecher Stowe: A Reference Guide* provides succinct annotations for materials published before 1974. Ongoing bibliographic information is available in the *MLA Bibliography*, *American Literary Scholarship: An Annual*, and the *Bibliography of American Literature*.

General Studies of Stowe and Her Times

At least three broad but often overlapping historical contexts inform Stowe studies: slavery and the antislavery movement, domestic ideology and the status of women, and literary historical developments in the middle of the nineteenth century.

For short selections on slavery, nineteenth-century race ideology, and abolition, teachers can rely on the Norton Critical Edition of *Uncle Tom's Cabin* (ed. Ammons), which contains some slave sale announcements and fugitive slave posters, excerpts from slave narratives by Josiah Henson (said to be a model for Tom), Solomon Northup, William Wells Brown, and Harriet Jacobs; correspondence by Stowe about abolition; selections from her *Key to* Uncle Tom's Cabin; and excerpts from modern historians' writings about nineteenth-century race theory. For comprehensive historical accounts of slavery and the American South, teachers should consult Edmund S. Morgan, *American Slavery, American Freedom*; James Oakes, *Slavery and Freedom*; David M. Potter, *The Impending Crisis, 1848–1861*; and John McCardell, *The Idea of a Southern Nation*. More specific historical material about race and Stowe's antislavery politics can be found in Thomas Gossett's two excellent volumes *Race: The History of an Idea in America* and Uncle Tom's Cabin *and American Culture*. Along with biographical information, this second study discusses Stowe's ideas about race, Northern and Southern reactions to her novel, the development of anti–Uncle Tom literature, the reception of the novel in England, the proliferation of Tom shows, and attitudes toward the book during Reconstruction and beyond. Also important to an understanding of race in *Uncle Tom's Cabin* is George M. Fredrickson's chapter on Stowe and romantic racialism in *The Black Image in the White Mind*. For an excellent recent analysis of racism in popular American culture, including discussion of the continuing vitality of Stowe-inspired stereotypes, see Patricia A. Turner's *Ceramic Uncles and Celluloid Mammies: Black Images and Their Influence on Culture*.

On the topic of women and slavery, informative historical accounts can be found in Jacqueline Jones's *Labor of Love, Labor of Sorrow: Black Women, Work, and the Family from Slavery to the Present*; Angela Y. Davis's *Women, Race, and Class*; Vincent Bakpetu Thompson's *The Making of the African Diaspora in the Americas, 1441–1900*; and David Barry Gaspar and Darlene Clark Hines's edited volume, *More Than Chattel: Black Women and Slavery in the Americas*. Also valuable are Elizabeth Fox-Genovese's *Within the Plantation Household: Black and White Women of the Old South* and Victoria E. Bynum's *Unruly Women: The Politics of Social and Sexual Control in the Old South*. In addition, slave narratives provide indispensable information, with the best known and most often read being Frederick Douglass's *Narrative of the Life of Frederick Douglass, an American Slave* and Harriet

Jacobs's *Incidents in the Life of a Slave Girl*. Scholarship about slave narratives offers valuable historical insights, as is true of William L. Andrews's *To Tell a Free Story: The First Century of Afro-American Autobiography, 1760–1865* and of the volume edited by Charles T. Davis and Henry Louis Gates, Jr., *The Slave's Narrative*, which includes an essay by Robin W. Winks, "The Making of a Slave Narrative: Josiah Henson and Uncle Tom—A Case Study."

For primary texts containing antislavery rhetoric and argument for comparison with *Uncle Tom's Cabin*, teachers can turn to well-known tracts such as David Walker's famous *Appeal to the Coloured Citizens of the World*; speeches by William Lloyd Garrison; Frances Ellen Harper's antislavery poetry such as "The Slave Mother," "The Tennessee Hero," and "Free Labor"; and Lydia Maria Child's *Appeal in Favor of That Class of Americans Called Africans*. William Wells Brown's *Clotel* and Harriet E. Wilson's *Our Nig*, two novels of the 1850s by African Americans, provide significant comparison and contrast.

To understand the kind of proslavery arguments that Stowe wrote against, teachers might consult Josiah Priest's *Bible Defence of Slavery*, a popular antebellum work advancing standard racist assumptions about African Americans' not experiencing pain when beaten, not having the same family feelings as whites, and not truly being human according to the Bible. Also instructive are Thomas Jefferson's *Notes on the State of Virginia*, particularly his disparaging discussion of black people's mental abilities and artistic capacities, and Caroline Lee Hentz's proslavery novel, *The Planter's Northern Bride*. Useful as well in revealing proslavery sentiments are hostile Southern reviews of Stowe's novel such as those reprinted in *Critical Essays on Harriet Beecher Stowe*, edited by Elizabeth Ammons.

The Limits of Sisterhood: The Beecher Sisters on Women's Rights and Woman's Sphere, a collection of documents and analyses edited by Jeanne Boydston, Mary Kelley, and Anne Margolis, represents a fruitful place to start thinking about Stowe and nineteenth-century domestic ideology, the growing movement for women's rights, and prevailing assumptions about (white) female human nature and the feminine "sphere." Also useful on gender relations and white ideology in the middle of the nineteenth century are Gillian Brown's *Domestic Individualism: Imagining Self in Nineteenth-Century America*, which includes a chapter entitled "Domestic Politics in *Uncle Tom's Cabin*"; Mary Kelley's *Private Woman, Public Stage: Literary Domesticity in Nineteenth-Century America*, which helps place Stowe in context with other white women writers; and Ann Romines's *The Home Plot: Women, Writing, and Domestic Ritual*, the first chapter of which discusses Stowe. For discussion of the gap between black and white women's reality and representation, see Bettina Aptheker's *Woman's Legacy: Essays on Race, Sex, and Class in American History*; Hortense Spillers's important essay on the gendering of the African American woman in captivity, "Mama's Baby, Papa's Maybe: An American Grammar Book"; and the volume edited by

Shirley Samuels, *The Culture of Sentiment: Race, Gender, and Sentimentality in Nineteenth-Century America*, especially Harryette Mullen's essay "Runaway Tongue: Resistant Orality in *Uncle Tom's Cabin, Our Nig, Incidents in the Life of a Slave Girl*, and *Beloved*." Background on the growing women's rights movement, including the historic Seneca Falls Convention in 1848, can be found in Nancy F. Cott, *The Grounding of Modern Feminism*, and in Eleanor Flexner and Ellen Fitzpatrick's edited volume, *Century of Struggle: The Women's Rights Movement in the United States*. Additionally important to an understanding of the gendered intellectual context in which Stowe wrote is Marie Caskey's *Chariot of Fire: Religion and the Beecher Family*.

Many early-twentieth-century literary historical overviews of the period in which *Uncle Tom's Cabin* appeared gave significant attention to Stowe. But after World War II, discussions of Stowe disappeared from literary history, until feminist challenges to the canon and to literary history called for fresh examinations of the many contributions of women writers to nineteenth-century literature. Preeminent among volumes that restore Stowe to her place in literary history are Jane P. Tompkins's classic *Sensational Designs: The Cultural Work of American Fiction, 1790–1860*, which changed Stowe scholarship permanently by placing *Uncle Tom's Cabin* in a rich and important tradition of sentimental writing; Nina Baym's *Woman's Fiction: A Guide to Novels by and about Women in America, 1820–70*, which talks in detail about Stowe's contemporaries, arguing that her famous novel was anomalous; and Joyce W. Warren's excellent collection of essays by various scholars, *The (Other) American Traditions: Nineteenth-Century Women Writers*, which, although its essay on Stowe does not discuss *Uncle Tom's Cabin*, outlines key issues in the study of nineteenth-century women writers. Also valuable are David S. Reynolds's *Beneath the American Renaissance: The Subversive Imagination in the Age of Emerson and Melville*, which devotes a few pages to *Uncle Tom's Cabin*, and Lawrence Buell's *New England Literary Culture: From Revolution through Renaissance*, which includes the chapter "Hawthorne and Stowe as Rival Interpreters of New England Puritanism." Particularly accessible and convenient are the overview essays on early- and mid-nineteenth-century literary historical topics in *The Columbia Literary History of the United States* and *The Columbia History of the American Novel*, both edited by Emory Elliott, and *The Cambridge History of American Literature*, edited by Sacvan Bercovitch. Contributed by scholars such as Cathy Davidson, Eric Sundquist, Nellie McKay, Nina Baym, Michael Davitt Bell, Jonathan Arac, and Carolyn Porter, essays in these volumes provide concise, introductory discussion of the early American novel, the literary marketplace, Romanticism, writing and race, domesticity, fiction and reform movements, women writers, and types of nonfiction.

Critical Commentary on *Uncle Tom's Cabin*

Book-length studies of Stowe's novel include J. C. Furnas's *Goodbye to Uncle Tom*, an overwrought, misogynist, yet still instructive attack on Stowe's racism and the novel's racist legacy; Thomas F. Gossett's rich historical analysis, Uncle Tom's Cabin *and American Culture*, described earlier; E. Bruce Kirkham's focus on Stowe's composition process, *The Building of* Uncle Tom's Cabin; and Josephine Donovan's consideration of the novel's vision of reform and social change, Uncle Tom's Cabin: *Evil, Affliction, and Redemptive Love*.

Three anthologies offer important critical essays. Elizabeth Ammons's *Critical Essays on Harriet Beecher Stowe* reprints selected nineteenth-century and pre-1980s views, including positive commentary by Charles Dudley Warner, Paul Laurence Dunbar, Constance Mayfield Rourke, and Langston Hughes. Also reprinted here, as well as in the Norton Critical Edition of the novel, is what is probably the single most famous essay ever written on it, James Baldwin's "Everybody's Protest Novel," a sexist, scathing, yet nevertheless brilliant 1949 attack on Stowe's racism, particularly her emasculation of Tom. In addition, this collection contains an excerpt from Leslie A. Fiedler's discussion of Stowe's sexual sadism and prurience in *Love and Death in the American Novel*, published in 1960, and Elizabeth Ammons's essay about Tom and Eva as feminine Christ figures, "Heroines in *Uncle Tom's Cabin*."

Eric Sundquist's collection, *New Essays on* Uncle Tom's Cabin, offers six excellent analyses of the novel, beginning with Sundquist's long, informative introduction. Next comes Richard Yarbrough's "Strategies of Black Characterization in *Uncle Tom's Cabin* and the Early Afro-American Novel," which provides detailed discussion of Stowe's novel alongside work by Richard Wright, Martin Delany, Frances Ellen Harper, and Victoria Earle Matthews. Jean Fagan Yellin's "Doing It Herself: *Uncle Tom's Cabin* and Woman's Role in the Slavery Crisis" reads the novel against views espoused by Stowe's sister, Catharine Beecher, and the well-known white Southern abolitionists, the Grimke sisters. Karen Halttunen's "Gothic Imagination and Social Reform: The Haunted Houses of Lyman Beecher, Henry Ward Beecher, and Harriet Beecher Stowe" persuasively locates the book in a family and Calvinist horror tradition. Robert B. Stepto's "Sharing the Thunder: The Literary Exchanges of Harriet Beecher Stowe, Henry Bibb, and Frederick Douglass" brings together Stowe's novel and African American abolitionist tradition. Elizabeth Ammons's "Stowe's Dream of the Mother-Savior: *Uncle Tom's Cabin* and American Women Writers before 1920" examines the paradigm of the maternal Christ in the work of Stowe and subsequent white and black women writers such as Louisa May Alcott, Angelina Grimke, Frances Ellen Harper, Sarah Orne Jewett, Elizabeth Stuart Phelps, and Harriet E. Wilson.

The collection *The Stowe Debate: Rhetorical Strategies in* Uncle Tom's Cabin, edited by Mason I. Lowance, Jr., Ellen E. Westbrook, and R. C. De Prospo, provides perspectives on the cultural conditions that produced *Uncle Tom's Cabin* and Stowe's rhetorical strategies. With one section devoted to race and slavery, the volume continues critical debate about Stowe's relation to racist ideology. Sarah Smith Duckworth, for example, argues that Stowe's real concern was white, not black, salvation, while Michael J. Meyer and Susan Marie Nuernberg analyze the novel's positive contribution to abolitionism.

So many illuminating articles and essays have appeared in the 1980s and 1990s that only a few can be mentioned here. Most influential, without question, has been Jane Tompkins's defense of Stowe's artistry in her groundbreaking "Sentimental Power: *Uncle Tom's Cabin* and the Politics of Literary History," reprinted in her already mentioned *Sensational Designs* and in the Norton Critical Edition of *Uncle Tom's Cabin* (ed. Ammons). Equally major is the critique of Stowe's representation of slavery in Hortense J. Spillers's complex juxtaposition of *Uncle Tom's Cabin* and Ishmael Reed's *Flight to Canada*. Entitled "Changing the Letter: The Yokes, the Jokes of Discourse, or, Mrs. Stowe, Mr. Reed," the essay is reprinted in the Norton Critical Edition. Also reprinted there is Robert S. Levine's helpful examination of early African American reactions to the novel, "*Uncle Tom's Cabin* in *Frederick Douglass' Paper*: An Analysis of Reception," which can aid teachers in answering questions about early black views. For discussion of Stowe and sentimentality that is highly critical, see Ann Douglas's influential book, *The Feminization of American Culture*, which argues that sentimentalism and commercialism in America have worked together to vitiate the culture. For analysis of Stowe's creative process and the culture of serial publication in mid-nineteenth-century America, see Susan Belasco Smith's "Serialization and the Nature of *Uncle Tom's Cabin*."

Most contemporary articles on *Uncle Tom's Cabin* continue to explore three major themes: Stowe's perspectives on race, her depiction of slavery, and her investment in nineteenth-century domestic ideology. In "De-authorizing Slavery: Realism in Stowe's *Uncle Tom's Cabin* and Brown's *Clotel*," Peter Dorsey examines the reception granted Stowe's novel and argues that Stowe profoundly changed the development of American fiction with regard to race. In "White Slaves: The Mulatto Hero in Antebellum Fiction," Nancy Bentley concentrates on Stowe's Haitian references and the terrorism symbolized by racially mixed figures. In "Racial Essentialism and Family Values in *Uncle Tom's Cabin*," Arthur Riss argues that the progressive politics of the novel ironically derive from its racial essentialism.

Concentrating on Stowe's deployment of domesticity are articles such as Lora Romero's "Bio-political Resistance in Domestic Ideology and *Uncle Tom's Cabin*," a Foucauldian reading of the discourses governing the bodies of white women and slaves, and Myra Jehlen's "The Family Militant: Domesticity versus Slavery in *Uncle Tom's Cabin*," which argues that the book is both conservative and revolutionary. As these brief descriptions suggest, the best contemporary gender-focused analyses understand that race (including whiteness) and gender are inseparable and therefore that discussion of domesticity as an ideology requires simultaneous attention to race issues.

Perhaps a good place to end this sketch is with Lori Askeland's "Remodeling the Model Home in *Uncle Tom's Cabin* and *Beloved*," an essay yoking the two most famous novels to date about slavery in the United States. As this pairing of texts reveals, critical perspectives, like approaches in the classroom, continue to find Stowe's novel complex and provocative.

Visual, Sound, and Internet Resources

Harriet Beecher Stowe regarded herself as a painter who created pictures of slavery about which there could be no argument, and certainly *Uncle Tom's Cabin* is a novel in which the detailed depiction of persons and places and the development of scenes are prominent. It is therefore highly appropriate to incorporate a variety of resources into the teaching of the novel. An excellent place to begin is Uncle Tom's Cabin *and American Culture* (<http://jefferson.village.virginia.edu/utc>), a Web site for teachers and students developed by Stephen Railton, which includes an impressive array of images, illustrations, music, and relevant texts, such as period news stories, reviews, and sources for the novel.

Teachers can also use photocopies of the *National Era* and other antislavery newspapers of the day, such as the *Liberator*. In addition, consulting the many illustrations that have been used throughout the publication history of *Uncle Tom's Cabin* can show students how different artists saw and interpreted the action of the novel. John Jewett published seven illustrations with the first edition in 1852, and the famous illustrator of Dickens's novels, George Cruikshank, illustrated the first British edition. All of Jewett's illustrations and several of Cruikshank's are reproduced in the Norton Critical Edition (ed. Ammons) and the *Uncle Tom's Cabin* Web site. In the twentieth century, there have been notable illustrated editions of the novel; see especially R. F. Fenno and Company's 1904 edition and the 1938 Heritage Press edition with the illustrations of Miguel Covarrubias. In this volume Paul C. Gutjahr suggests ways to use the various illustrations of the novel to present major themes.

Photographs and paintings illustrating slavery and life in the mid–nineteenth century are also helpful; Eric Foner and Olivia Mahoney, *A House Divided: America in the Age of Lincoln*, the catalog for a 1992 exhibit of the Chicago Historical Society, includes reproductions of early photographs, artifacts, and posters, as well as descriptions of life on farms and plantations. Early parts of the PBS series *The Civil War*, by Ken Burns, as well as the companion text for this series, *The Civil War: An Illustrated History* by Geoffrey C. Ward, Ric Burns, and Ken Burns, provide a wealth of visual and sound resources.

Two resources especially developed for classroom use are *Harriet Beecher Stowe's* Uncle Tom's Cabin, a forty-five-minute videotape that is an abridged version of the script of George Aiken's original 1852 production of *Uncle Tom's Cabin* (#ASU933), and *The Civil War,* two fifteen-minute filmstrips that investigate and compare various writers' contributions in the antebellum period (#ASU317). Both are available from Films for the Humanities and Sciences (PO Box 1053, Princeton, NJ 08543-2053).

While there appear to be no recorded readings of *Uncle Tom's Cabin,* some sound recordings can usefully augment classroom discussion or independent study. Examples include Robert William Fogel's *The Economics of Slavery* (Encyclopedia Americana–CBS News Audio Resource Library, 1974); *Great Black Speeches,* by F. M. Stewart, H. H. Garnet, and B. T. Washington, read by Claudia McNeil and Norman Matlock (Caedmon, 1974); and *Slave Voices: Things Past Telling,* a compilation made by National Public Radio in 1987 of recordings of former slaves originally created in the 1930s.

In *I'll Make Me a World: A Century of African American Arts,* a series produced by Blackside, Inc., and WNET, New York, for PBS in February 1999, a section of the final two hours is devoted to scenes from a modern dance production, *Last Supper at Uncle Tom's Cabin / The Promised Land.* This dance, written and choreographed by the Bill T. Jones–Arnie Zane Dance Company, was first performed at the Next Wave Festival, the Brooklyn Academy of Music, in 1990. *I'll Make Me a World,* which includes several discussions of *Uncle Tom's Cabin* by contemporary African American writers and artists, is available on videotape for purchase or rental. There are a number of versions of *Uncle Tom's Cabin* dramatized for the stage, most of which are adapted from Aiken's early play. In addition, "Uncle Tom" vignettes were a staple of vaudeville performances and musical theater, especially in the early part of this century. In this volume, Susan Belasco discusses contemporary dramatic versions, including *I Ain't Yo' Uncle,* produced by the San Francisco Mime Troupe and the Lorraine Hansberry Theatre, and the 1997 New York production *Uncle Tom's Cabin; or, Life among the Lowly,* a compilation of several versions of the play interwoven with slave narratives, directed by Floraine Kay and Randolph Curtis Rand. The Internet Movie Database (http://us.imdb.com) lists eight film versions of *Uncle Tom's Cabin* produced between 1903 and 1927, some of which are available in libraries and on videotape for purchase. The 1903 version, produced by Edwin S. Porter, was among the earliest movies ever filmed. The 1956 film version of *The King and I,* the musical by Richard Rodgers and Oscar Hammerstein II, with Deborah Kerr and Yul Brynner, contains the famous "Uncle Thomas" ballet, choreographed by Jerome Robbins. In 1987, a made-for-television movie starring Avery Brooks as Uncle Tom, Bruce Dern as St. Clare, and Phylicia Rashad as Eliza was directed by Stan Lathan; this movie, which earned mixed reviews, is available on videotape. Although there has been no recent big-screen movie version of *Uncle Tom's Cabin* (such as there has been of *Little Women* or even *The Scarlet Letter*), there are good companion movies about the period, including *Glory* and *Gettysburg*. As essays in this volume suggest, teachers of *Uncle Tom's Cabin* might encourage students to consider how the legacy of slavery and racism and the characters of Simon Legree, Uncle Tom, Little Eva, and Topsy persist in contemporary literature, movies, and television programs.

NOTE

Throughout this volume references to Stowe's *Uncle Tom's Cabin* are to the Norton Critical Edition (ed. Ammons).

Part Two

APPROACHES

Introduction

Because *Uncle Tom's Cabin* is a novel that presents many challenges for teachers and students, we have divided this volume into three sections emphasizing, respectively, the novel's historical context, late-twentieth-century debate and controversy, and current theoretical and critical approaches. However, since many issues, such as the question of racism, analyses of the book's gender politics, and discussion of Stowe's artistry, necessarily cut across all three sections of the anthology, readers may wish to skim or read the whole collection.

The six essays in the first section, *"Uncle Tom's Cabin* in Context," address the centrality of the literary, social, and historical context of the novel. Susan Belasco describes the circumstances of the writing, reception, and enduring reputation of the novel, suggesting that students can more easily discuss the complex issues of race and gender in the book if they have a clear understanding of the literary milieus in which Stowe was writing.

The remaining five essays deal with the history of racial attitudes, domesticity, religion, abolition, colonization, and the literary marketplace of the nineteenth century. Surveying the prevailing attitudes and ideas on race in the nineteenth century and providing information about the antislavery movement in the United States, Susan M. Nuernberg explores the conflicting views about race that emerge in the novel. Lisa Logan takes up the context of domestic ideology for the novel and discusses two central texts of the period, Catharine Beecher's *A Treatise on Domestic Economy* (1841) and Lydia Maria Child's *The American Frugal Housewife* (1830), in relation to *Uncle Tom's Cabin*. The complicated religious background of the novel is explored by Stephen R. Yarbrough and Sylvan Allen, who outline the conflicts that the rhetoric of religion exposes for both nineteenth-century and contemporary readers with an emphasis on Stowe's wish to write her novel to save the souls of whites and blacks, Southerners and Northerners. Situating the novel in a global context of international power relationships, Elizabeth Ammons examines Stowe's controversial endorsement of Liberian colonization and describes how students might come to an awareness of the book's imperial project. The final essay in this section, by Paul C. Gutjahr, places *Uncle Tom's Cabin* within the context of an emerging literary marketplace and an American public eager for new materials to read and focuses attention on the production of the book itself—marketing, technological innovations, illustrations, and textual decisions.

The second section, "Controversy and Debate," includes essays that help teachers examine the difficult issues of race, gender, and class that must emerge during any classroom discussion of the novel. We begin this section with a challenge to the entire project of teaching *Uncle Tom's Cabin*. Interested in comparing the novel with *The History of Mary Prince* and Harriet Wilson's *Our Nig* in order to interrogate, in part, the issue of appropriation, Sophia Cantave raises hard questions about Stowe's legacy to American culture that all teachers should consider before they begin discussions of the text with their students. Stephen Railton explores what he calls the "excursionary" aspect of *Uncle Tom's Cabin*, the ways in which the novel depicts black slaves for the benefit of white readers, creating a racist dynamic even as the novel argues against slavery. Considering race in conjunction with the construction of gender, Gillian Brown challenges the principle of sentimental power, as applied to *Uncle Tom's Cabin* by Jane Tompkins and other feminist critics, and links racism with sentimentalism in the novel. Defining Stowe's particular sentimentalism as "sentimental possession," Brown encourages teachers and students to examine what she calls the "troubling effect" of the novel: its endorsement of domesticity, feminism, antislavery, and racism. In the next essay, David Leverenz sharply defines the racial, gender, and class dichotomies offered in the novel. He outlines a pedagogy of liberal pluralism that explores the contradictions and "nonnarratable plots" of the novel by encouraging close reading, careful analysis of key passages, and extensive classroom discussion. Connected to the issues of race, class, and gender, another controversial topic that often emerges in discussions of *Uncle Tom's Cabin* is violence. In an essay that pairs Stowe's novel with Harriet Jacobs's *Incidents in the Life of a Slave Girl*, Kristin Herzog compares the treatment of violence in these two works—a novel and an ex-slave narrative—that are often taught together. In the final essay of this section, Mary Jane Peterson makes a case for teaching *Uncle Tom's Cabin* to less experienced readers at the secondary and undergraduate levels. Peterson suggests specific student-centered strategies and methods designed to assist those who may themselves feel marginalized within their own educational communities.

In the third section, "Critical Approaches to the Novel," five essays illustrate various theoretical or methodological strategies. Marianne K. Noble's reader-response study examines the norms of passionlessness imposed on middle-class women in the mid–nineteenth century and the ways in which repression leads to what she sees as a masochistic eroticism in *Uncle Tom's Cabin*. In the next essay, Sharon Carson moves *Uncle Tom's Cabin* away from the central position it is beginning to occupy in mid-nineteenth-century American literature written by whites and places it instead in relation to theoretical and conceptual frameworks that are important in African American studies. Blending new historicism with rhetorical criticism, Harold K. Bush, Jr., discusses his use of the Declaration of Independence as a key commentary text on *Uncle Tom's Cabin* and suggests ways to engage students in understanding Stowe's rhetorical strategies. Taking Topsy as her focal point, Kimberly G. Hébert provides a cultural studies approach to *Uncle Tom's Cabin*, linking the concept of "black performance" to two twentieth-century characters, Shirley Temple, the 1930s child star, and Pecola Breedlove, in Toni Morrison's *The Bluest Eye*. The final essay in this section charts an interdisciplinary course for teaching the novel. Jamie Stanesa suggests that *Uncle Tom's Cabin* is not about a single issue or even a group of them but about the intersection of politics, religion, domesticity, and literature in nineteenth-century American culture.

The Writing, Reception, and Reputation of *Uncle Tom's Cabin*

Susan Belasco

Unlike other frequently taught novelists of the nineteenth century, Harriet Beecher Stowe is primarily known for one book, her best-selling *Uncle Tom's Cabin*, regarded by many as a major cause of the Civil War. The popularity of the book—as well as its prominent place in American literary culture—has tended to overshadow her many other accomplishments, about which most students know little or nothing. Stowe was a prolific journalist who wrote for a variety of periodicals in the emerging and lucrative American literary marketplace; a popular lecturer who toured Europe, New England, and the West; a productive novelist and essayist; and a well-known champion of important reform movements other than abolition, such as temperance and women's suffrage. In fact, Stowe was a celebrity and something of a media personality by the late nineteenth century. For her seventy-first birthday in 1882, the editorial staff of the *Atlantic Monthly* hosted a party of over two hundred people: the guest list included major literary luminaries of the day. Oliver Wendell Holmes, John Greenleaf Whittier, Lucy Larcom, Elizabeth Stuart Phelps, and William Dean Howells were all in attendance, and others who were invited but unable to attend included Julia Ward Howe, Mark Twain, Thomas Wentworth Higginson, and James Russell Lowell (see Hedrick, *Stowe* 394; F. Wilson 609–19).

The internationally famous woman writer honored by the magazine whose founding she had assisted was already well known in 1851 when she began to write *Uncle Tom's Cabin*.[1] Helping students understand Stowe's central position in the literary marketplace of the nineteenth century, as well as the rich historical, political, social, and literary context of the novel, is a useful first step toward meaningful discussions of the complex moral questions that it so effectively raises. A good beginning for an investigation of the context is the history of the periodical in mid-nineteenth-century America and especially the emergence of the *National Era*, the weekly newspaper in which *Uncle Tom's Cabin* first appeared in forty-one installments from 2 June 1851 through 1 April 1852. Some questions to consider are, What was the nature of the literary marketplace in the 1850s, and how did that marketplace shape the writing of *Uncle Tom's Cabin*? What was the relation between abolitionism and the explosion of periodical literature? What in Stowe's background helped her gain her success as a writer and then as a novelist? When I teach *Uncle Tom's Cabin*, I begin by devoting a class period to these questions.

The new interest in periodicals in American literary studies has encouraged students to understand the role that the market played in the development of texts now considered classics. Many important American writers wrote occasionally or frequently for the periodical press, including Herman Melville, Edgar Allan Poe, Nathaniel Hawthorne, Walt Whitman, Margaret Fuller, Frances E. W. Harper, Frederick Douglass, Fanny Fern, Lydia Maria Child, Ralph Waldo Emerson, Henry David Thoreau, and Elizabeth Barstow Stoddard. These authors wrote poems, stories, serialized fiction, and articles and essays that appeared in papers like the abolitionist *Liberator*; Horace Greeley's influential newspaper, the *New York Tribune*; the monthly women's magazine *Godey's Lady's Book*; or in literary journals like *Harper's Monthly*. The production and distribution of periodical literature had a profound effect on the culture and society of mid-nineteenth-century America. By 1850, the era was marked by the spirit of enlargement and extension; the population grew significantly, and literacy rates rose. In that year, for example, the population of New York was over 500,000 while the population of Boston was 136,000. The growth in the number and range of periodicals reflected the mood of the country and made it possible for numerous magazines, journals, and newspapers to succeed, though it also led to numerous failures, as editors and publishers slowly learned the vagaries of an evolving marketplace. In the 1830s a variety of technological developments in papermaking and the development and use of the cylinder press had altered the course of publication. Cheaper postal routes further contributed to wider distribution and a larger potential audience for printed materials. In addition, railroads were connecting various parts of the country very quickly. By 1840, there were nine thousand miles of track; by the beginning of the Civil War, the figure reached over thirty thousand. Not only did the railroads provide more efficient transportation for goods and mail, they also provided opportunities for travel and a new outlet for selling portable reading materials. Periodical publication soared as demand increased. According to the census of 1840, there were over six hundred ongoing periodicals of various kinds in the country; by 1869, there were four thousand (see Smith and Price).

The periodical quickly came to play a central role in communication, information, and entertainment. Not everyone, of course, agreed that the rise of the periodicals and the expansion of the publication industry in general were positive cultural developments. Although Henry David Thoreau did publish work in numerous journals, he felt some bitterness about his inability to obtain the interest of the general periodical audience. In *Walden* (1854), for example, he was specifically critical of family newspapers, such as the Boston-based *Olive Branch*: "If we will read newspapers, why not skip the gossip of Boston and take the best newspaper in the world at once?—not be sucking the pap of 'neutral family' papers, or browsing 'Olive Branches' here in New England. Let the reports of all the learned societies come to us, and we will see if they know any thing" (109 [ed. Shanley]). Despite Thoreau's reservations about their intellectual quality, periodicals—in all their many nineteenth-century forms and formats—quickly became a central feature of the American literary landscape.

Others embraced the periodical early in their careers and worked to establish an audience. For example, Whitman greatly admired the *United States Magazine and Democratic Review* (Oct. 1837–Dec. 1851), a monthly designed to promote the expansionist and anti–big government politics of the Democratic party, as well as to provide a forum for contemporary American writers. Hawthorne published twenty-five essays and tales in the magazine, including "Rappaccini's Daughter" and "The Artist of the Beautiful." Other contributors included Poe, James Fenimore Cooper, William Cullen Bryant, James Russell Lowell, and William Gilmore Simms. Eager to find new outlets for his own work, especially in a magazine of such quality, Whitman published ten pieces in the *Review* from 1841 to 1845, most of which were undistinguished, melodramatic tales such as "Death in the School-Room (a Fact)" (Aug. 1841). Whitman also published "A Dialogue [against Capital Punishment]" (Nov. 1845), his contribution to the progressive campaign to abolish the death penalty. Later, he published in the *United States Review* one of his several self-reviews of *Leaves of Grass*, "Walt Whitman and His Poems" (Sept. 1855), proclaiming that its author was an American bard, "self-reliant, with haughty eyes, assuming to himself all the attributes of his country." The rapid development of the periodical press in mid-nineteenth-century America invited both the pointed criticism of Thoreau and the shameless exploitation of Whitman.

In addition to providing news, entertainment, and advertisements for an increasingly consumer-oriented society, the periodical also proved to be an invaluable tool for the antislavery movement. William Lloyd Garrison's *The Liberator*, Frederick Douglass's *North Star* (later called *Frederick Douglass' Paper*), and Lydia Maria Child's *National Anti-slavery Standard* are but three examples of successful abolitionist newspapers created to support the campaign against slavery in the United States. There were many more. Established by the American and Foreign Anti-Slavery Society in Washington, DC, the *National Era* existed from 7 January 1847 through 22 March 1860 (see Harrold 81–107, 139). The editor, Gamaliel Bailey, who had formerly edited the controversial

Cincinnati *Philanthropist* (sponsored by the Ohio Anti-Slavery Society), had a strong record as a journalist and as an abolitionist. The backers of the *Era* chose as an associate editor the poet John Greenleaf Whittier, who was specifically engaged to handle the literary contributions to the paper and to contribute articles and poems himself. In keeping with the practice of the newspapers of the day, the *Era* presented much more than news to its readers, offering literature as well. Its declared purpose was "to represent the class of anti-slavery men [. . .] and to lay before the Southern men [. . .] such facts and arguments as may serve to throw further light upon the question of slavery, and its disposition" (qtd. in Harrold 87). Ironically, the *Era* used the works of numerous women writers who well-represented the "class of anti-slavery men." To present "such facts and arguments," Bailey further announced in a preliminary article that "the *National Era* would not be confined to the discussion of one subject. Political questions of general interest will be freely examined in its columns. The cause of Literature will receive a large share of attention; a record of current events will be carefully kept up and a full, though condensed report of Congressional proceedings, will be given" (qtd. in Harrold 88–89). In the prospectus of the *Era* (published on 10 April 1851), Bailey further announced that Grace Greenwood, a very popular writer of the day, would write exclusively for the newspaper, that another well-known woman writer, E. D. E. N. Southworth, had also agreed to participate, and that other contributors would include "Alice and Phoebe Carey, and Mrs. H. B. Stowe—names familiar and attractive" (*Era* prospectus 3) and notably female. In this announcement, Bailey and Whittier were making it clear that their newspaper had well-respected names behind it. As diverse as the articles, stories, and features in the paper were, the underlying purpose of all the coverage was nonetheless to promote the antislavery cause, often through the domestic imagery of the union as a "house" and the American citizenry as a "family."[2]

To accomplish the goal of promoting abolition among Southerners, Bailey and his writers had to make the antislavery argument moderate and persuasive. Bailey had been specifically chosen for the editorship of the newspaper because of his reasonable, diplomatic personality, as well as for his belief that Southerners and Southern slaveholders might be persuaded that slavery was more than a sectional issue. While William Lloyd Garrison and his followers called for disunion and cared little about offending readers—Southern or Northern—Bailey's paper directly addressed Southern readers. According to his biographer, Stanley Harrold, Bailey wanted to treat Southerners as reasonable beings whom he might involve in a "national campaign against a moral, social, political, and economic evil" (85). To that end, he decided to offer "further light" on the question of slavery for a distinctly Southern audience. Bailey chose steady persuasion in a variety of forms, and the hundreds of articles, essays, reviews, continuing stories, and poems published in the *Era* all had a common purpose: to subvert the ideology of slaveholding.

Although it is nearly impossible to locate and use hard copies of the *Era*, having students examine the microfilms—and even copy and reconstruct issues of the four-page paper with its seven columns of small print—is quite instructive. To read *Uncle Tom's Cabin* column by column in issue after issue is a very different experience from reading the novel in book form, in part because one is constantly reminded of the presence of the many other voices, and speakers competing for attention on the pages of the newspaper. In the *Era*, aesthetic and political materials occupy the same pages and sometimes the same columns. The interrelation of these texts, their languages and voices, is suddenly clarified. For instance, the *Era* for 2 June 1851, published not only the first installment of *Uncle Tom's Cabin* but also notices of articles appearing in other periodicals, such as *Blackwood's* and *Harper's*; the latest publisher's lists, such as John P. Jewett's The Best of School Books series; and an array of advertisements for cold remedies, such as Ayer's Cherry Pectoral and Wistar's Balsam of Wild Cherry. In addition, this issue includes pointed letters to the editor from a variety of American citizens protesting the Fugitive Slave Law and linking Congress with civil despotism; "A Reminiscence," a sketch by a popular writer, Patty Lee, about the sad death of a young girl (with more than a passing resemblance to Little Eva); a report of the murder of a master by a slave girl in North Carolina (suggestive of the course of action Cassy decides not to take); a description of a disturbance at a festival involving several thousand German immigrants in Hoboken, New York, which was clearly designed to contradict the accounts by the Southern press, who widely reported the incident as a riot; the text of a speech by Louis Kossuth, the Hungarian revolutionary, demanding his release from enforced exile in Turkey; the prospectus for a new weekly journal, the *National Monument*, published by the Washington National Monument Society to raise funds for the "erection of the noble column now rising on the bank of the Potomac in honor of the Father of his Country"; a blistering review of Daniel Webster's attitudes toward slavery; and finally, a regular feature, the "Letter from Cincinnati," detailing the population growth of this increasingly important city in the free state of Ohio. The presence of these texts points up the extent to which *Uncle Tom's Cabin* was just one part of the program undertaken by the *National Era* to raise the complex and related issues of freedom and slavery in a variety of ways.

When Stowe agreed to write a new story for Bailey in the spring of 1851, she was already quite familiar with the antislavery agenda of the *Era*—in large part because of her family background and history. After I have introduced students to the newspaper itself, I often ask them to investigate Stowe's family, education, and introduction into the antislavery movement. Students are frequently surprised to learn that Stowe was a member of one of the most famous American families of the time. The family members were so pervasive in their influence that according to a contemporary, Dr. Leonard Bacon, "this country is inhabited by saints, sinners and Beechers."[3] Stowe's father, Lyman Beecher, was considered by many to be the most powerful preacher—as well as the last

Puritan—in America. He was a strong supporter of the temperance movement, an advocate of colonization as the solution to slavery, and an educational
reformer who was the first president and professor of theology of the Lane
Theological Seminary, a new Presbyterian school established in 1830 in Cincinnati. Although Beecher opposed slavery, he had serious reservations about the
abolition movement and feared the violence that he thought would surely be
generated by fervent abolitionists. His advocacy of colonization exerted an
important influence on Stowe (especially evident in the final chapter of *Uncle
Tom's Cabin*) and caused a great deal of debate in the family and among students at Lane. While Lyman Beecher remained committed to colonization to
his death in 1863, other members of his family were less sure; however, all of
them were strongly abolitionist in outlook.

Stowe's siblings also became powerful forces in nineteenth-century America,
and she remained in close contact with them throughout her life. Like her
father, her brother Henry Ward Beecher was a famous minister; he was also a
journalist who wrote for a variety of periodicals and later edited the *Christian
Union*. Other brothers had careers as ministers, educators, and authors:
Thomas K. Beecher performed the marriage of Samuel Clemens and Olivia
Langdon on 2 February 1870, Edward Beecher became the president of Illinois College, and Charles Beecher published sermons and sketches throughout his life, including *The Incarnation; or, Pictures of the Virgin and Her Son*
(1849), for which Stowe wrote an introduction. Stowe's sister Catharine
Beecher was arguably the most famous woman in America in the early 1850s.
Her *Treatise on Domestic Economy* (1841) was a widely read and profoundly
influential book that firmly defined and defended the ideology of middle-class
domesticity. Catharine Beecher's influence on Stowe is a crucial one, since
many of the domestic standards of *Uncle Tom's Cabin* can be traced to her sister's views. In addition, Harriet attended and later taught at her sister's Hartford Female Seminary, where she met women who either were or would be
popular writers, including Fanny Fern and Lydia Sigourney. Harriet's half-sister Isabella Beecher Hooker became deeply involved in women's rights and
wrote for a number of periodicals, including *Putnam's Monthly* and the *Nation*.
In short, Harriet Beecher Stowe was a member of a prominent, activist, and
influential family. On 6 January 1836, Harriet married Calvin Stowe, a professor and librarian at Lane who was friendly with Gamaliel Bailey in Cincinnati
and sympathetic to the abolitionists. Not only was Stowe well prepared to write
for Bailey's *Era*, she was an insider in the antislavery movement and well aware
of the powerful role a writer might play.

Stowe had already published four pieces in the paper, one of which, "The
Freeman's Dream: A Parable" (1 Aug. 1850), was specifically antislavery in
tone. The others were mild sketches of family life, designed to appeal to the
family readership of the newspaper. Bailey invited Stowe to publish for the *Era*
because he knew her other work; since the mid-1830s, she had published
numerous articles and stories in the very popular *Godey's Lady's Book*, edited

from 1837 to 1877 by Sarah Josepha Hale. The highly visible *Godey's* maintained a list of 70,000 subscribers by 1851 and reached 150,000 just before the Civil War. Although Hale envisioned a primarily female audience and actively promoted women writers in the pages of her magazine, her contributors included Edgar Allan Poe, Nathaniel Hawthorne, and Nathaniel P. Willis. In addition to *Godey's*, Stowe also wrote for the *New-York Evangelist*, becoming well established as a writer of articles, sketches, and stories by 1850. Bailey was consequently delighted to have the well-respected Stowe writing for his own newspaper.

Following this class meeting or two on the periodical background of mid-nineteenth-century America, I often find it useful to introduce the immediate historical context of Stowe's new project for the *Era*: the revolutions and rebellions in Europe in 1848–50 and the passage of the Fugitive Slave Law in the United States in 1850. As even a glance at the periodicals at the end of the 1840s shows, the upheavals in Europe received wide coverage in the United States and were the most important international news of the day. Large city newspapers such as the *New York Tribune* and even much smaller papers like the *Era* kept readers well informed about such events as the abdication of King Louis Phillipe in February 1848, the repeal of the Corn Laws in England, the Italian revolt against Ferdinand II, and the dozens of rebellions that erupted in Austria, Prussia, Spain, and Hungary.[4] While the rebellions captured the imaginations of Americans who championed the cause of the oppressed, abolitionists were quick to appropriate what they perceived as an instructive analogy between the despots of Europe and the slaveholders of the American South. Bailey, in particular, took up the cause of Louis Kossuth, the Hungarian revolutionary, who had unsuccessfully tried to liberate his country from the Austrian monarchy in 1848–49. After living unhappily in exile in Turkey, Kossuth in 1851 was invited to the United States, where he was celebrated as a hero and sponsored by eminent men such as Stowe's brother Henry Ward Beecher. In the *Era*, Bailey ran story after story about Kossuth and the Hungarian cause, designed to underscore the similarities between despotic rule in Austria and America.

Just as the European rebellions began to be repressed, the Fugitive Slave Law was passed in 1850. Abolitionists immediately seized the opportunity to sharpen the analogy between Europe and the American South, pointing not just to despotism but also to the chaos and disruption of societies in the midst of revolutions. While American students can certainly enrich their understanding of many of Stowe's allusions in *Uncle Tom's Cabin* by exploring some unfamiliar European history, I always take this opportunity to suggest that a thorough investigation of the American Fugitive Slave Law is crucial to understanding the immediate political context for Stowe's decision to enter wholeheartedly into the antislavery cause with a story for the *Era*. In the spring of 1850, Stowe had moved with her husband and children from Cincinnati to Brunswick, Maine, away from immediate proximity to slavery in nearby Kentucky. But the passage of the Compromise of 1850 substantially changed the boundaries of slavery. The hope of many, especially nonabolitionists, was that the compromise would remove the topic of slavery from the agenda for national political debate. However, the compromise, which was widely viewed in the North as a capitulation to southern slaveholders, admitted California into the Union as a free state and abolished the slave trade in the nation's capital. At the same time, the New Mexico and Utah territories were organized with no prohibition of slavery. Even worse in the eyes of many, the Fugitive Slave Law made all a party to slavery. While citizens in free states had always been required by law to return fugitive slaves (the first Fugitive Slave Act was passed in 1793), the new law suspended due process. Slaveholders or their representatives simply presented certificates of ownership to federal agents, who were empowered to declare a slave free or to return him or her to the avowed owner. The law provided fees of $10 to agents for every fugitive returned to slavery and $5 for every fugitive who was judged to be legitimately free. Abolitionists immediately charged that the fee structure encouraged agents to return any black person to slavery; free blacks were especially at risk under the new system. In addition, anyone who gave food, shelter, or assistance to fugitive slaves was liable to a fine of $1,000 and six months in prison. Stowe and the members of her family were aghast. Henry Ward Beecher constantly opposed the Fugitive Slave Law from his pulpit and wrote editorials and articles for a variety of periodicals. Her brother Edward's wife, Isabella, wrote to Stowe, urging her to write something about slavery: "Now Hattie, if I could use a pen as you can, I would write something that would make this whole nation feel what an accursed thing slavery is" (qtd. in Hedrick, *Stowe* 207).

Stowe decided that it was time for her to take what action she could. In fact, she had recently received $100 from Bailey as an advance on additional articles for the *Era*. When she wrote to him on 9 March 1851 to advise him of her progress on her new project, she explained that she was "occupied upon a story which will be a much longer one than any I have ever written, embracing a series of sketches which give the lights and shadows of the 'patriarchal institution'" (Van Why and French 17). She further commented:

> Up to this year I have always felt that I had no particular call to meddle with this subject, and I dreaded to expose even my own mind to the full force of its exciting power. But I feel now that the time is come when even a woman or a child who can speak a word for freedom and humanity is bound to speak. The Carthagenian women in the last peril of their state cut off their hair for bow-strings to give the defenders of their country; and such peril and shame as now hangs over this country is worse than Roman slavery, and I hope every woman who can write will not be silent. (17)

In the same letter, Stowe explained that she expected the serial to extend for three or four numbers and that the manuscript would be ready in two or three weeks. But she was unable to keep to her projected timetable, and the first installment did not appear until 5 June. Although it is not known how much of the manuscript Bailey initially received, he certainly did not have all of it, nor did he know how long the novel would be. And neither, clearly, did Stowe. Following the practice of Dickens, Thackeray, Grace Greenwood, and a whole host of other serial novelists, Stowe did not have her entire narrative in hand, nor did she likely have a complete cast of characters in mind. The story unfolded—week by week and episode by episode—in the pages of the *Era*, and the author responded to requests from both her private and public audiences to extend and further develop the narrative.

Few letters survive from this period of Stowe's life, probably because she was very busy and engaged with her writing of the novel. At the time that she was preparing the installments of *Uncle Tom's Cabin*, her own house was particularly full. She was a professor's wife who was expected to entertain her husband's colleagues and visitors to Bowdoin College, she was a mother of six small children, and she was a part-time journalist and tutor trying to make an extremely inadequate income cover the many expenses of the Stowes' new home in Brunswick. According to her biographer, Joan Hedrick, Stowe took many opportunities to read her work to family members and friends and even the students she taught in small private classes in her home. Stowe also shared her writing with her sister Catharine, who was living in her home during this time. Given the circumstances of composition, it is not surprising that *Uncle Tom's Cabin* is a profoundly domestic novel (see Kelley). Stowe's first auditors were the friends and family members who made up the Stowe household.

Her second audience was the increasingly large readership of the *Era*. When Bailey began the *Era* in 1847, his weekly circulation was just 8,000, quite substantial compared with other antislavery newspapers. By early 1853, the circulation peaked at 28,000, which meant not only that it surpassed all other abolitionist papers but also that it was among the largest selling newspapers in the country (Harrold 139). Certainly the phenomenal success of *Uncle Tom's Cabin* had a great deal to do with the success of the newspaper, but even before 1851 Bailey was attracting good audiences with the general high quality of his paper. An array of well-informed correspondents covered national and international affairs quite competently, and Bailey published a range of good literature. Taking justifiable pride in the literature he published, Bailey commented that the twenty-one books that had been issued from material first appearing in the *Era* constituted a "pretty fair contribution to American Literature, for one newspaper" (qtd. in Harrold 189).

Bailey announced on 8 May 1851, that a new serial would begin soon, entitled *Uncle Tom's Cabin; or, the Man that Was a Thing*. By the time the first installment appeared on 5 June, the title had changed to *Uncle Tom's Cabin; or, Life among the Lowly*. The reason for the change in title is not clear; the second suggests a religious piety that neatly captures within the title both the radical and the conservative elements in the book. I have suggested elsewhere that the effect of serialization carried with it the necessity of a broad focus for the work itself and pressure on a writer to create a large cast of characters (S. B. Smith, "Serialization"). Like Dickens, who invented multiple characters and plotlines in his serials, Stowe provided not just a story about the growth of a single character but also a series of incidents in the lives of slaves and slaveholders. Her second subtitle points directly to the ensemble of characters that make up the scenes of *Uncle Tom's Cabin*. Instead of following the linear progress of a single character, Stowe imagined a variety of memorable characters—Uncle Tom, Eliza, George, Mrs. Shelby, Augustine St. Clare, Little Eva, and Topsy—whom readers could recall in subsequent episodes, even if they did not appear for weeks at a time. This creation of striking characters was crucial to the serial novelist, who was more concerned with scenes that had to work as independent installments than with the full integration of plot lines.

Beyond the obvious difficulties of writing and publishing a novel serially, Stowe also had to deal with sending her work to Washington, DC, on a regular basis. *Uncle Tom's Cabin* appeared in installments of roughly a chapter a week, evidently according to an agreement between Bailey and Stowe. But variations of several kinds sometimes altered the publication schedule. One no doubt resulted from the difficulty of getting mail from Brunswick, Maine, to Washington, DC, in a timely fashion. On 21 August and 30 October, Bailey announced that chapters 12 and 19 arrived too late for inclusion, and on 18 December, he explained that he had received no word from Stowe about chapter 27. At other times chapters were published together (as in the first installment which includes chapters 1 and 2) or were split in parts and came out as separate installments, as space in the *Era* dictated. These complications placed additional demands on the editor, writer, and reader, effectively extending the time with which all were engaged in the production and reception of the text.

From the beginning, determining the length of the work concerned Stowe. Her editor naturally wanted a sufficient sense of the structure and plan of the serial in order to manage space in the newspaper; later, when Stowe sold the copyright of the novel to John P. Jewett in the spring of 1852 before the serial had completed its run, Jewett urged her to conclude the novel quickly because he worried that the novel would be too long and therefore unprofitable to publish. But readers of the serial did not want the story to end too quickly. Bailey occasionally published enthusiastic letters of praise from readers; on 27 November 1851, a subscriber wrote to say that "we hope she will not be in a hurry to finish it," while another prayed "that she may keep it going all the winter." These and other letters suggest the intimacy of serialized publication; much like the television serials of today, literature became a part of the day-to-day lives of readers.

Throughout 1851 and 1852, the ongoing installments of *Uncle Tom's Cabin* were a stunning success for Bailey, the *Era*, and for Stowe. By the time Jewett contracted to publish the novel in 1852, Stowe was the most popular novelist of the day. Because of his wife's keen interest in *Uncle Tom's Cabin*, Jewett (who had not read the novel as it appeared in the *Era*) offered Stowe a contract of ten percent of the sales for the book, which was not unusual in the mid–nineteenth century. Calvin Stowe, who handled the negotiations on his wife's behalf, was uncertain of how the book would sell (F. Wilson 277; an early biography of Stowe suggests that Calvin hoped his wife would be able to buy a good silk dress with the money from the book). In the first week of publication, the book sold over 10,000 copies; the numbers quickly rose to 300,000 by the end of the year.[5] *Uncle Tom's Cabin* was the runaway best-seller of the nineteenth century, heavily promoted by Jewett in a well-executed advertising campaign and spurred on by the many responses and imitators that quickly followed.

From the beginning, response to the novel divided into oppositions. Good questions for students to pursue include, Is the book art or propaganda? How did Northern and Southern readings of the book differ? What were the different responses of black and white readers? What was the social and historical effect of the book?

The responses to the first question—whether the novel was literature or not—captured the attention of many commentators (see Gossett, *American Culture* 164–211; Railton 74–89). Reading an advance copy that Stowe sent, Charles Dickens considered the book "a fine one with a great and gallant purpose in it, and worthy of its reputation," although he also felt that there were various defects in the novel, especially in characterization (808). Elizabeth Ammons brings together a collection of nineteenth-century reviews in the Norton Critical Edition of *Uncle Tom's Cabin*, which students can examine easily. Among the most interesting is that of George Sand, who found that the great merits of the work overshadowed the faults and who indeed suggested that Stowe's novel revealed the shortcomings of contemporary definitions of literary talent. In a letter to Bailey outlining the progress on the serial, Stowe had commented:

> My vocation is simply that of a painter, and my object will be to hold up in the most lifelike and graphic manner possible slavery, its reverses, changes, and the Negro character, which I have had ample opportunities for studying. There is no arguing with *pictures*, and everybody is impressed by them, whether they mean to be or not.
>
> (qtd. in Van Why and French 17)

To Sand, writing for *La Presse* (17 Dec. 1852), the book certainly fulfilled that aim; Sand commented, "In matters of art there is but one rule, to paint and to move. And where shall we find creations more complete, types more vivid, situations more touching, more original, than in 'Uncle Tom'" (461). Prominent American writers had mixed reactions to the literary merits of the novel. Emerson seems to have found it appealing, while Henry Wadsworth Longfellow was enthusiastic about the way in which the book captured his attention and imagination. Although not an early admirer, James Russell Lowell wrote in 1859 that Stowe had "creative genius" (qtd. in F. Wilson 442). While it is probable that other literary figures of the day such as Louisa May Alcott, Whitman, Dickinson, and Melville read the book (they would certainly have known about its success), they did not comment on it publicly or even in extant letters (see Gossett, *American Culture* 165–68; Baym, *Novels* 220–23). Even Thoreau, who undoubtedly did not read *Uncle Tom's Cabin* or any other novel of the day, owned a figurine of Uncle Tom and Little Eva, given to him by a fugitive slave he helped to escape.[6] Few writers would have gone as far, however, as an editor at *Harper's* who praised it as a "work of high literary art" with "qualities of permanent literary value" (qtd. in Baym, *Novels* 221). Fanny Fern (Sara Willis Parton), Stowe's fellow student at Catharine Beecher's school, was just beginning her journalism career when she reviewed *Uncle Tom's Cabin* on 28 May 1853 for the *Olive Branch*. In a witty commentary that neatly exposes the jealousy of many literary figures who responded negatively to Stowe's book, Fern asked:

> Do you suppose that you can quietly take the wind out of everybody's sails, the way you have, without having harpoons, and lampoons, and all sorts of *miss*—iles thrown after you? No indeed; every distanced scribbler is perfectly frantic; they stoutly protest that your book shows no genius, which fact is unfortunately corroborated by the difficulty your publishers find in disposing of it; they are transported with rage in proportion as *you* are translated.   (Fern 256)

Depending on the amount of time that a teacher wishes to take on the art and propaganda question, students might also be asked to read sections of George Orwell's essay "Charles Dickens," in which Orwell asserts that "all art is propaganda" (56); this can serve as a departure point for a discussion about how that statement undercuts the traditional distinction that has placed novels like *Uncle Tom's Cabin* or *Bleak House* into an inferior literary category. Teachers might also wish to refer to the section on literary narratives in *The Cambridge History of American Literature* (Bercovitch 607–777) for a discussion of how art and propaganda are linked in a variety of narratives in the nineteenth century.

Questions of art aside, students should clearly understand that the great majority of the reviews and reactions to *Uncle Tom's Cabin* depended upon the writer's political and geographic orientation. Among white Northern abolitionists, the book happily revived what some saw as a lagging interest in the antislavery cause after the first flush of anger over the passage of the Fugitive Slave Law had waned. One enthusiastic admirer was the Unitarian clergyman William Henry Channing, who wrote that the book had inspired him to further action in the antislavery cause (qtd. in Gossett, *American Culture* 167). In one of the longest reviews of the book, William Lloyd Garrison wrote ardently about the book in his *Liberator* and sympathized with the abuse that Stowe was suffering at the hands of the Southern press. Some abolitionists, however, had reservations about the book. For example, the reviewer for the *National Antislavery Standard* objected to colonization as the solution to slavery (Review).

Inviting students to compare the Northern abolitionist response to the novel with the Southern opposition can be very fruitful and can be easily accomplished by assigning George F. Holmes's review in the *Southern Literary Messenger* (18 Oct. 1852). This long review, readily available in the Norton Critical Edition (ed. Ammons) and other collections, is especially useful since Holmes offered objections that other Southerners would also voice. He said that Stowe knew little or nothing of the actual conditions of slavery, nothing of the economy of the South, and nothing of blacks as a race inferior to whites.

Understandably, the questions of the artistic merit of the novel were of rather less importance to black readers deeply concerned about the issue of slavery and their future in the United States. However, many black reviewers welcomed the power of the novel as an antislavery weapon yet had serious reservations about other issues in the novel, especially Stowe's advocacy of colonization.[7] Although Frederick Douglass strongly opposed colonization, he enthusiastically supported both Stowe and her book. As editor of *Frederick Douglass' Paper* in Rochester, New York, he published reviews and dozens of letters about the novel. William J. Wilson, in his regular column signed "Ethiop," observed, "Mrs. Beecher Stowe has deserved well of her country, in thus bringing *Uncle Tom's Cabin*, and all its associations [. . .] into these Northern regions, and placing it upon the Northern track, and sending it thence round the land" (466). William Wells Brown, at this time an exile living in England in order to escape the Fugitive Slave Law, wrote a letter that Douglass published in which he says that the novel "has come down like a morning's sunlight, unfolding all eyes upon the 'peculiar institution,' and awakening sympathy in hearts that never before felt for the slave" (qtd. in Banks 214). For many, however, the colonization solution offered in Stowe's "Concluding Remarks" could not be erased from the book, and Douglass published letters and even a poem in his *Paper* deploring the notion that blacks could simply be returned to Africa. On 11 May 1852, the American and Foreign Anti-Slavery Society of Rochester passed a resolution specifically condemning Stowe's favorable treatment of colonization. Examining the debates that Douglass hosted in the pages of his *Paper* is a good place for students to learn a great deal about black responses to *Uncle Tom's Cabin* and to begin to understand the questions that this book raised for the future of blacks in America.

No introduction to the contextual history of *Uncle Tom's Cabin* is complete without some attention to the dramatic adaptations that began to appear virtually as soon as the novel was published and the serial ended in the *Era*. These adaptations had an enormous influence on society in the 1850s and clearly did a great deal to keep the antislavery issue alive. As Thomas F. Gossett has observed, even more people saw a performance of *Uncle Tom's Cabin* than read the book, and the dramatic versions strongly affected the general reaction and response to Stowe's novel (*American Culture* 261–83). The popularity of stage adaptations of *Uncle Tom's Cabin* also changed the history of theater in America. According to historians of American drama, English actors and English plays—especially Shakespeare—largely dominated the stage from the mid-eighteenth century through much of the nineteenth century (Hodge 22–23). Margaret Fuller, in her essay "American Literature" (1846), had complained of this dominance, criticizing the "staleness" of a play entitled *Town and Country* (134). Following such criticism by Fuller, Emerson, and other powerful literary voices, there were many efforts to introduce plays by American writers with native themes. For instance, numerous plays about the hardships of frontier life and about the Revolutionary War were performed quite successfully. But the most popular plays of the period with American themes were about Indians. From 1825 until 1850, some forty plays that included central roles for actors depicting Native Americans were performed in the major theaters of Boston, New York, Saint Louis, Atlanta, and New Orleans; these plays constituted a significant part of the total performed during this period and drew, by all accounts, large and enthusiastic audiences. (See Moody; Sitton; Hodge.)

While the Indian dramas as a whole tended to be romantic depictions of the tragic end of a way of life, the general interest in social reform in the mid-century prompted a new wave of American themes for the theater. William Henry Smith's *The Drunkard* (1844) was perhaps the most popular of the temperance plays, and the controversial issue of slavery was perceived to have dramatic possibilities in the context of the antislavery movement. Since George Aiken's successful *Helos, the Helot; or, The Revolt of Messene* (1852) concerned slavery in ancient Sparta, not surprisingly, he was among the first to adapt a version of *Uncle Tom's Cabin* for the stage.[8] When it opened in Troy, New York, on 15 November 1852, it ran for one hundred performances, and for the next thirty-five years the play toured the country. Aiken was strongly antislavery, and abolitionists immediately recognized the effect the stage could have. There are, nonetheless, a number of mixed messages that run throughout the various versions of the *Uncle Tom's Cabin* plays. How does a playwright handle the action of a book that is very long, controversial, and composed of many different characters and plots? In an early version, for instance, Aiken ends with the death of Eva. In another, he begins with the death of Eva and concludes with the death of Uncle Tom. Aiken's final version includes scenes from both. Asking students to examine the focus of a particular adaptation and compare it with others can effectively introduce the larger question of what constitutes the center of the novel itself. Black actors were never used in the performances, and tracing the various adaptations of the play throughout the nineteenth century can readily show students the history of racial attitudes. Although Aiken's version was among the best, and truer to Stowe's text than most, there were dozens of adaptations and revisions, including one that Stowe wrote in 1856 for Mary Webb, an English actress. Uncle Tom, Little Eva, and Topsy became stock characters in tableaux and short dramatic sketches; some of the more ambitious versions of the entire novel included music, dance, and live animals. P. T. Barnum staged a version for his American Museum with a set of the Mississippi River that included a steamboat spewing real smoke.

Apart from examining the nineteenth-century history of dramatic versions of *Uncle Tom's Cabin*, students might also be encouraged to investigate how the novel has continued to influence and entertain us. The early part of the twentieth century brought more adaptations of *Uncle Tom's Cabin*. One of the first movies made in America was *Tom*, a silent film produced by the Edison Company in 1902. As Misha Berson points out in a useful article about recent productions, the legacy of theatrical adaptations of *Uncle Tom's Cabin* is "a melodrama-minstrel aesthetic that is still prevalent, and a gallery of African-American stereotypes that have stuck fast to the collective psyche and are with us despite the attempts of many social critics to exorcise them" (21). Teachers who wish to explore theatrical adaptations of *Uncle Tom's Cabin* have a wealth of new materials available to them, since four new versions appeared in the 1990s. Perhaps the most unusual is *Last Supper at Uncle Tom's Cabin / The Promised Land*, a modern dance, written and choreographed by the Bill T. Jones–Arnie Zane Dance Company. The dance was first performed at the Next Wave Festival, the Brooklyn Academy of Music, in 1990 and won two Bessie awards. The San Francisco Mime Troupe and the Lorraine Hansberry Theatre produced *I Ain't Yo' Uncle*, adapted from the original Aiken script by Robert Alexander. On 5 March 1993, *I Ain't Yo' Uncle*, played to Los Angeles audiences anxiously awaiting the outcome of two important trials—the federal trial of the the three police officers who arrested and assaulted Rodney King on 3 March 1991 and the state trial of the three men who assaulted Reginald Denny, a truck driver, during the Los Angeles riots. These trials, in the aftermath of the 1992 riots in Los Angeles, directly involved issues of racism and civil rights. Consciously linking the play with current events in Los Angeles and several other American cities, stills of contemporary, racially charged incidents occasionally illuminated the stage set, including one from the videotaped beating of Rodney King. Another new dramatic version of Stowe's novel is *Unkle Tomm's Kabin: A Deconstruction of the Novel by Harriet Beecher Stowe*, a collaborative creation of Seattle's Empty Space Theatre and the Alice B. Theatre, a gay and lesbian acting troupe. The most recent dramatization, *Uncle Tom's Cabin; or, Life among the Lowly*, appeared in New York in the fall of 1997. The work is a compilation of several versions of the play interwoven with slave narratives, and it was directed by Floraine Kay and Randolph Curtis Rand (M. Jefferson E1). Attention to the influence of Stowe's novel on popular entertainment today and in the past clearly demonstrates the power of *Uncle Tom's Cabin*.

In the end, any teacher of *Uncle Tom's Cabin* must decide how much time to devote to the social, cultural, historical, and political background of the novel. It has been my experience, however, that a grasp of some contextual essentials better prepares students to understand the novel and to debate the larger questions of race, gender, and class that it raises. Indeed, *Uncle Tom's Cabin* is a very good example of a book that is deeply embedded and implicated in the context in which it was written. To consider the novel's original timeliness and then to think about how it speaks to us today represent important steps in understanding the way literature is shaped by both the writer's and the reader's expectations and experiences.

NOTES

[1]Stowe contributed *The Minister's Wooing* to the *Atlantic* as a serial novel that ran from December 1858 until December 1859.

[2]I am drawing here on my essay "Serialization and the Nature of *Uncle Tom's Cabin*" (see S. B. Smith). For another view of the context of the *Era* and the composition of *Uncle Tom's Cabin*, as well as an excellent discussion of the novel in relation to other frequently taught narratives about slavery, see Robbins, especially 535–41.

[3]See Kirkham 3n1 for a discussion of this quotation and Bacon's account of the Beechers' fame. Kirkham is also the standard source for details of the textual history of *Uncle Tom's Cabin*.

[4]For an indispensable guide to the complicated history of the European revolutions, see L. Reynolds; see also Reynolds and Smith 2–35.

[5]See Hedrick, *Stowe* 223–24, and Kirkham 140–49 for details of Stowe's relationship with Jewett.

[6]See Thoreau, *Journal 4* 630 for a photograph of the figurine.

[7]For indispensable surveys of black responses to *Uncle Tom's Cabin*, see Banks; R. Levine.

[8]A new edition of Aiken's play appears in Wilmeth 181–246.

Stowe, the Abolition Movement, and Prevailing Theories of Race in Nineteenth-Century America

Susan M. Nuernberg

We all know that one cannot be for slavery and for racial equality at the same time. We often assume that the reverse holds true as well, when, in fact, acceptance of racial equality is *not* a necessity for being antislavery. Recall, for example, that African Americans in this country did not achieve civil rights until one century after emancipation.

Readers who reject *Uncle Tom's Cabin* because it portrays African Americans in an offensive way should know that Harriet Beecher Stowe did not write it to advocate racial equality in the secular and social sphere. She aimed to put an end to slavery, to what stood in opposition to her notions of Christian morality, which required the abolition of slavery to purify the nation of sin. Deriving not from ideas about earthly equality but from the concept of equality before God, Stowe's ideology is progressive on abolition but conservative on race because it calls for a retreat to traditional religious and moral values. While she spoke out in *Uncle Tom's Cabin* against the injustices of slavery, she avoided the subject of racial equality on the economic and political level.[1]

To help clarify Stowe's views, teachers can acquaint students with the prevailing attitudes and ideas on race during Stowe's period. In the first half of the nineteenth century, racial thought in the United States developed along two separate currents: the realm of science and the realm of romanticism and religion. Pre-Darwinian scientific theories of racial difference started with the premise that blacks and Native Americans were inferior to whites and then proceeded to provide explanations for the racial dominance of whites. Regardless of whether differences were labeled innate (polygenesis) or the product of environment (monogenesis), the fictitious superiority of the white race was constantly confirmed and substantiated with apparent scientific objectivity and authority—that is, with selective facts and evidence that supported this thesis. Proslavery advocates used science when claiming that blacks benefited from a protective social status or deserved animal-like treatment because of their inferiority to whites or their subhuman status. In contrast, romantic racialism, a term coined by George M. Fredrickson, acknowledged that blacks were different from whites but saw them in flattering terms as exhibiting Christian virtues (that whites lacked) by remaining childlike, affectionate, docile, and patient under the exceedingly degrading conditions and provocations of slavery (see Fredrickson, *Black Image*). It accepted inherent diversity over racial environmentalism, it was compatible with Christian humanitarianism, and it was opposed to slavery. Abolitionists voiced romantic racialist views in proclaiming that it was a sin to take advantage of the blacks' naturally amiable qualities by keeping them in servitude.

The dominant view of eighteenth-century science on the origin of racial differences was single creation, or monogenesis, the idea that all races were members of the same species and had a common remote ancestry and that attributed differences in color, anatomy, intelligence, temperament, and morality to environment. One of the most vigorous champions of monogenesis was Samuel Stanhope Smith, a Presbyterian minister and president of the College of New Jersey (now Princeton University), who argued in his 1787 book *Essay on the Causes of the Variety of Complexion and Figure in the Human Species* that differences could be attributed to differing physical and social environments, especially to climate and to ways of life produced by "savagery" and "civilization" (Fredrickson, *Black Image* 72). Like most other eighteenth-century advocates of the unity of the human species and of white racial superiority, he reiterated the specious assertion that the white race was the original human norm from which other races had degenerated.[2] Willy-nilly he exposed the absurd logic of environmentalism by insisting that a literal transformation of one race into another must be possible through the power of environment. Since no one had ever observed whites turning into blacks or blacks turning back into whites, the dominant eighteenth-century justification of racial difference toppled into disrepute.

Most early-nineteenth-century learned people agreed that racial differences were innate rather than the product of environmental forces, and they rationalized white superiority by declaring that there must have been separate and unequal creations. One of the first Americans to espouse the notion of polygenesis, that blacks and Native Americans were members of separate and permanently inferior species of the genus *Homo* and not simply "savage" or "semicivilized" varieties of the same species, was Charles Caldwell, a native of South Carolina who practiced medicine in Philadelphia. Using the accepted biblical chronology of Archbishop James Ussher, he argued in his 1830 book, *Thoughts on the Original Unity of the Human Race*, that blacks were known to have existed 3,445 years ago, which was only 743 years after Noah's ark—not enough time for environmental forces to shape a new race. Nor, in his estimation, could environment have produced the vast intellect of the Caucasian; that must have been, he contended, a "gift of nature" that had been withheld from inferior races (qtd. in Fredrickson, *Black Image* 73). The doctrine of polygenesis, which had emerged in the eighteenth-century scientific revolution,[3] was popularized anew in the 1840s and 1850s by ethnologists. The "American school of ethnology" affirmed on the basis of cranial measurements and other archaeological evidence that blacks were permanently inferior to whites.

The theory of polygenesis developed by leading exponents of the new scientific ethnology, such as Josiah C. Nott of Mobile, Alabama, amounted to a scientific apology for black slavery, Indian extermination, and imperial expansion. Although recognized as a leading scientist in his day, Nott was stridently proslavery and described his questionable and biased research in letters to James Henry Hammond in the summer of 1845 as "the nigger business" or "niggerology"

(Fredrickson, *Black Image* 78).[4] Nott and other members of the school of ethnology, including Samuel George Morton, a Quaker from Philadelphia, and George R. Gliddon, an Egyptologist originally from England, were respected practitioners of a mode of knowledge that we no longer accept; however, their views are indicative of the racial preconceptions of many scientists and intellectuals of the period who defended America's racial status quo. *Types of Mankind*, the eight-hundred-page study of separate species of humankind by Nott and Gliddon, sold out immediately in 1854. Its main thesis is that pure-blooded nonwhite races are incapable of high intelligence or of civilization without the infusion of some white blood. The typing of the races, as discussed in Nott and Gliddon's book, originated in the eighteenth-century scientific revolution and was detailed by a number of writers, including the Swedish botanist Karl von Linné, who established the binomial method of designating plants and animals.

While science disagreed on the question of how the races had originated (as different species or as degenerations or varieties of the same), it never questioned the assumption of a racial hierarchy. Of course, not everyone who believed that the races differed fundamentally embraced scientific racial determinism and its attendant stereotype of blacks as lacking the enterprise and intellect of whites. Scientists tended to see only the "practical fact" of inherent black inferiority; meanwhile, others had discovered redeeming virtues and even evidences of black superiority. Those who subscribed to the priority of feeling over intellect and construed black-white differences in terms of relativism rather than the hierarchy sanctioned both by Romanticism and by evangelical religion came up with a strikingly different concept of black differences. Instead of conceiving of blacks as "savage" or "semicivilized," romantic racialists tended to endorse the "child" stereotype of the most sentimental school of proslavery plantation romances and to reject slavery itself because it took unfair advantage of the blacks' innocence and good nature.[5] Coexisting as a separate tradition alongside mainstream racist thought, romantic racialism was widely espoused by Northern humanitarians who, like Stowe, were antislavery.

Notions of white or Anglo-Saxon superiority were common among white abolitionists. The famous Unitarian preacher Theodore Parker names the supposedly hereditary traits of the Anglo-Saxon in his sermon "The Nebraska Question" of 12 February 1854. These traits include the Anglo-Saxon's "restless disposition to invade and conquer other lands; his haughty contempt of humbler tribes which leads him to subvert, enslave, kill, and exterminate; his fondness for material things [. . .]; his love of personal liberty [and his] most profound respect for [. . .] established law [. . .]. And his [. . .] inflexible, industrious, and unconquerable will" (qtd. in Fredrickson, *Black Image* 100). Such descriptions of the Anglo-Saxon were being formulated and popularized at the very time when the slavery controversy focused attention on the African character as being either subhuman, as in Caldwell's view, or morally superhuman, as perceived by the romantic racialists.

Writing to admonish whites to abolish slavery and purify the religion of sin, Stowe shows herself to be a romantic racialist by having certain black characters represent all that whites are not. Tom becomes a symbol of the Christian virtue and piety lacking in white America, as evidenced by passage of the Fugitive Slave Law in 1850 that forced the North to police and return the South's black runaways. Tom is excessively meek, patient, and humble. He is affectionate, forgiving, compassionate, attached to family, nonviolent, and trusting. Stowe's treatment of black characters is so ambivalent that it is impossible for us to determine how much of Tom's meekness is due to his religious virtues and how much to his racial heritage. Stowe describes him as "a large, broad-chested, powerfully-made man, of a full glossy black, and a face whose truly African features were characterized by an expression of grave and steady good sense, united with much kindliness and benevolence" (18). When he realizes that he will be sold away from his family, he responds not with resentment or anger. "I'm in the Lord's hands," he says; "nothin' can go no furder than he lets it;— and thar's *one* thing I can thank him for. It's *me* that's sold and going down [the river], and not you [his wife] nur the chil'en. Here you're safe;—what comes will come only on me, and the Lord, he'll help me,—I know he will" (81).

Although Stowe forges a link between alleged Negro virtues and Christian ones, she was not the first romantic racialist to do so. This was the theme of a series of lectures given in Cincinnati, where Stowe lived, during 1837 and 1838 by Alexander Kinmont and published in 1839 as *Twelve Lectures on Man*. Blacks were destined to develop a "far nobler civilization" than whites, Kinmont reasoned, because the white's "innate love of dominion" rendered him or her "almost constitutionally unable to be a true Christian" (qtd. in Fredrickson, *Black Image* 105). Stowe appropriates Kinmont's rhetoric of the black as a natural Christian in her portrayal of Uncle Tom as childlike, affectionate, docile, and patient. In addition, George Harris's claim that "the African race has peculiarities, yet to be unfolded in the light of civilization and Christianity, which, if not the same with those of the Anglo-Saxon, may prove to be, morally, of even a higher type" (375–76) clearly echoes Kinmont's vision of millennial perfection for blacks.[6]

Kinmont's rhetoric of the moral superiority of the enslaved black appealed not only to Stowe but also to other white abolitionists, among them William Ellery Channing, who in his 1840 essay "Emancipation" emphasized the idea that since the African nature was "affectionate and easily touched," blacks were peculiarly susceptible to religious experience. Channing argued that the Africans were natural candidates for Christian perfection because they "carr[y] within [them], much more than we, the germs of meek, long-suffering, loving virtue" (qtd. in Fredrickson, *Black Image* 106). Although the condition of the slave was permanent and even hereditary, there has never been a germ or gene for "loving virtue" or for "meekness" in any race or individual. Passivity was a survival-oriented reaction to social and economic strife and not an innate racial characteristic as Stowe, Channing, and Kinmont imply. Many slaves accepted their fate with docility and apparent resignation; however, such passivity is a form of resistance, cultivating patience and waiting for the right opportunity to ignite. History belies the myth of black passivity by providing countless examples of discontented slaves who escaped to the North or to Canada via the Underground Railroad and of revolts and insurrections involving groups of slaves whose aim was personal freedom.

The most controversial aspect of Stowe's rhetoric of race, aside from Tom's excessive meekness, and the one that twentieth-century students as well as scholars feel they cannot afford to let pass uncriticized, is her endorsement of emigration when she depicts George Harris relocating his family to Liberia in search of "an African nationality" at the end of the book. The rationale for this cultural and fictional endorsement is rooted in the period's confusion of social reality and racial differences.

Stowe, like Kinmont, saw Africa millennially as the home of a future high civilization. She argues through the character of George that blacks *ought* to return to Africa. In the chapter "Results," Stowe quotes a letter of George's in which he embraces colonization and rejects social equality as his goal. George writes, "The desire and yearning of my soul is for an African *nationality*. I want a people that shall have a tangible, separate existence of its own" (374). The American Colonization Society, founded early in the nineteenth century, was supported largely by Protestant clergy who hoped to establish a colony of converted former slaves in Liberia to contribute to the conversion and redemption of Africa.[7] The aim of colonization, besides the physical removal of free blacks, was the gradual elimination of slavery. This goal was to be accomplished by encouraging voluntary manumission and by offering a way of freeing slaves without augmenting the number of free blacks on American soil. Many of the members of colonization societies believed that blacks could not be assimilated into American society and, if freed, would remain an alien and troublesome presence. Free blacks, however, would thrive in Liberia because their efforts to improve themselves would no longer be hampered by white prejudice and discrimination, which were seen as fundamental facts of American life that could not be changed.

Stowe embraces this stance when she has George renounce social equality with white Americans. George's letter continues:

> But, you will tell me, our race have equal rights to mingle in the American republic as the Irishman, the German, the Swede. Granted, they have. We *ought* to be free to meet and mingle, —to rise by our individual worth, without any consideration of caste or color; and they who deny us this right are false to their own professed principles of human equality. We ought, in particular, to be allowed *here*. We have *more* than the rights of common men; —we have the claim of an injured race for reparation. But, then, *I do not want it*; I want a country, a nation, of my own.
> (375)

Stowe appropriates the ideas and language of the colonization movement to talk about the desirability, in George's perspective, of expatriation for free blacks. The most "white" of her black characters, George chooses a return to Africa over social equality with whites in America. By having the victim disavow any desire for social justice, Stowe resolves the conflict for those who support abolition but *not* racial equality in the social sphere.

Many abolitionists shared Stowe's stand on colonization, as evidenced in their wide acceptance of her novel. Her position, however, was only one among many articulated within the abolitionist movement of her day. Clear alternatives are presented in the writings of Frederick Douglass and Martin R. Delany, both of whom, like Stowe, criticized the Fugitive Slave Law but, unlike her, opposed the aims and methods of the colonization movement. Frederick Douglass rejected colonization, as he bluntly told Stowe in a letter of 8 March 1853, which he published in *Frederick Douglass' Paper* in December 1853, because "we are *here*, and we are likely to remain. Individuals emigrate—nations never. We have grown up with this republic, and I see nothing in her character, or even in the character of the American people as yet, which compels the belief that we must leave the United States" (qtd. in R. Levine 535). Douglass saw a real need to "elevate" blacks in America through practical education in industrial and mechanical skills from their condition of poverty, ignorance, and degradation and from their forced dependency on merely servile occupations (R. Levine 530).

Douglass's fellow African American, Delany, however, felt that blacks could overcome white racism only by developing a separate course of action for themselves. This action was necessary because he saw the primary goal of whites to be the subjugation of blacks. He envisioned black economic self-determination through the development of large-scale cotton, sugar, and rice enterprises in the Caribbean that would successfully compete against and destroy the economy of the Southern states where these goods were produced with slave labor. Delany's embrace of the back-to-Africa movement differs from Stowe's in that Delany saw the regeneration of Africa as thwarting white racial domination, whereas Stowe saw it as fulfilling a prophesy of millennial perfection on earth. Most African Americans, however, such as Douglass, felt that blacks should continue to work for equality in America (Griffith 28).

Likewise differing significantly from Stowe, William Lloyd Garrison, the most radical of the famous white American antislavery advocates, questioned her stance on nonresistance, which, like colonization, legitimately troubles many readers. Garrison points out that for her and other whites it is acceptable to return blow for blow, but they expect blacks to turn the other cheek. He found her use of different standards of conduct for whites and blacks objectionable, as well as her use of religious principles to discuss social injustices. "When [blacks] are spit upon and buffeted, outraged and oppressed, talk not then of a non-resisting Savior—it is fanaticism! Talk not of overcoming evil with good—it is madness! Talk not of peacefully submitting to chains and stripes—

it is base servility! Talk not of servants being obedient to their masters—let the blood of the tyrants flow" (qtd. in Gossett, *American Culture* 170). Garrison's critique of Stowe's elevation of black character through the portrayal of Uncle Tom as a flawless and "non-resisting Savior" anticipates the most devastating criticism *Uncle Tom's Cabin* would receive in the twentieth century.

Reminding us that the issue of *Uncle Tom's Cabin* and race theory is by no means simply a nineteenth-century one, James Baldwin in his now famous 1949 essay, "Everybody's Protest Novel," correctly remarks that Uncle Tom is not a human being but an inspiring myth. Baldwin attacks Stowe for robbing Tom of his humanity and his sex and declares:

> Here, black equates with evil and white with grace; if being mindful of the necessity of good works, she could not cast out the blacks—a wretched, huddled mass, apparently, claiming, like an obsession, her inner eye—she could not embrace them either without purifying them of sin. She must cover their intimidating nakedness, robe them in white, the garments of salvation; only thus could she herself be delivered from ever-present sin, only thus could she bury, as St. Paul demanded, "the carnal man, the man of the flesh." (498)

Baldwin gives us insight into the sexual dynamics of the nineteenth-century white race theory that spiritualized blacks. Baldwin shows us that what is at stake sexually is the idea of neutering black men. Nowhere is this better illustrated than in Stowe's characterization of Tom as devoid of carnal need, while George Harris's neutering comes in the form of his being sent to Africa to preclude him from mixing and begetting in America.

Stowe's book broadcast and perpetuated notions of race that were simply wrong. As J. C. Furnas notes, however, those same notions of race "plague us today" ("Goodbye" 105). Stowe's ideas are confused and contradictory, they were debated in her own time, and they are representative in general of ideas and attitudes held by others in the abolitionist movement and in antebellum American culture. Once those facts are established in the classroom, the questions I believe we need to raise with students are, Do we downgrade Stowe because she shared many of the misconceptions about race common in her day? How do her views affect our estimate of her humanitarian point of view?

Of course, there are many answers, each depending on who is reading, who is teaching, and how discussion is framed and guided. I emphasize that Tom does in fact have religious traits that Stowe admired—and not just in blacks. He represents Stowe's idea that the highest virtue is Christian love. Stowe herself claims to have had a vision while taking communion in church in February 1851 of a saintly black man being mercilessly flogged and praying for his torturers as he died, a vision of a black Christ that inspired both the character of Uncle Tom and the story's climax in his death/victory.[8] Tom *is* too noble, meek, and forgiving to be a realistic character, and Stowe does present him as if these spiritual qualities were racial attributes. In *A Key to* Uncle Tom's Cabin, she states her attitudes on the spiritual character of blacks explicitly: "The Negro race is confessedly more simple, docile, childlike and affectionate, than other races," she says, "and hence the divine graces of love and faith, when in-breathed by the Holy Spirit, find in their temperament a more congenial atmosphere" (41 [1853 ed.]). Obviously this description was meant as a compliment, but if blacks have these qualities because of their racial character, why credit them for it? Stowe did not hold the "good" whites in the novel to any such standard of virtue and holiness. Gossett is correct in noting that Stowe's white characters are presented as "all the more admirable because they do not take the blows of fate meekly" (*American Culture* 107). In spiritually elevating the black as thoroughly virtuous, she is depicting the spiritual shortcomings of whites to make the abolition of slavery palatable to white readers.

What does *Uncle Tom's Cabin* accomplish in the social milieu of the period? Does it argue for social justice and the promotion of racial equality? No! Does it contest white political supremacy? No! Does it concern itself with the place of free blacks in American society? No! It does, however, vilify slavery and by so doing help the cause of abolition. Like other abolitionists, Stowe tended to see herself as a moral and religious reformer, not a social reformer. She writes in the preface to *A Key* that her goal in writing is "to bring this subject of slavery, as a moral and religious question, before the minds of all those who profess to be followers of Christ in this country" (iv). In doing so, we might note, she could fulfill her own religious responsibilities and help to reassert Christian influence over the nation at large. She was the daughter of the preacher Lyman Beecher, one of the most powerful rhetoricians of the Second Great Awakening in New England; the wife of Calvin Stowe, a minister and professor of religion at Bowdoin College in Maine; and the sister of six ministers. It is certain that she understood the moral force of her evangelical argument against slavery and that she was sensitive to the power of language to represent eternal values and to change human hearts.

Stowe writes about innate virtue and an alleged disposition to being religious in the black race to emphasize what the white race lacks or must acquire: precisely those virtues and the inclination to worship God the way blacks could. Her goal of helping to free blacks from slavery doubled as an argument in favor of purifying the Christian religion. At the same time, she alleviates the white fear of a racially mixed society by offering the image of a free black, who is at home only in Africa—an idea that was rightly criticized in her own time just as it is today.

NOTES

Initial research for this essay was conducted during a summer seminar sponsored by the National Endowment for the Humanities in 1992. An earlier version of this essay appears in Lowance,Westbook, and De Prospo.

[1]For more information on the reception of *Uncle Tom's Cabin*, see Ammons, *Critical Essays*, and R. Levine.

[2]For excellent discussion of S. S. Smith's views, see Jordan's introduction to Smith's *Essay* and Fredrickson, *Black Image* 71–76.

[3]One of the first scientists to view the human being as an object of study in the same fashion that other animals were and to recognize the "historicalness" of nature was Johann Friedrich Blumenbach (1752–1840), the founder of scientific anthropology (see Baron).

[4]For more information on the American school of ethnology and on Nott's views, see Fredrickson, *Black Image* 77–82.

[5]For an exhaustive discussion of concepts of blacks in proslavery plantation romances, see Tracy. For more information on romantic racialism, see Fredrickson, *Black Image* 97–102.

[6]For more information on Kinmont and his ideas, see Fredrickson 104–07, and Gossett, *American Culture* 83–85.

[7]For more information on the colonization movement, see Fredrickson, *Black Image* 8–11, and Griffith 109–12.

[8]For an account of Stowe's vision, see Douglas 8; for a discussion of Tom as a black Christ, see Ammons, "Stowe's Dream."

Uncle Tom's Cabin and Conventional Nineteenth-Century Domestic Ideology

Lisa Logan

Students usually come to *Uncle Tom's Cabin* knowing only that Stowe's book was an antislavery tract, a protest novel. Without an understanding of nineteenth-century domestic ideology, however, they miss many of the implications and the popular sweep of Stowe's critique. I often begin discussion by asking students what arguments the book makes for slavery's abolition. Their answers—that slavery makes legal the objectification of human beings, violates democratic principles, destroys families, and undermines Christianity—suggest the scope of the slavery debate in nineteenth-century America, its power to enter not just the lives of those directly involved in the debate but also the homes of everyday citizens. Like the book itself, which bulges with subplots and minor characters, Stowe's arguments against slavery can seem wide-ranging and disconnected unless understood through her main argument: that slavery undermines domestic ideology and, therefore, threatens the foundation of American society.

My approach is first to introduce students to a historical sense of the "cult of true womanhood" and the idealized status of the home in the nineteenth century as a separate sphere or haven from the public world of industry and capital. I then encourage students to examine the tensions present in such an apparently binary system, one that opposes home and market, spirit and body, heart and head. Last, we discuss how these tensions work themselves out (or not) in *Uncle Tom's Cabin*.[1]

By exploring the economic, religious, and political contexts and implications of domestic ideology, students are able to connect Stowe's antislavery arguments with her ambitious, woman-centered agenda. As many historians have argued, transformations in industry, commerce, and agriculture throughout the late eighteenth and the nineteenth centuries led to alterations in the family itself; it functioned less and less as a unit of production, and the duties and status of women in the home also shifted. Especially in the middle and upper middle classes, men worked outside the home as women and their labor were increasingly dissociated from the public domain. The work women performed also shifted from domestic production (weaving, spinning, milking cows, laundering, soap and candle making, food preparation, etc.) to household management and child rearing (for discussion of the rise of domesticity, see Bloch; Cott, *Bonds* 19–62; Matthews; B. Welter). Because of these changes at a time when free women conceivably could have pursued their own independence, woman's work was elevated to a "profession" or "vocation," giving rise to the domestic ideology that Stowe and her sister Catharine Beecher espoused. The home, which came to represent a separate and feminine sphere, was idealized as a haven from the public world and its capitalist values. Proponents of this ideology viewed women's work not as drudgery, scrubbing and scouring, but as building democracy and praising God.

For students who come to the text without having interrogated dominant cultural assumptions about and definitions of the family, the gendered divison of labor idealized by Stowe and other advocates of domestic ideology often seem a "natural" result of "progress." For this reason, the difficulty of teaching about domestic ideology lies not in student comprehension but in convincing them that traditional or conventional organizations of family life in the United States are products of cultural constructions and not a natural or inevitable state of affairs. To demonstrate this point, I bring to class nineteenth-century domestic manuals, including Lydia Maria Child's *The American Frugal Housewife* (1830) and Catharine Beecher's *A Treatise on Domestic Economy* (1841), and twentieth-century women's magazines, such as *Good Housekeeping* and *Family Circle*. Comparing the contents pages in these texts can lead to discussions about surface similarities and underlying differences; and noticing specific differences helps students to link domestic advice to specific cultural moments.

Given the naturalized status and seeming innocence of the division of labor in their own homes, many students also need to see how women's work might be appropriated by a writer such as Stowe for political reasons in an age when the middle class espoused domestic ideology.[2] To demonstrate domesticity's political intent, I point students to Catharine Beecher's *Treatise on Domestic Economy*, in which she introduces systems of domestic order as a "remedy" for American women's "peculiar" situation (26). Explaining that Beecher advocated domesticity as a "branch of study" (41) and that her book was read by thousands of young women, I emphasize that Beecher's book is not mere advice to the homemaker. She argues that "the principles of democracy [. . .] are identical with the principles of Christianity" (2). She specifically links the necessity of a domestic system, especially "systematic housekeeping," to the fluctuating "state of things in this country. Every thing is moving and changing. Persons in poverty, are rising to opulence, and persons of wealth, are sinking to poverty" (16). For Beecher, this "flow of wealth" (17) makes the stability that middle-class domestic ideology imparts even more essential to the nation. Further, her remarks that "the people of this Country are under the influence of high commercial, political, and religious stimulous [sic]" and that "women are made the sympathizing companions of the other sex" (20) suggest the centrality of this ideology to the nation's moral fiber and woman's vital democratic role. Beecher implies that the country is "ill" from fluctuating socioeconomic stimuli and shifting values and that the only national remedy is a good dose of domestic order.

Stressing Stowe's (and Beecher's) political agenda is important because the values that underpin domestic ideology often seem to some students irreproachable. According to Beecher's ideal, the home represents a world governed by spiritual rather than material forces, and, within it, woman's most important charge is the religious and moral instruction of children, future democratic citizens. Beecher writes:

> the success of democratic institutions [. . .] depends upon the intellectual and moral character of the mass of people [. . .]. The formulation of the moral and intellectual character of the young is committed to the female hand. The mother writes the character of the future man [. . .]. Let the women of a country be made virtuous and intelligent, and the men will certainly be the same.   (13)

Immune to the self-serving values and caprices of industrial capitalism, the ideal or "true woman" opposed the moral degeneracy of the market with Christian values and gentle, self-sacrificing, and virtuous maternal influence. (For discussion of Beecher's work, see Sklar, Introduction v–xviii; G. Brown, *Domestic Individualism* 18–25.) I often illustrate the breadth and political import of this conception of woman's sphere with one of Beecher's house plans; in each plan, the adjacency of parlor, nursery, and kitchen constructs the home as a physical and disciplinary space (see Beecher 276, fig. 11). Beecher writes, "Thus, the mother can have her parlor, nursery, and kitchen under her eye at once" (278). I encourage students to read these rooms as sites in a national discourse. Woman, while appearing to concern herself only with her own household, actually oversees and influences the nation's future citizens (the nursery) and mediates the public and private spheres through the parlor or front room, in which all visitors are received.[3]

I also introduce students to the feminist aims of conventional domesticity by using Jane Tompkins's chapter "Sentimental Power: *Uncle Tom's Cabin* and the Politics of Literary History" in *Sensational Designs*, which I always assign. According to Tompkins, domestic ideology allotted women their own sphere and made them answerable to the ultimate authority—God. Further, Tompkins argues, the political agenda of domestic ideology had "millennial" goals: to place women at the head of a Christian kingdom on earth. In other words, Stowe, through domestic ideology, sought to "reorganize culture from the woman's point of view" (124). In such a world, the home, religion, and even those in the public sphere would derive their authority from the family and, in particular, the mother. Tompkins sees Beecher's vision as feminist both in its desire to locate power in women and in its imperialist drive. In their coauthored work, *The American Woman's Home* (1869), Beecher and her sister Harriet Beecher Stowe articulate their vision of domestic empire: "The family state then is the aptest earthly illustration of the heavenly kingdom, and in it woman is its chief minister" (Beecher and Stowe 19, qtd. in Tompkins 143). To make this point in class, I usually supplement Tompkins with Beecher and emphasize my own view that while domestic imperialism *is* political, some might not necessarily view it as feminist. Certainly, Beecher's vision makes woman the primary agent in "accomplishing the greatest work that ever was committed to human responsibility":

> It is the building of a glorious temple, whose base shall be coextensive with the bounds of the earth, whose summit shall pierce the skies, whose splendor shall beam on all lands; and those who hew the lowliest stone, as much as those who carve the highest capital, will be equally honored, when its top-stone shall be laid, with new rejoicings of the morning stars, and shoutings of the sons of God.   (*Treatise* 14)

Beecher seems to place women at the center of a new colonial power. Her vision replaces nineteenth-century industrial capitalism and manifest destiny with a boundless Christian empire that extends across the entire world and that operates according to the "womanly" values of cooperation, community, and loving nurture. (For discussion of domesticity's political implications, see the essays in Samuels, *Culture*).

Having presented this overview of domesticity and its political and feminist implications, I next begin to introduce students to some of the tensions this ideology generates. Specifically, I ask them to think about who has access to these values and to what extent self-sacrifice, virtue, piety, and submissiveness can stand as ideals for slaves. These questions arise naturally if the class has read Harriet Jacobs's *Incidents in the Life of a Slave Girl* (1861) beforehand. If not, one might assign chapter 21, "The Loophole of Retreat," in which Jacobs describes her years of confinement in a nine- by seven-foot garret. This tiny, bug- and rat-infested space preserves her from her master's pursuit and affords her the "freedom," for the first time since she was a small child, to indulge in the everyday acts of reading and sewing, which white women of the North probably took for granted. The cost of her escape cannot be called "domesticity," however, since she may not mother her children. This chapter effectively disputes the applicability of domestic values to enslaved black women, whose experiences under slavery can never approximate the ideals of virtuous mothering and home management. I have also used some of the photographs in Elizabeth Fox-Genovese's *Within the Plantation Household*, which demonstrate visually and with little explanation required the contrast between white ideals of womanhood and black women's daily realities in the South.

The process of reading domesticity in Stowe's text might begin by inviting students to create a scale of "true womanhood" and to position Stowe's female characters along it. As we discuss each woman's relationship to this ideology, we raise questions about domesticity's tensions, including its inherent racism and classism in opposing market and home, body and spirit.[4] Eventually, we reframe Tompkins's argument: From which woman's viewpoint does the novel aim to reorganize American culture? To what extent does Stowe succeed in replacing material values with spiritual ones? a market economy with a domestic one?

I often begin by asking students to constellate Stowe's white women around a domestic paradigm, which the novel frames in terms of system and economy:

> South as well as north, there are women who have an extraordinary talent for command, and tact in educating. Such are enabled, with apparent ease, and without severity, to subject to their will, and bring into harmonious and systematic order, the various members of their small estate,—to regulate their particularities, and so balance and compensate the deficiencies of one by the excess of another, as to produce a harmonious and orderly system.   (178–79)

Rachel Halliday is such a woman, and the chapters on the Quaker settlement make sense to students in a new way once they understand them in the context of nineteenth-century domestic ideology. As Jane Tompkins has astutely pointed out, Mrs. Halliday's home represents the ideal domestic state:

> The home is the center of all meaningful activity; women perform the most important tasks; work is carried on in a spirit of mutual cooperation; and the whole is guided by a Christian woman who [. . .] rules the world from her rocking chair.   ("Sentimental Power" 142)

Halliday's gentle influence seems intended as a model for loving action, and her home is an image of how the world might look if organized according to maternal values. I then ask students to consider the feasibility of this ideal; I point out that, just as Stowe's gentle suasion was said to have provoked a nation to war rather than to reform, so the pacifist Quakers resort to force to win the day. Such discussion emphasizes the utopianism underlying domesticity and shows that the domestic sphere really is constructed as a haven from the public one—a heaven on earth. By considering domesticity as an ideal, we also contextualize Stowe's work in other forms of American Romanticism, such as transcendentalism, and view these two intellectual traditions in conversation.

Students immediately notice that Mrs. Shelby embodies Beecher's ideal as well; she is described as

> a woman of a high class, both intellectually and morally. To that natural magnanimity and generosity of mind [. . .] she added high moral and religious sensibility and principle, carried out with great energy and ability into practical results.   (9)

Her irreproachability assures her influence over her slaveholding husband, who "reverenced and respected the consistency of hers, and stood, perhaps, a little in awe of her opinion [and] gave her unlimited scope in all her benevolent efforts for the comfort, instruction, and improvement of her servants" (9). The problem for Stowe, however, is that Mr. Shelby's traffic in slaves renders his wife's philosophy inconsistent with its application. Forced into an "open acknowledgment that we care for no tie, no duty, no relation, however sacred, compared with money" (29), Mrs. Shelby in essence becomes her husband's accomplice; in response, however, she undermines her husband and aids Eliza's escape. This turn of events emphasizes that, in a slave economy, domesticity is under assault and that the nation's legal structure subordinates feeling, benevolence, piety—indeed, women themselves—to the authority and shifting fortunes of capitalist patriarchy. By narrating this incident so that readers identify with Mrs. Shelby's decision and root for Eliza's safe passage, Stowe reverses the power dynamics and promotes domestic values.

Unlike Rachel Halliday and Mrs. Shelby, Marie St. Clare represents the antithesis of a mother (see Ammons, "Stowe's Dream" 164), a "woman with no heart," a "yellow, faded, sickly woman, whose time was divided among a variety of fanciful diseases, and who considered herself, in every sense, the most ill-used and suffering person in existence" (134, 135). Like the slave economy that supports her self-absorbed idleness, Marie is presented as capricious and sick. Her "Christian" principles are limited to mere parroting of biblical justifications of slavery. According to Stowe, Marie is not a "whole woman" (133).

In a chapter devoted entirely to housekeeping, Stowe opposes Marie's luxurious yet chilling languor with Ophelia's frenetic activity. But Miss Ophelia, too, falls short, if only because of her rigidity. She is "square-formed, and angular. Her face was thin, and rather sharp," her "lips compressed," her movements "sharp, decided, and energetic." Ophelia is a "living impersonation of order, method, and exactness. In punctuality, she was as inevitable as a clock, and as inexorable as a railroad engine" (137). She is governed by systematic principles of moral rightness in her campaign against domestic "shiftlessness" and in her "theological tenets [that] were all made up, labelled in most positive and distinct forms" (137). Ophelia fails to live up to the domestic ideal, however, because of her inability to "feel" and because she acts on intellect and reason instead of emotion.[5] Stowe's point is that slavery will be abolished not through the application of rhetoric but through the reforming power of domesticity. She believes that people should privilege feeling over reason and maternal, Christian values—values that are nourished at home—over those of the market and intellect.

Students might be asked to compare the various homes in the book in the same way they have considered its mistresses. Such a comparison underlines Stowe's point about slavery's assault on domestic values: the further south one gets, and the deeper into a slave economy, the more dysfunctional domestic arrangements become. Again, I use Rachel Halliday's home, with its gently tinkling teaspoons, musical coffee cups, and the "cheerful and joyous fizzle" of frying food as a touchstone (122). Students might look at the Shelby and St. Clare homes, which exhibit inconsistency and disorder at the very least. Gillian Brown suggests that we read Dinah's kitchen in the St. Clare household as a central metaphor for slavery's threat to domesticity ("Getting in the Kitchen"). Legree's plantation, as Karen Halttunen ("Gothic Imagination") and Jennifer

Jenkins have argued, represents the antihome, slavery's devastating effect on domesticity. Significantly, Stowe refers to Legree's dwelling not as a home but an as "establishment." In the sitting room, the wallpaper is "mouldering, torn and discolored," and the place has a "peculiar sickening, unwholesome smell, compounded of mingled damp, dirt and decay" (320). The pseudomistress of this domestic haunt is Cassy, a slave/woman with a "wild and insane" light in her eyes (321).[6] The force of Stowe's argument rests not only in the literal terrors of Legree's gothically isolated "home," itself a mockery of a separate haven, but also in Cassy's advice to Emmeline:

> What use is it for mothers to say anything? You are all to be bought and paid for, and your souls belong to whoever gets you. That's the way it goes. I say, *drink* brandy; drink all you can, and it'll make things come easier. (326)

This advice conveys the connection between the loss of maternal and domestic values and the loss of the soul.

In chapter 4, "An Evening in Uncle Tom's Cabin," Stowe portrays a slave home that strives to achieve the domestic ideal but is undercut by the system of slavery itself. Uncle Tom's cabin is a site of physical, emotional, and spiritual nourishment; a "plump" and "beam[ing]" Aunt Chloe presides over this "snug territor[y]," and husband Tom labors over his Bible (17). Unlike Beecher's ideally designed home, in which a mother oversees several large rooms through open doors, the slave cabin is bedroom, kitchen, and parlor all in one, with its inhabitants spilling all over one another in seemingly benign confusion. A portrait of the revolutionary hero General Washington adorns one wall. While this passage suggests Stowe's democratic desire to extend the domestic ideal to slaves, this scene, as the presence of our first president's portrait in a slave hovel suggests, is narrated ironically, emphasizing slavery's threat to this small and lowly haven. As Tom and friends sing hymns with the master's young son, Mr. Shelby completes the sale of his best slave.

A classroom strategy that examines the various homes and mistresses in the novel leads naturally into a discussion of how domesticity relies on sentimental codes of reading. These codes raise questions about domestic ideology's inherent racism and classism, questions that often arise as students debate the efficacy of Stowe's antidote and critique. I often point out how our discussion thus far has relied on readings based on the *appearances* of people and things. Students are quick to notice what Karen Sanchez-Eppler has called the "bodily grammar" of the novel, the notion that readers can judge characters' inner states through physical clues (102).[7] Stowe announces this strategy of reading as her novel opens, when we meet Haley, a "short, thick-set man, with coarse, commonplace features" (1). Through this reading, one can address the ways that Stowe stereotypes black characters throughout the novel and how these stereotypes complicate her abolitionist argument.

As Sanchez-Eppler has argued, domestic ideology naturalizes gender by constructing women as morally and emotionally superior. By attributing these faculties to women's biology, domestic ideology—and the sentimental discourse that it uses—relies on the very body that it purports to transcend (100–14). To emphasize the ways that this discourse depends on the body to signify the self, I use illustrations from *Godey's Lady's Book*, drawing students' attention to the physical appearance of hairstyles, dresses, and even facial expressions; and I invite students to extrapolate from these illustrations nineteenth-century ideals of beauty and domesticity.[8] I also point to the invention of pessaries, uterine support devices that women resorted to wearing because of the effects of sentimental dress—specifically, corsets—on reproductive organs. Most students have never heard of these devices, which show dramatically the relationships among domesticity, sentimental costuming, and the female body. One look at these contraptions suggests that women wearing them would be rendered incapable of physical labor even as they were acutely aware of their bodies each time they moved.[9]

The relationships among domestic ideology, sentimental discourse, and the body provide a good context from which students can discuss Stowe's use of stereotypes and her argument that domesticity offers a solution to slavery.[10] From this perspective, students see that Stowe's use of light-skinned blacks is a strategy for appealing to a popular audience. As Carolyn Karcher argues, the use of the "tragic mulatto" allows writers to ally their black characters with the "sensibilities, tastes, and moral standards of white readers" and yet still include the exploitation and abuse of black women that antislavery writers must depict in their fiction (63). Again, however, Jacobs's *Incidents in the Life of a Slave Girl* challenges domesticity as an abolitionist strategy. Like Stowe's Cassy and Eliza, Jacobs's Linda Brent exhibits characteristics of true womanhood that invite readers' sympathy. Linda, too, dreams of a home for herself and her children but must "follow the condition" of her mother, a slave. While *Uncle Tom's Cabin* ignores or covers over the difficulties black women face in accessing the domestic ideal, Jacobs's narrative addresses them. Jacobs depicts the way legal constructions of race permit whites to invade her free black grandmother's home. A white mob searches her home following Nat Turner's rebellion, rifling through her most private possessions; Dr. Flint repeatedly violates the domestic sanctum and physically abuses Linda and her child; and, finally, Linda's cramped attic hideaway of seven years, from which she watches but cannot be with her children, is a scathing parody of domesticity under slavery. Once in the North, Linda longs for a home of her own but instead serves as a domestic servant in the home of a white woman. Her situation dramatizes the ways that domesticity—here the physical structure of a home—relies on industrial capitalism and privatization even as it purports to be a haven from market systems. The contrast between *Uncle Tom's Cabin* and *Incidents* illustrates the problems black women have in accessing domesticity in practice. Jacobs's narrative demonstrates how the United States legal system, capitalism, and even sentimental discourse read the black body, maintaining white male power.

Understanding domesticity's reliance on sentimental discourse also illuminates Stowe's problem in depicting the dark-skinned Tom and Topsy. Stowe has little literary precedent for her black hero, whom she describes as "a large, broad-chested, powerfully-made man, of a full glossy black, and a face whose truly African features were characterized by an expression of grave and steady good sense, united with much kindliness and benevolence" (18). She displaces Tom's Africanism, his threatening otherness, with the feminine qualities of "kindliness and benevolence."[11] Again, placing Stowe's book next to a slave narrative is illuminating. William Lloyd Garrison's preface to Frederick Douglass's *Narrative of the Life of Frederick Douglass, an American Slave* (1845) emphasizes the author's intellect and his "gentleness and meekness" (247; ed. Gates), while the narrative proper defines Douglass in terms of intellect and manliness, a manliness that is explicitly linked to violence. By contrast, in his Christ-like death and apotheosis, Tom's "white" soul displaces his African body. Stowe not only has difficulty imagining a heroic black man who is not feminine but also can locate no cultural place to which to rescue him. To illustrate this limit of domesticity, teachers might ask students to imagine an alternative ending to Tom's story, one that would work within Stowe's parameters.

Stowe's solution to the problem of what to do with slaves once they are set free also illustrates domesticity's (and Stowe's own) limited vision. She suggests in her "Concluding Remarks" that slaves be educated in the North and then sent to Liberia to teach all they have learned. According to Marva Banks, Stowe's position on African colonization provoked concern and rage among her contemporary black readers, who read in the novel's ending and racist stereotypes her alliance with the American Colonization Society, "whose chief aim was to export blacks to Africa (or elsewhere) to protect white supremacy in the United States" (211). Although Stowe denied this charge, according to Banks, her novel *Dred* (1856) portrayed colonization positively as well. This solution to educate and export blacks evinces one imperialist component of Stowe's domestic vision, which she seeks to extend over people and continents.

A productive way to examine Stowe's colonization solution and the inherent racism and classism of her domesticity is by looking at Topsy's fate. After the death of her only friend, the sainted Eva, Topsy is spirited away to be educated in the North under the direction of Miss Ophelia, who has promised to do her best to "learn" to love her. But what is the content of Topsy's education to be? Such education supports the very middle-class ideals and maternal values that a black woman will not have the time, privilege, or money to practice in the United States, at least according to Stowe's conclusion.[12] As Jacobs's *Incidents* illustrates, black women can expect to work in the homes of whites and, regardless of their financial situation, to live as second-class citizens, to ride in "a filthy box, behind white people" on a train and to "pay for the privilege" (162). In other words, Stowe's domesticity argument seems to run aground when applied to free black women in the United States.

In her own dealings with Jacobs, Stowe was guilty of racism and classism as well. According to biographer Joan D. Hedrick, Stowe's racist politics were a result of "domestic settings in which her position as white mistress to black servants radically compromised her perceptions." Hedrick writes that although Stowe "over identified with [her servants] as women, she distanced herself from their race and class" (Stowe 209). Stowe's failure to extend domestic ideology to black women emerges in her treatment of Harriet Jacobs. Seeking a white woman's support in publishing her narrative, Jacobs reluctantly allowed Amy Post to reveal her history in a letter to Stowe. Stowe responded, astonishingly, by writing to Jacobs's employer, Mrs. Willis, to ask if such a story were true. Stowe's insensitive actions represented a breach of confidentiality and left Jacobs in the embarrassing situation of having to explain her past. Moreover, while Jacobs wished to write her own book, Stowe offered to appropriate her history for the sequel to *Uncle Tom's Cabin*. Mrs. Willis and Jacobs herself wrote many letters to Stowe, begging her not to do so, and their letters went unanswered. These examples of Stowe's racist and classist attitudes are further reinforced by her response to Jacobs's request that Stowe take Jacobs's daughter Louisa to England to further the abolitionist cause. According to Jacobs, Stowe felt that Louisa's "situation as a slave [. . .] would subject her to much petting and patronizing [. . .] and she was very much opposed to it with this class of people" (Jacobs 235). Jacobs's treatment in the North, even by Stowe herself, illustrates the problems black women had in accessing domestic ideals.

While my reading of Stowe's domestic politics—and her correlating solution of colonization—suggests a far less objectifying vision of black women than slavery offers, I argue that black readers might embrace these politics only with reservation and revision. Domesticity, the informing ideology underlying *Uncle Tom's Cabin*, is a crucial intervention into nineteenth-century political discourse. While advancing abolition, Stowe's ideology of domesticity attempts the installation of a racist, white, middle-class, privileged ideal tempered by maternal values and Christian love. Finally, this ideology is political not only in its attempts to reorganize culture but also in its installation of white, middle-class privilege as the ideal. Once students understand domesticity as both reformist and imperialistic, feminist and conservatively classist, abolitionist and racist, spiritual and material, a literary method and a political agenda, they begin to see that Stowe's book is big as well as complex. They can then interpret her stereotypes and metaphors more accurately and talk back to them with a sounder awareness of nineteenth-century culture.

NOTES

[1]For a discussion that complicates these binaries, see the special issue of *American Literature*, *No More Separate Spheres* (Davidson).

[2]Students frequently object to analyzing divisions of labor in their own homes. For example, they maintain that their mothers "enjoy" cleaning and laundry duties because

this work offers them a vehicle through which to express their love. The relation between love and laundry is, of course, open to scrutiny.

[3]Brodhead argues that *Uncle Tom's Cabin* and other antebellum fiction traces the middle-class desire to redefine itself in terms of "disciplinary intimacy, or simply discipline through love" (70). Antebellum fiction, he maintains, aimed at a disciplinary model that consisted in the "sentimentalization of the disciplinary relation" (71).

[4]For a fuller discussion of the racist and classist meanings of domesticity, see the essays by Wexler, Karcher, Lang, Samuels, and Sanchez-Eppler in Samuels, *Culture*.

[5]For an important discussion of the chapter "Miss Ophelia's Experiences and Opinions" in the context of domestic economy, see G. Brown, "Getting in the Kitchen." She argues that Dinah's sporadic housekeeping is a metaphor for the presence of the marketplace in the kitchen and, therefore, for slavery's undermining effects on domesticity. Brown argues that Legree's plantation, with its absence of a feminine and nurturing influence, represents the antithesis of home. Viewing domestic values as at once transgressive and subversive, Brown contends that, for Stowe, abolition begins at home.

[6]Sanchez-Eppler traces the parallels between abolition and feminist rhetoric. Her comments seem especially relevant here, where the "wife" is also literally enslaved.

[7]For a historical discussion of the ways that nineteenth-century pseudosciences, including phrenology and physiognomy, operated as "technologies of race" (23) by situating racial differences in the human body, see Wiegman.

[8]Lehuu argues that, in their very theatricality and visibility, the illustrations in *Godey's Lady's Book* both "underwrote and undermined" sentimental discourse (74).

[9]Gillian Brown discusses the stillness of domestic women's bodies (*Domestic Individualism* 63–95). For illustrations of various pessaries and their function see H. Green 122–24.

[10]According to Samuels, "Representing slavery in nineteenth-century America involved either fixing the slave's identity in the body as a matter of 'blood' or 'skin' or unfixing the identity of slavery by understanding identity as transcending the body" ("Identity" 157). In either case, representations of the slave's body, like the sentimental discourse in *Uncle Tom's Cabin*, struggle with the biologically based assumptions about gendered and racialized bodies.

[11]Ammons argues that Tom's feminine and maternal qualities resemble those of a Victorian heroine ("Stowe's Dream").

[12]For good discussions of domesticity's educational implications, see Brodhead; Wexler.

Radical or Reactionary? Religion and Rhetorical Conflict in *Uncle Tom's Cabin*

Stephen R. Yarbrough and Sylvan Allen

Why, although Harriet Beecher Stowe never intended to encourage war, did *Uncle Tom's Cabin* dispose its readers to violence? Students in an American literature class at the University of North Carolina, Greensboro, raised this question, and when one student, Sylvan Allen, received an undergraduate research assistantship, she and the professor, Stephen Yarbrough, decided to pursue it with the specific aim of contributing an essay to this volume.

Because the question the class had raised required determining what Stowe had intended her book to accomplish, the project took as its starting point a brief section of a volume Yarbrough had coauthored with John C. Adams, *Delightful Conviction: Jonathan Edwards and the Rhetoric of Conversion* (85–93), which considered how Stowe had modified Edwards's conversion rhetoric to suit the purposes of her benevolent moralism. Allen and Yarbrough then set out to locate specific episodes in the novel that might illustrate such a rhetoric of conversion. Numerous conferences followed, determining what secondary research they would need to support their claims about the author's intentions and her initial audience's responses, what previous critical research they would need to address, what collateral issues they would need to emphasize, and so forth. The authors then worked out a tentative outline, divided the writing, and began to draft. Over the course of a year, numerous revision sessions followed until they sent a draft to the editors of this volume. This essay is the result.

The concept of the plurality of meaning is a difficult one to teach to undergraduates. How can it be that the statements "Stowe was a reactionary" and "Stowe was a radical" are both true and false? When developing scholars encounter opposing statements like these, they tend to assume that an argument is in store, and that the most convincing argument will be the best answer. They seldom consider the possibility that the different statements may answer different questions and that each may be appropriate to each. The students' rite of passage into the "scholarly conversation" requires learning how to use the answers others have found for other questions without losing sight of their own questions, because the past, unacknowledged, can arise like a ghost to pursue its own ends. Ironically, we found, that is what befell Stowe: the very rhetorical power she drew from the answers given by her traditional religious past distorted the answers she intended to offer her audience.

Apparently, Stowe herself thought of *Uncle Tom's Cabin* as both asking a question and answering it. According to her *Key to* Uncle Tom's Cabin, her "great object" in writing the novel was "to bring this subject of slavery, as a moral and religious question, before the minds of all those who profess to be followers of Christ, in this country" (iii–iv; Jewett ed.). Few have accepted as an answer to the question of Stowe's intent that she wanted her readers simply to consider the question. Most critics, much as Wendy Rader-Konofalski has stressed, believe that Stowe advocated individual action in the form of "active resistance against the law of the land" (159). Yet no one denies that Stowe never, before the war began, advocated forcing the South to abolish slavery. Like Hawthorne in his campaign biography of Franklin Peirce and like Thoreau in "Civil Disobedience," she did not promote forced abolition through either legal or military means. However, more so than Hawthorne's or Thoreau's, her motives were religious. She intended not to provoke a war but to save souls—and in so doing to bring about a peaceful end to slavery. As Jean Fagan Yellin describes Stowe's motivation, what Stowe found wrong with slavery was that it "entrusts the souls of black slaves to whoever can afford to buy their bodies, thus endangering their salvation and almost certainly condemning white America to everlasting hellfire" (*Knot* 135).

When Yellin uses *Uncle Tom's Cabin* as an answer to her questions about white Americans' attitudes toward slavery before the Civil War, Stowe does not appear very radical. But when critics use the novel as the answer to a different set of questions, the novel seems to take on a different meaning (raising this issue is a good way to bring research into class discussions). For instance, by asking how this nineteenth-century novel might contribute to twentieth-century feminism, some critics have found in *Uncle Tom's Cabin* a more radical intent than saving souls in order to end slavery.

As Dorothy Berkson notes, ever since Elizabeth Ammons suggested in "Heroines in *Uncle Tom's Cabin*" that the violent acts within the novel are "the signs of patriarchy's most chilling system—slavery," critics have repeatedly taken for granted "the subversive and radical role women consistently play in that novel" ("Mothers" 102). Jane Tompkins, for instance, describes the novel as "the most dazzling exemplar" of a myth elaborated by sentimental novelists of the nineteenth century, a myth "that gave women the central position of power and authority in the culture" ("Sentimental Power" 125). Although Tompkins agrees that the novel further "insists on religious conversion as the necessary precondition for sweeping social change," *Uncle Tom's Cabin*, says Tompkins, is a "politically subversive" book because it promotes establishing a "new matriarchy" like that Stowe's half-sister Isabella Beecher Hooker "had dreamed of leading" ("Sentimental Power" 132, 142).

The claim that *Uncle Tom's Cabin* is politically subversive has been challenged numerous times, however. Yellin, for instance, aligns the novel much more closely with the views of Stowe's sister Catharine Beecher, who insisted that "Heaven has appointed to [woman] the subordinate station" and that "woman is to win every thing by peace and love [. . .]. But this is to all be accomplished in the domestic and social sphere" (qtd. in "Doing It Herself" 87). Just as Stowe "opposed the active resistance of black and white abolitionists and insurrectionists," she celebrates "not feminism and abolitionism but 'domestic feminism' and colonization" ("Doing It Herself"102).

In a related argument, Myra Jehlen suggests that although feminist critics "have tended to find their authors and characters grouped about the pole of subversion" (398), such subversion does not exist in *Uncle Tom's Cabin*. Rather, in this novel Stowe "did not seek to advance the cause of women's self-rule; in fact she reaffirmed their feudal placement, at the same time establishing an equivalent place of subservience for blacks." Stowe did indeed envision "a second American revolution," but it was to be one "much like the first which left existing hierarchies of power and property essentially intact, in fact preserving them through strengthening reforms" (399).

We followed a line of questioning different from those of any of the critics discussed above. Even so, at the end of our questioning process, we agreed with Yellin and Jehlen that Stowe's aim was not revolutionary but really quite "reactionary."[1] We arrived at this conclusion by exploring a question that had been raised in our class: What is the relation of Stowe's rhetoric to an earlier rhetoric the class had studied, that of the American Puritans? We found that the rhetoric Stowe employed suggested that she wanted to restore her world to a system in which patriarchal powers—law, order, reason, authority—no longer conflicted with legal, benevolent, responsible action. We believe we would not be far amiss to claim that Stowe desired to reinstate the encyclopedic social order promulgated by Puritan New England ministers for hundreds of years.

What was this order? Jonathan Edwards described it as one of mutual dependency in *The Nature of True Virtue* (1765): "There is a beauty of order in society [. . .]. As, when the different members of society have all their appointed office, place and station, according to their several capacities and talents, and everyone keeps his place and continues in his proper business" (568). Within this order were three governing institutions—family, church, and state—each with its prerogatives and peculiar responsibilities (see Morgan, *Visible Saints*). In Edwards's time, this order had already begun to break down. In Stowe's, it was completely asunder. The capitalist free-market system, the republican separation of church and state, and most especially the slavery system had made it impossible to behave consistently and coherently within the three areas traditionally governed by the three major institutions.

In such a degenerate system, Stowe implies, good people must live in a paradox, a brief example of which occurs in chapter 13 when young Simeon Halliday, revolted at the thought that his father may be imprisoned for doing a benevolent act, calls the law "a shame." The elder Simeon rebukes his son:

> Thee mustn't speak evil of thy rulers, Simeon [. . .]. The Lord only gives us our worldly goods that we may do justice and mercy; if our rulers require a price of us for it, we must deliver it up.   (122)

The elder Simeon, like all the good people represented in the novel, must both respect authority and disobey it. Stowe simply wanted to resolve this paradox and restore the moral coherence of the old way of life, romanticized and stripped of certain elements she found distasteful.[2] The path to that restoration was neither political persuasion nor war but the old path, conversion.[3]

Teaching the rhetorical strategies of *Uncle Tom's Cabin* is much easier when students are already familiar with the Calvinist sermon tradition in which Stowe was raised. A comparison of Stowe's novel with the sermons, particularly those of Jonathan Edwards, reveals that her novel, like the sermons, sometimes seeks to convert readers rather than persuade them. The problem, for Stowe, is that while her chief aim is to elicit the readers' sympathy for others different from themselves—to persuade readers toward a sense of identity—the conversion strategies she sometimes borrows were designed to separate the sheep from the goats—to heighten a sense of difference.[4]

Traditional Puritan conversion rhetoric assumes that although members of a community may share the same opinions, attitudes, ideas, and language, they may in substance (that is, in their souls) be fundamentally different. Moreover, the superficially shared surface may conceal that crucial difference. Accordingly, conversion rhetoric entails a systematic undermining of the grounds on which individuals base their values and purposes, revealing the inadequacy of those grounds and the incapacity of the individual to establish proper grounds, thus preparing the individual to surrender unconditionally to an exterior, transcendent authority. Edwards's conversion sermons, for instance, both with imagery (as in "Sinners in the Hands of an Angry God") and with logic (as in "True Grace Distinguished from the Experience of Devils"), strive persistently to undercut the individual's confidence in his or her opinions, values, and especially attitudes. The sermons do not attempt to persuade listeners to choose rightly but to undermine their confidence in their ability to choose rightly, leaving them with no recourse but to obediently submit to God's will.

Similarly, in her novel Stowe continually seeks to undermine her audiences' reasons for maintaining slavery. What Stowe wished her audience to submit to, however, was poles apart from the Calvinist God of Jonathan Edwards. Although, as Vernon Louis Parrington points out, Stowe's "particular hero and saint was Jonathan Edwards" (215), she nevertheless found abhorrent the essential Calvinist doctrines Edwards had strenuously defended, particularly that of election. Henry F. May describes Stowe's life as "a long and agonizing struggle with the religion of her fathers, and more particularly with the religion of her father" (4). Edward Wagenknecht similarly writes that "before her heart could find rest, even in God, she had to fight her way out from her inherited Calvinism" (*Stowe* 195). Eventually, she found her way "from Lyman Beecher's Calvinism toward a theology of Christocentric liberalism, which emphasized not the judgment of God but the love of Christ and the availability of salvation for all" (Halttunen, "Gothic Imagination" 127). By the time she wrote *Oldtown Folks* (1869), she was fully comfortable with Arminianism, "a theological position that granted individuals more power to effect their own salvation" (Berkson, Introduction xxv), a position from which Calvinism appears "as a subtle poison" having "the power of lacerating the nerves of the soul, and producing strange states of morbid horror and repulsion" (qtd. in Berkson, Introduction xxviii). And, indeed, *Uncle Tom's Cabin* works on the assumption that there is something the individual can do to effect his or her salvation and so contribute to an end to slavery.

In the "Concluding Remarks" of *Uncle Tom's Cabin* she addresses her readers directly, telling them exactly what they can do:

> But, what can any individual do? Of that, every individual can judge. There is one thing that every individual can do,—they can see to it that *they feel right*. An atmosphere of sympathetic influence encircles every human being; and the man or woman who *feels* strongly, healthily and justly on the great interests of humanity, is a constant benefactor to the human race. See, then, to your sympathies in this matter!   (385)

Instead of the Calvinist God, Stowe wanted her readers to submit to their own hearts. Stowe believed in a natural, God-created principle of "disinterested benevolence," a seat of sympathy and compassion, a divine principle informing the conscience. She also believed in free will, which enabled individuals to contradict their self-interest. A heart kept free of self-interest could *feel* the difference between virtue and vice.

This and similar views developed during the eighteenth century by David Hume, Francis Hutcheson, William Wollaston, and others came to Stowe primarily through her father and earlier New Divinity ministers. Wollaston's description in his *The Religion of Nature Delineated* (1724) is typical:

> There is something in *human* nature [. . .] which renders us obnoxious to the pains of others, causing us to sympathize with them [. . .]. It is grievous to see or hear (and almost to hear of) any man, or even any animal whatever, in *torment* [. . .]. It is therefore according to *nature* to be affected with the sufferings of other people and the contrary is *inhuman* and *unnatural*.   (qtd. in Fiering 249)

Eighteenth-century Calvinists like Edwards countered that conscience and sympathy can be misplaced and self-serving. In *Some Thoughts concerning the Revival* (1742), Edwards linked dependence on sympathy and conscience to spiritual pride:

> There is no sin so much like the Devil as this, for secrecy and subtlety [. . .]. We had need therefore to have the greatest watch imaginable, over our hearts, with respect to this matter, and to cry most earnestly to the great Searcher of hearts, for his help. "He that trusts his own heart is a fool" [Prov. 28.26].   (416–17)

Thus, the main difference between Calvinism's pietist rhetorical aims and benevolent moralism's aims is that where pietism stresses the need to *change* one's heart, benevolent moralism stresses the need to *submit to* one's heart.

This difference in aims produced an important distinction between the way Puritans saw their relationships to other human beings and the way benevolent moralists like Stowe did. Puritans believed that true unity with others had to come by way of their common subordination to God's will. Benevolent moralists believed that achieving unity with others *was* God's will. Further, the pietist end of conversion is a subordination to God, or God's earthly representatives, in which the question of the rightness or fairness of mundane institutional laws is completely a nonissue.[5] In class, the example of Anne Hutchinson, who was excommunicated for breaking the Fifth Commandment, not heresy, helps show how important the principle of social subordination was. Roger Williams's exile provides another. But in Stowe's era, social justice was the chief issue to benevolent moralists. Piety specifically prohibits active alteration of the conditions in which God has placed the individual, as you can demonstrate to your class by having them read John Winthrop's "A Model of Christian Charity." In contrast, benevolent moralism prohibits passive acquiescence in those conditions when they demand a sympathetic response. Stowe wanted her readers to act against slavery, to act on the sympathy she believed they already felt. Unfortunately, neither Stowe nor anyone else could convince an audience to act on its feelings when precisely those convictions—those rational beliefs—are preventing that action.

Accordingly, insofar as it was modeled upon Calvinistic conversion rhetoric, Stowe's strategy of conversion to sympathy sought to undermine any grounds for overriding the basic, immediate, sympathetic response to others' distress that she assumed all individuals but the most corrupt felt. Although she borrowed a pietistic strategy, her intended ends were moralistic, for Stowe assumed that her readers, white Southerners included, possessed fundamentally and originally good inclinations. She therefore believed that two related forces had worked against her readers' natural sympathy. One was the force of habit and tradition that allowed Southern whites, who witnessed the horrors of slavery daily, simply not to feel with their hearts what they saw with their eyes. The other was the force of distance and abstraction that prevented Northerners from recognizing the basic humanity of slaves and allowed them to ignore the slaves' plight.

Stowe explores the first force working against her readers' natural sympathy—Southern white indifference created by habit and tradition—through her portrait of Augustine St. Clare. Although a Louisiana slaveholder, St. Clare's kindness and generosity toward his slaves indicate a native capacity for sympathy stained only by his complacent acceptance of the South's oppressive economic and cultural foundations.

Because of his capacity for sympathy, this master assumes the role not of a bullwhipping driver but of a doting uncle, freely patting slave children on the head and distributing small pieces of change. St. Clare even indulges his slaves' eccentric and inefficient behaviors. Nevertheless, as a white man in a privileged position within a complex pattern of economic relations, St. Clare has never considered infringement on slaves' basic human liberty to be inherently unjust. Grounding his beliefs on the rational tenets of his education and tradition, he views slavery as a potentially mutually beneficial system of labor and patronage, even if it is actually prone to abuse and inhumanity. Stowe blames St. Clare's ability to privilege his "rational" acceptance of the slavery system over his native sympathy for the slaves' plight on his religious cynicism. Only after the death of his daughter, Eva, whose benevolence and purity had made the relationship of owner and slave seem comfortable, if not entirely beneficial, does St. Clare appear to surrender to a more righteously ordered perception of society and his place in it.

If Stowe's rhetoric uses St. Clare as an example of a white Southerner whose economic need and habitual perceptions have permitted him to subordinate his sympathy to a false rationality, her example of a Northern white who ignores his natural sympathy and rationalizes slavery is Senator Bird. Chapter 9, "In Which It Appears That a Senator Is But a Man," opens to a domestic scene involving the Ohio state senator, who has recently returned from the legislature after arguing and winning the case for "a law," as his wife describes it, "forbidding people to give meat and drink to those poor colored folks that come along" (68). On the senate floor, Bird, we learn later, had been

> as bold as a lion about [the act], and "mightily convinced" not only himself, but everybody that heard him;—but then his idea of a fugitive was only an idea of the letters that spell the word,—or, at the most, the image of a little newspaper picture of a man with a stick and bundle, with "Ran away from the subscriber" under it. The magic of the real presence of distress,—the imploring human eye, the frail, trembling human hand, the despairing appeal of helpless agony,—these he had never tried.   (77)

Stowe's employment of Edwards's distinction between speculative and sensible knowledge is obvious here,[6] as you can illustrate in class by having students read all or part of Edwards's "A Divine and Supernatural Light," available in most survey anthologies. Stowe's use of Edwards's distinction implies that the senator's entire legal, rational argument is founded on the concept of the fugitive as a mere sign and that "the real presence" of one would confound all his logic.

This, in fact, is exactly the tactic Mrs. Bird uses in her "argument" against her husband's position, which is a refusal to argue at all. When the senator tells her, "I can state to you a very clear argument, to show—," she interrupts, "O, nonsense, John! you can talk all night, but you wouldn't do it. I put it to you, John,—would *you* now turn away a poor, shivering, hungry creature from your door, because he was a runaway?" (69). "Clear argument" is "nonsense." The senator's contention that "we must put aside our private feelings" is overturned by Mrs. Bird's reply that "obeying God never brings on public evils" (69). The issue becomes simply whether her husband is the kind of person who could act on mere law and reason in the face of human distress. Mrs. Bird refuses to believe that he could. She counters his every attempt to defer his *personal* feeling, whether to duty ("You know it isn't a duty,—it can't be a duty!") or to reason ("I hate reasoning, John,—especially reasoning on such subjects") (70). The husband is silenced; his status as a good Christian is, in his wife's eyes, on the line.

Shortly after this conversation, Eliza and her child appear at the Birds' home seeking asylum. The senator sheds tears, hiding them of course, at the sight of the slaves' misery. He has, as the novel has told us, "a particularly humane and accessible nature" (69), so we are not surprised that without being asked he arranges to convey Eliza to safety. "Your heart is better than your head, in this case, John" (75), his wife assures him, yet the reader is well aware that John's heart is in turmoil. As he sinks into "deep meditation" while "anxiously" putting on his boots before leaving with Eliza and her son, he mutters, "It's a confounded awkward, ugly business [. . .] and that's a fact! [. . .] It will have to be done, though, for aught I see,—hang it all!" (74). Because he "feels right," he has been thrown into the role of a hypocrite and criminal, and about that he cannot feel right. His "conversion" cannot be complete and satisfying because of the evil of the system he serves.

While St. Clare's portrait illustrates Stowe's conviction that most Southern whites were basically good people, if misguided by habit and convention and trapped by a cruel system, the predicaments of Senator Bird typify those of Stowe's entire Northern audience. The Fugitive Slave Act made what was once a Southern problem incontrovertibly an American problem, as Stowe stressed in her novel's conclusion:

> Nothing of tragedy can be written, can be spoken, can be conceived, that equals the frightful reality of scenes daily and hourly acting on our shores, beneath the shadow of American law, and the shadow of the cross of Christ. (384)

The North could no longer deny the slavery on *our* shores; it could no longer psychologically separate itself from the South. As John William Ward says, "No longer could it be maintained that it was 'they,' the Southerners, who supported slavery; it was 'we,' the people of the United States, who did" (488).

Why, then, if the novel encourages white Northerners to see white Southerners as part of "us" rather than as "them," could it also have encouraged these Northerners to exert violence toward their Southern counterparts? The answer lies simply in the conversion rhetoric's demand to be "born again" and so to reject violently those characteristics of oneself that one cannot openly condone, as expressed, for instance, in the biblical injunction "If thy right eye offend thee, pluck it out [. . .]: for it is profitable for thee that one of thy members should perish, and not that thy whole body should be cast into hell" (Matt. 5.29). By this logic, if one finds one's identity in belonging to a group (as one does in pietist Christianity), then the stronger the identity between two persons (or groups), the more violent must be the rejection of the undesirable characteristics of those who belong to the same group. In Stowe's novel, a characteristic of those who are capable of sympathy is that they respond passionately and sometimes violently toward those who act unsympathetically. Mrs. Bird, for example, was ordinarily a quiet, restrained woman:

> There was only one thing that was capable of arousing her, and that provocation came in on the side of her unusually gentle and sympathetic nature;—anything in the shape of cruelty would throw her into a passion. (68)

Once, on finding out that her sons had been involved in "stoning a defenseless kitten," Mrs. Bird "whipped" them and "tumbled" them off to bed without any supper. The moral was that the "boys never stoned another kitten!" (68).

Beyond implying that cruelty can be stopped only if violent punishment is enforced on those who cause it, this little tale also suggests that the violence is even more understandable when the cruel party is part of oneself, part of the sympathetic one's family. Just as Edwards's conversions produced self-loathing toward the convert's sinful self, Stowe's, too, produced self-loathing, but toward that part of "us" that necessitated the Northern sympathetic response—the Southern slave owners. In effect, through episodes like this one Stowe's novel implicitly demands that its Northern readers obey the biblical injunction and *force* an end to slavery.

White Southern readers of *Uncle Tom's Cabin* seem to have sensed this underlying, if unintended message. Publications record a general assumption that *Uncle Tom's Cabin* was a call to arms. A contributor to *Southern Ladies Book*, for example, accused Stowe of dealing in the "pernicious intrigues of sectional animosity" (Roppolo 360), while an editor of the New Orleans *Daily Picayune* said the novel was "provocative of mischief beyond her power to check" (Roppolo 349). Southern whites could not help but understand that Stowe's novel provided Northern whites with a motive to exert violence against them, a motive very much like Northerners' Puritan ancestors' motive for flogging Quakers, exiling dissenters, and executing witches: the motive to save their own souls. Despite Stowe's repeated assertion that white Southerners were generally good people caught up in a bad system,[7] Stowe used pietist conversion rhetoric throughout the novel, and pietist conversion rhetoric implies that a person's identity is determined by the system with which that person allies.[8] From the pietist perspective of Stowe's Calvinist rhetoric, no one could long tolerate belonging to an evil system without becoming an evil person. Southern whites sensed from the rhetoric that they too would be condemned if they did not submit to the demands of sympathy.

Stowe's conversion rhetoric in *Uncle Tom's Cabin* sought to undermine her opposition's grounds for belief—to deny that their reasons for their beliefs about slavery could have grounds. Therefore her rhetoric eliminated the possibility of finding a common ground or compromise solution. While explicitly she declared that those who supported slavery were basically decent people, the way she tried to convert them implied that they were actually the evil portion of a larger whole. Explicitly she declared that everyone had an equal capacity to "feel right" and therefore do right; implicitly her rhetoric suggested that their not doing right signified that they were not feeling right, and so they should subordinate their feelings to the feelings of those who could still feel. Even though in this novel the people with proper feelings are often women, *Uncle Tom's Cabin* in no way promotes matriarchy or any other radical change in the social structure. The hierarchy of patriarchy is in fact reinforced. Explicitly, Stowe may have preached that readers should submit to their own hearts, but implicitly she measured those hearts against the authoritative heart of the Son of God, as represented by the novel's exemplary true father, Tom.

NOTES

[1]We use the term *reactionary* here in much the same sense as Craig Jackson Calhoun, who argues "that 'reactionary radicals' have been at the center of most modern revolutions and many other radical mobilizations in which revolutionary outcomes were precluded" (888).

[2]These elements include not only the Calvinist rejection of good works and benevolent feeling as signs of regeneration but also the New Divinity tenet espoused by Samuel Hopkins that interprets disinterested benevolence as a "willingness to be damned" (qtd. in Ahlstrom 408). As we show, it was precisely such an unwillingness to be damned that served as a major motivation to war.

[3]For detailed accounts of Stowe's religious views, see Buell, "Calvinism"; Caskey; and Hedrick, "Fruits." For a different analysis of Stowe's conversion strategy, see King.

[4]For a good account of Stowe's use of identity rhetoric, see Rader-Konofalski. For accounts of conflicting rhetorical strategies in *Uncle Tom's Cabin*, see MacFarlane; Sanchez-Eppler.

[5]For Edwards, morality is purely circumstantial and contingent—"there is no action [that] is either moral or immoral but considers things with their circumstances"—and circumstances alter: "Thus the action of killing a man is in no wise a moral evil abstracted from its circumstances" (*Philosophy* 208). To Edwards and most pietists, to do the "right thing" in any absolute sense is impossible for finite beings. Authority serves as the symbolic representative of the truth, justice and goodness available to God's comprehension; therefore, obedience to authority for God's sake is the rule. Not *what* one does but *for whom* one does it determines the state of the soul.

[6]For Edwards, "speculative knowledge" is always mediated by signs, usually in the form of logical or inferential conclusions; "sensible knowledge" is immediate and sensory. His most famous example stresses the difference between merely "knowing" that honey is sweet from testimonial or other evidence and knowing that it is sweet from

actually having tasted honey. It can be argued that Edwards's entire theology of "experimental religion" rests on this distinction. Mrs. Bird uses the distinction here much as Edwards used it, to destroy an auditor's confidence in the certainty of his or her rationally determined beliefs, not by demonstrating logical inconsistency but by undermining their foundation.

[7]Wagenknecht (*Stowe* 183), Fisher (96), Sarson (40), and many other critics stress that Stowe intended to attack the slavery system rather than the enslavers themselves. Her theory of benevolence, her belief in the inherent goodness of human beings, her discounting of original sin, and her faith in the moral efficacy of domestic harmony all worked toward locating the cause of evil in the individual's circumstances.

[8]For a fuller discussion of the pietist conception of identity, see Yarbrough and Adams (esp. 47–49).

Uncle Tom's Cabin, Empire, and Africa
Elizabeth Ammons

> For two hundred and twenty-eight years has the colored
> man toiled over the soil of America, under a burning
> sun and a driver's lash—plowing, planting, reaping, that
> white men might roll in ease, their hands unhardened
> by labor, and their brows unmoistened by the waters of
> genial toil, and now that the moral sense of mankind is
> beginning to revolt at this system of foul treachery and
> cruel wrong, and is demanding its overthrow, the mean
> and cowardly oppressor is mediating plans to expel the
> colored man entirely from the country. Shame upon
> the guilty wretches that dare propose, and all that
> countenance such a proposition. We live here—have
> lived here—have a right to live here, and mean to
> live here.
> —Frederick Douglass, *The North Star*, 26 January 1849

This essay examines Stowe's endorsement of African colonization in *Uncle Tom's Cabin*, a narrative position embedded in nineteenth-century worldwide capitalist, race, and colonial issues. Because I believe that my students' need to think about global power relations will only increase in the foreseeable future, attention to the novel's imperial implications, especially *Uncle Tom's Cabin* and Africa, strikes me as a crucial classroom focus.

During the decade that led to Stowe's antislavery novel, the world saw major upheavals as Western imperial powers invaded what seemed to be every corner of the earth in the name of trade, Christianity, and "civilization." In 1842, the Treaty of Nanking declared Hong Kong part of the British Empire, and the Boers stole land in southern Africa to create the slaveholding Orange Free State. Two years later, the Treaty of Tangier ended the war in Morocco by solidifying French imperial power in northern Africa, and in 1846 the first Anglo Sikh War concluded with the British victorious and the East India Company secure in India. In 1848, the United States, having invaded Mexico, annexed what is now Texas, New Mexico, California, Utah, Nevada, Arizona, and parts of Colorado and Wyoming. In response to such imperial activities, militant resistance and revolutions erupted. In New Zealand, the Maori repeatedly rose up against the British. In Hungary, people rebelled against Austrian rule. In China, the beginnings of what would become the Tai P'ing Rebellion stirred. In the United States, Native Americans fought to repel white theft of Indian lands.

To illustrate even more specifically the turbulence and shifting global context in which Stowe conceived *Uncle Tom's Cabin*, consider 1848. Karl Marx and Friedrich Engels published the *Communist Manifesto* in London. The first woman's rights convention in the United States was held at Seneca Falls, New York. The second Sikh War of resistance to British rule began in India, while riots broke out in Ceylon in response to new taxes levied by the British occupiers there. The Treaty of Guadalupe Hidalgo approved the United States confiscation of half of Mexico, and revolutions advocating constitutional rule by the middle classes erupted in so many places in Europe—France, Spain, Italy, Prussia, Hungary—that 1848 became known as the year of revolutions. The discovery of gold in California started the rush that would see sixty thousand people from all over the world, including China, enter the state by the end of the next year. Britain claimed yet more land in southern Africa; the first English settlers headed out to take possession of New Zealand; and the potato famine in Ireland, exacerbated by colonial rule, went into its third year, killing tens of thousands of people and turning even larger numbers into desperate emigrants.[1]

Uncle Tom's Cabin clearly shows that Stowe was aware of world events. Asked by Ophelia to read the future, Augustine St. Clare observes: "One thing is certain,—that there is a mustering among the masses, the world over; and there is a *dies irae* coming on, sooner or later. The same thing is working in Europe, in England, and in this country" (202). Reiterating the point to his brother, Alfred, he draws analogies to the French Revolution, the Haitian Revolution, and contemporary rebellions in Italy and Hungary. He reminds Alfred that the masses "took *their* turn once, in France," and continues ironically with reference to the successful slave rebellion in Haiti in 1804: "It makes a terrible slip when they get up [. . .] —in St. Domingo [Haiti], for instance" (233). To Alfred's boast that he is willing to "sit on the escape-valve, as long as the boilers are strong," Augustine replies, "The nobles in Louis XVI.'s time thought just so; and Austria and Pius IX. [in Italy] think so now; and, some pleasant morning, you may all be caught up to meet each other in the air, *when the boilers burst*" (233–34). Global revolution hovers in Stowe's novel.

Most directly invoked is the Hungarian Revolution, which inflects Stowe's description of George Harris's militance.

> If it had been only a Hungarian youth, now bravely defending in some mountain fastness the retreat of fugitives escaping from Austria into America, this would have been sublime heroism; but as it was a youth of African descent, defending the retreat of fugitives through America into Canada, of course we are too well instructed and patriotic to see any heroism in it; and if any of our readers do, they must do it on their own private responsibility. When despairing Hungarian fugitives make their way, against all the search-warrants and authorities of their lawful government, to America, press and political cabinet ring with applause and welcome. When despairing African fugitives do the same thing,—it is—what *is* it? (172)

As Susan Belasco Smith points out, Stowe's brother Henry Ward Beecher published a long article on the Hungarian Revolution in the *Independent* in 1851, a portion of which ran in the *National Era* in the same issue as chapter 19 of *Uncle Tom's Cabin*. Not surprisingly, as Smith puts it, "To Stowe, busily writing the middle chapters of *Uncle Tom's Cabin*, the Hungarian revolution could [. . .] serve as a convenient analogy to the situation in the United States" (81).

Given Stowe's references to the Haitian Revolution, the French Revolution, and various struggles for freedom in Europe, particularly the Hungarian Revolution, why did she support emigration to Liberia in *Uncle Tom's Cabin*? Why should people living in the United States, the supposed haven from oppression—witness her own reference to Hungarian refugees—leave to find a freedom that, ironically, involved depriving others of theirs?

From the beginning, Liberia was controversial. Founded by the American Colonization Society in 1822 for settlement by free African Americans and manumitted slaves, the West African colony was preceded by other colonization and "repatriation" ideas and attempts. As Benjamin Brawley explains in what remains an excellent summary of pre-Liberia thinking in the United States, prominent white Americans proposed Sierra Leone, the West Indies, and the North American Southwest and Northwest as resettlement sites for American blacks. For example, afraid that escaped or freed slaves would lead armed rebellions, the General Assembly of Virginia early in 1805 asked the federal government to designate a part of the Louisiana Purchase "to be appropriated to the residence of such people of color as have been, or shall be, emancipated, or may hereafter become dangerous to the public safety" (Brawley 122). Four years earlier President Thomas Jefferson had written to the governor of Virginia, James Monroe, for whom the capital of Liberia would later be named: "Africa would offer a last and undoubted resort, if all others more desirable should fail" (Brawley 121). In 1811 Jefferson continued to hope for a colony in Africa that could serve as both refuge and dumping ground for African Americans. "Nothing is more to be wished than that the United States would themselves undertake to make such an establishment on the coast of Africa." Problems existed, however, as Jefferson conceded:

> But for this the national mind is not yet prepared. It may perhaps be doubted whether many of these people would voluntarily consent to such an exchange of situation, and very certain that few of those advanced to a certain age in habits of slavery, would be capable of self-government. This should not, however, discourage the experiment, nor the early trial of it. (Brawley 122–23)

Evidently, public support for the idea and black people's desire to emigrate amounted to minor details for Jefferson.

Inspired by the example of Sierra Leone, founded by the British in 1791 as a refuge for "recaptives" (Africans liberated from captured slave ships) and for free blacks and escaped slaves living in Canada, Liberia was primarily the idea of racist white Americans who wished to remove African Americans. The American Colonization Society (ACS), founded by Southern slaveholders, aimed "to rid the country of free blacks by colonizing them in Africa" (J. Smith 2). As one ACS member said of the growing class of free blacks in the United States: "I dread for [Virginia] the corroding evil of this numerous caste, and I tremble for a danger of disaffection spreading through their seduction, among our servants." Others maintained, "African colonization [. . .] is our only security from social and political death" (J. Smith 2).

If Southern planters wanted to exile threatening free blacks, many Northerners expressed support for colonization because it would Christianize Africa. For others, both black and white, pragmatism ruled. Unable to obtain justice in the United States, free blacks, they argued, might follow in the tradition of the New England Pilgrims and seek freedom far from home. The 1847 Declaration of Independence of Liberia—a nation with a red, white, and blue starred-and-striped flag and its very name meaning liberty—emphasized the parallel by deliberately echoing the Declaration of Independence of its 4,500 African American immigrants' homeland. The document reads in part:

> We, the people of the Republic of Liberia, were originally inhabitants of the United States of North America.
>
> In some parts of that country, we were debarred by law, from all the rights and privileges of men; in other parts, public sentiment, more powerful than law, frowned us down.
>
> We were everywhere shut out from all civil office.
>
> We were excluded from all participation in the government.
>
> We were taxed without our consent.
>
> We were compelled to contribute to the resources of a country which gave us no protection.
>
> We were made a separate and distinct class, and against us every avenue of improvement was effectually closed. Strangers from all lands, of a color different from ours, were preferred before us.
>
> We uttered our complaints; but they were unattended to, or met only by alleging the peculiar institution of the country.
>
> All hope of a favorable change in our country was thus wholly extinguished in our bosoms, and we looked with anxiety abroad for some asylum from the deep degradation.

From the beginning, Liberia testified to America's failure to grant blacks the same rights and freedoms as whites.

Not surprisingly, bitter debate surrounded the idea of Liberia in the United States. Like Frederick Douglass, quoted in my epigraph, most African Americans opposed colonization as a racist scheme to remove Americans whose heritage and labor justified their citizenship every bit as much as, if not more than, that of anyone else in the United States. Philadelphia Bethel Church leaders in 1816, for example, called colonization "a circuitous route" back to slavery, a scheme to banish free blacks "into the wilds of Africa" (Liebenow 19). Martin Delany, though supportive of emigration to other parts of West Africa, called Liberia a "poor miserable mockery—a burlesque on a government [. . .] a mere dependency of Southern slaveholders" (Sundiata 3). Most abolitionists vigorously opposed colonization. William Lloyd Garrison, attacking the idea repeatedly, published *Thoughts on African Colonization* in 1832 and, as Brawley summarizes, charged the ACS in an editorial one year earlier

> first, with persecution in compelling free people to emigrate against their will and in discouraging their education at home; second, with falsehood in saying that the Negroes were natives of Africa when they were no more so than white Americans were natives of Great Britain; third, with cowardice in asserting that the continuance of the Negro population in the country involved dangers; and finally, with infidelity in denying that the Gospel has full power to reach the hatred in the hearts of men.
>
> (126–27)

African American emigrationists such as Edward Blyden and Bishop Henry McNeal Turner argued, however, that colonization offered American blacks freedom from oppression along with the great work of spreading Christianity, the missionary task of "African redemption" (Sundiata 3). Other Liberian settlers voiced much the same reasoning. Lott Carey of Richmond, Virginia, declared, "I am an African. I wish to go to a country where I shall be estimated by my merits, not by my complexion; and I feel bound to labour for my suffering race" (Liebenow 20). Writing back to the United States from Liberia in the 1870s, Scott Mason stated, "The Colored man never is free, and never will be until he plants his foot on the land of his forefathers"; Alonzo Hoggard said, "I am well satisfied here in this place. I have no more use for America" (Belcher et al. 1).

Others, however, regretted emigrating to Liberia. The climate hosted fatal diseases to which Americans had no immunity; the land would not support crops they knew how to cultivate; the geography confined them to a thirty- to forty-mile coastal strip; and the African people did not want to be colonized, which often resulted in armed conflict. Returning to the United States in the early 1930s, the former immigrant Elizabeth McWillie stated that many Americo-Liberians were "so fed up on Liberia that they would kiss a Mississippi cracker if he could only get them away from there." Another immigrant wrote to L. K. Williams of the National Baptist Convention in 1934, "I have never in my life seen black people hate other black people as this Administration and the so called leading people in Liberia hate the American Negroes; they do not want any American Negroes out here in large numbers" (Sundiata

112). A century of colonial rule, regardless of the invaders' skin color, had not made Africans love their conquerors.

The relationship between Liberia and the United States was ambiguous from the start. Never an official United States colony, Liberia nevertheless functioned as one and yet—because its transplanted Americans were black— also found itself ignored and abandoned by the United States government. The early colonial settlers reproduced European imperialism, setting themselves up as a ruling elite and maintaining that the native population would benefit because of the exposure to western civilization and Christianity. Late in the nineteenth century, the Firestone Rubber Company established a long period of economic imperialism, blessed and protected by both the Americo-Liberian and the United States governments; and Western economic imperialism helped block the black emigration project of Marcus Garvey's anti-European Universal Negro Improvement Association in the 1920s, which unlike ACS efforts had wide support in the United States black community. Not until 1980 did Americo-Liberian elite one-party rule end. (For detailed discussions, see Liebenow; Shick; Sundiata.)

From the beginning, Africans identified Liberian colonization with European and white American imperialism. J. Gus Liebenow summarizes the irony:

> Liberia was founded so that those who—on the basis of skin color alone—had been denied the rights and privileges of full participation in American society could enjoy the benefits of freedom in the continent of their ancestors. Yet, in the experience of securing the blessings of liberty for themselves, their treatment of the tribal people during the tutelary period under the American Colonization Society (1822–1847), as well as during the tenure of the First Republic (1847–1980), resulted in the systematic denial of liberty to others who were forcibly included within the Republic. (5)

Liebenow observes, "It was not unusual to hear tribal people refer to Americo-Liberians as Kwee, or 'white' people, or to have them call Monrovia [the capital of Liberia] 'the America place'" (23). As in any colonial regime, cultural and imported class differences ran deep in Liberia.

A dictated letter to the ACS in 1910 provides an indigenous perspective on this history of colonization. King Gyude and a group of chiefs of the Grebos explain that their predecessors welcomed the first black American settlers in 1834, "pitying their condition and rejoicing in their anticipation that by their settlement among us the benefits of Christian enlightenment and civilization would be disseminated among the youth of our land." However, the authors assert, the newcomers "soon began to despise us, placing us in their room and they in their masters', just in the same fashion as in their slavery days in America." Then in 1856, while *Uncle Tom's Cabin* was being devoured throughout the Western world, the Americo-Liberian rulers burned the homes of the

Grebo people and expelled them from their ancestral land, initiating a long bitter history in which, according to the king and chiefs, "the Liberian colony [. . .]
has operated as a source of oppression and demoralization to our people"
(Richardson 31–32).

Conceived by Southern planters, unsupported by most African Americans,
opposed by abolitionists, and rapidly and repeatedly resisted by Africans,
Liberia was always a contested idea. How, then, does one read the endorsement of colonization in *Uncle Tom's Cabin*?

Stowe places her support for Liberian emigration in the mouth of George
Harris (374–76), her smartest, whitest, most militant black—which, of course,
goes a long way toward explaining her endorsement of an idea that abolitionists from Douglass to Garrison roundly condemned. Deportation conveniently
solves the problem of dealing with demands for racial equality in America. If
at the end of *Uncle Tom's Cabin* George Harris remained in the United States,
or even just across the border in Canada, how would Stowe contain his militant
voice not just for emancipation but also for black equality? Imagine Tom living
rather than dying, and the point becomes obvious. Tom would never be a problem because he would always be a servant. George Harris, however, does present difficulties. Educated, enraged, determined not to acquiesce in American
racism, he represents a character potentially out of the author's control: an
articulate advocate for racial equality in the United States. Similarly, Topsy,
"civilized" and educated, represents a threat, as do an independent Eliza, the
Harris children, Cassy, and, quickly mentioned at the very end, Cassy's son, an
educated "young man of energy" (377). Consequently Stowe, in the tested tradition of the ACS, packs them all off to Africa, the place for dangerous, ambitious, free American blacks.

Yet if Stowe's endorsement of emigration reflects her racism, and it does, it
also and paradoxically signifies her respect for African Americans' full equality
as fellow Christians, world missionaries, and, therefore, potentially glorious
imperialists. Even those opposed to Liberian colonization in the nineteenth
century did not oppose it because it was wrong to inflict Western religion, social
codes, and economic systems on people who already had their own cultural
practices and beliefs. For blacks and whites alike, imperialism was not the issue;
exiling African Americans was. Therefore we need to ask: Is it possible to think
of Stowe's endorsement of Liberian colonization both as a racist plot to deport
American blacks *and* as an idealistic imperialist project (hard as it is for us to put
those terms together), with black people rather than whites in the lead? The
opposition of leaders such as Douglass and Garrison, the history of Liberia, and
progressive condemnation of imperialism today make it difficult to find anything positive in Stowe's support for African American colonization of Liberia.
Nevertheless, we need to note that Stowe assigns to black Americans the same
respected nineteenth-century status enjoyed or aspired to by many white Americans, that of pioneer or settler, which is to say, imperialist. She includes African
Americans as primary actors in *the* nineteenth-century western drama of colo-

nizing the globe in the name of Christianity and Western civilization. To remind ourselves that, like Stowe, many of our predecessors viewed colonialism positively, or at the very least uncritically, consider the respected African American historian Benjamin Brawley's description of Liberian settlers:

> If we compare them with the Pilgrim Fathers, we find that as the Pilgrims had to subdue the Indians, so they had to hold their own against a score of aggressive tribes. The Pilgrims had the advantage of a thousand years of culture and experience in government; the Negroes, only recently out of bondage, had been deprived of any opportunity for improvement whatsoever. (191)

That Americans might take pride in not living up to the Pilgrim Fathers' brutal example reflects my, not Brawley's, view.

In the final analysis, however, there is no rationalizing the racism of Stowe's Liberian solution, which readers have rightly criticized from the beginning (see, e.g., Allen). Reacting to attacks, Stowe herself in a letter to the American and Foreign Anti-Slavery Society regretted sending George Harris to Africa (R. Levine 536); and, clearly, even as she wrote *Uncle Tom's Cabin*, she knew her position required strenuous defense. She has George Harris try to rebut the standard anticolonization arguments of her day. He concedes that "the scheme may have been used, in unjustifiable ways, as a means of retarding our emancipation" and acknowledges that emigrants could be seen as turning their backs on fellow African Americans. In response, he maintains that a sovereign black nation in Africa would have power to speak "in the council of nations" worldwide: "A nation has a right to argue, remonstrate, implore, and present the cause of its race,—which an individual has not" (375). Most important, his motive for leaving the United States is the same as that of Liberian immigrants I have quoted. George renounces the United States—"I have no wish to pass for an American, or to identify myself with them" (374)—and, Afrocentrically, chooses Africa as his home. While the rhetoric is Victorian, the sentiment anticipates Marcus Garvey and W. E. B. Du Bois. George says, "I go to *my country*,—my chosen, my glorious Africa!" (376).

But then Stowe tips her hand entirely. Immediately following George's proud, impassioned denunciation of United States racism, she dispatches every educated black American in her book to Africa (377). George's rhetoric simply establishes the pretext for removing all powerful black opponents of racism in *Uncle Tom's Cabin*. Completing the picture, she next shows us the uneducated, newly freed blacks on the Shelby plantation so grateful to their magnanimous young white master that they vow never to leave the plantation (379). Stowe wants slavery to end and racial inequality to remain. There is no other conclusion.

Discussion of *Uncle Tom's Cabin* and Liberian colonization opens up important classroom questions about American imperialism, the United States and Africa, African American colonists, changing attitudes toward capitalist expansionism and Christian missionary empire building, nineteenth-century Afrocentricism and black pride, Harriet Beecher Stowe's racism, and the ways in which the design of narrative speaks. It also raises illuminating questions about contemporary attitudes. Students might discuss, for example, why white immigrants to the United States who stole Native American land are heroized as "pilgrims" and "pioneers" while black people who left the United States, often in bitterness and despair at the nation's racism, are at best forgotten and at worst vilified. As we judge Stowe, as we should, we also need to look at ourselves.

NOTES

The epigraph is quoted in Shick.

[1]Useful surveys of world events can be found in compendiums such as Freeman-Grenville or R. Stewart, to which students might be sent to gather information. Also see Takaki.

Pictures of Slavery in the United States: Consumerism, Illustration, and the Visualization of Stowe's Novel

Paul C. Gutjahr

In the years directly before the Civil War, Samuel Goodrich—self-proclaimed "author and editor of about one hundred and seventy volumes, [of which] seven millions have been sold"—devoted a chapter in his autobiography to the topic of the seemingly immeasurable growth of American publishing in the first half of the nineteenth century (Hall 1). He writes, "Unfortunately we have no official resources for exact statistics upon this subject. The general fact of a vast development in all the branches of industry connected with the press, [however,] is palpable to all persons having any knowledge of the subject" (Goodrich 757). Goodrich had entered the American printing trade in the latter part of the eighteenth century. By the time he wrote his autobiography in the 1850s, he had participated in and witnessed a profound change in the print culture of the young United States.

In 1855, the publisher George Putnam underlined this changed state of affairs in American publishing in a speech he gave to the Association of New York Publishers. Reflecting with obvious pride on the growth of the industry of which he was a part, Putnam concludes a long list of impressive growth statistics by noting that original American works had increased "800 per cent in less than twenty years. As the average increase in the population of the United States in the same time,—great as it was—scarcely reached 80 per cent, it appears that literature and the bulk of the book trade advanced ten times faster than the population." Putnam goes on to note that when one compares "the numbers printed of each edition" between 1842 and 1853 "the growth is still greater; for 20 years ago who *imagined* editions of 100,000 or 75,000, or 30,000, or even the now common number of 10,000?" ("Authors").[1] (At the beginning of the nineteenth century, 2,000 copies was the normal press run for a book.) Putnam and his colleagues were celebrating one of the most dynamic growth spurts in the history of American publishing.

Within this vast growth perhaps no single genre experienced a more meteoric rise than the novel. The *North American* stated in 1827 that this was the "age of novel writing. [. . .] The press daily, nay hourly teems with works of fiction." Four years later it would continue the theme by stating that "novels have broken upon us in a deluge." In 1843, the *Knickerbocker* referred to the "great multitudes of novel-readers" as being so large "that no man can number" them (Baym, *Novels* 26).[2] Towering above all other works of fiction before the Civil War was, of course, Harriet Beecher Stowe's *Uncle Tom's Cabin*, first serialized in the *National Era* and then published as a two-volume book on 20 March 1852. Its first day in print, it sold 3,000 copies. Within a week, 7,000 more copies had been sold; by the end of the first year, 300,000 copies of *Uncle Tom's Cabin* were in print as the publisher, John P. Jewett, kept eight power presses going around-the-clock to meet demand.

Although Stowe's novel sold at an unprecedented rate in the United States, it was even more popular in England. Within the first year of its publication, no less than six London publishers had produced twenty-two different editions of *Uncle Tom's Cabin*. By the spring of 1853, one and a half million copies of the novel had been sold in England, roughly tripling the number of copies sold in the United States in the same period. The British were not the only ones enamored with Stowe's novel. Within a decade of its appearance, *Uncle Tom's Cabin* had been translated into dozens of languages so that Italians, Hindus, Wallachians, Finns, Armenians, and Javanese could all read the novel in their native tongues (Stowe, *Uncle Tom's Cabin*, ed. Lynn xxviii). It was a book that truly enjoyed worldwide appeal.

Amid the novel's extraordinary popularity, it is important to remember that after Jewett's first edition of *Uncle Tom's Cabin*, the novel was never a single, uniform entity. As it began to be produced on both sides of the Atlantic Ocean in 1852, it reached the hands of readers in editions that involved different bindings, type fonts, paper, introductions, illustrations, and even subtitles. *The National Union Catalog* of book imprints bears striking witness to the diversity of *Uncle Tom's Cabin* editions, listing over 250 editions of the book published between 1852 and 1980; the book remains in print today in an impressive nineteen English language editions. While these editions share the same central core text, the different ways in which a novel is manufactured and marketed can exercise a profound influence on how one might read and interpret that text. As the librarian and scholar Roger Stoddard reminds us, "Whatever they may do, authors do *not* write books. Books are not written at all. They are manufactured by scribes and other artisans, by mechanics and other engineers, and by printing presses and other machines" (4). In examining how different versions of *Uncle Tom's Cabin* were manufactured and marketed, one discovers that the material nature of a text is often pivotal to understanding that text's reception and influence in specified historical moments. The way a book is packaged, advertised, and distributed can have ideological and interpretive ramifications that rival the importance and impact of the book's intellectual design.

In my own teaching, I have found it helpful to concentrate on a single aspect of the book's production in relation to its textual narrative in order to explore how issues such as marketing, technology, available material resources, and economics might illuminate the varied reading experiences offered by different editions. The single aspect on which I focus is how the novel has been illustrated in the past century and a half. (Equally fruitful avenues for exploring how book production influences textual interpretation might be the ways that Stowe's novel has been bound, edited, and presented in different type fonts.) *Uncle Tom's Cabin* was considered such a long book when it came out that John Jewett feared that a two-volume edition would be too great a financial risk. Stowe was not well-known and producing unsuccessful two-volume editions could easily lead a smaller publisher like Jewett into bankruptcy. When he did decide to press ahead in publishing *Uncle Tom's Cabin,* he chose to release it with seven original illustrations, hoping to mitigate his risk by making the volume more attractive to potential buyers.

No one knows how much Stowe was involved in the production of the engravings that first accompanied her book. If she was a typical author of her age, she probably had little say. Nonetheless, long before Jewett decided to commission illustrations for his edition of *Uncle Tom's Cabin,* Stowe was intent on making her narrative as "visual" as possible. Wanting her words to paint pictures that made her story come alive, she reflected on writing the novel:

> My vocation is simply that of a painter, and my object will be to hold up in the most lifelike and graphic manner possible Slavery, its reverses, changes, and the negro character, which I have had ample opportunities for studying. There is no arguing with *pictures*, and everybody is impressed by them, whether they mean to be or not.
>
> (qtd. in Hedrick, *Stowe* 208).

Several British editions picked up on the graphic nature of the story by adding to the book's subtitle the words *Pictures of Slavery in the United States* (e.g., the Ingram edition). Just how Jewett and other publishers chose to complement Stowe's penchant for the visual with actual illustrations profoundly influenced the reader's experience and interpretation of the novel. Even with Stowe's desire to argue with *"pictures"* and dozens of publishers commissioning illustrations for her book, the interpretive importance of illustrations on the book's written text is frequently ignored. One clear indication of this neglect is that even scholars and publishers who have worked hard to preserve the original edition's verbal text have shown no concern for having Jewett's first illustrations accompany that text.[3] As a consequence, later publishers of *Uncle Tom's Cabin* have damaged their quest for an accurate reproduction of Jewett's 1852 text by leaving out that text's original artwork.

In studying book illustrations, recent scholarship has tended to treat a volume's visual and verbal texts as two completely separate entities. You either study a book's pictures or its written text, but little thought is given to how a separate, third text is created once visual and verbal texts are juxtaposed. Studying these third texts provides an often untapped way of exploring the variable meaning of *Uncle Tom's Cabin* in different historical and cultural moments. To see this third text, consider how the illustrated title page interacts with the text in Jewett's first edition (fig. 1). Here under the novel's title, a group of African Americans are pictured around a log cabin. The illustration is a simple woodcut, which bears a striking resemblance to countless similar woodcut title pages found on almost every religious tract distributed by the American Tract Society (ATS), an organization that produced millions of religious tracts that were

UNCLE TOM'S CABIN;

OR,

LIFE AMONG THE LOWLY.

BY

HARRIET BEECHER STOWE.

VOL. I.

BOSTON:
JOHN P. JEWETT & COMPANY.
CLEVELAND, OHIO:
JEWETT, PROCTOR & WORTHINGTON.
1852.

Fig. 1. Title page illustration from the 1852 Jewett edition of *Uncle Tom's Cabin*.

among the most widely distributed and read forms of printed material in ante-bellum America.[4] These tracts were touted as absolute nonfiction, intended to expose readers to the truth of the Christian Gospel. Surely Stowe, who was careful to emphasize the truth of *Uncle Tom's Cabin* (she never referred to the book as a "novel," and in 1853 she published a long apologetic on it as nonfic-tion, *A Key to* Uncle Tom's Cabin), benefited by the association that would be drawn in many reader's minds between the truth of religious tracts and the truth they were about to read in her depiction of slavery.

One can see examples of how the visual and verbal combine to form third texts in various British editions that sprang up in the 1850s. The fierce compe-tition among British publishers to sell their copies of Stowe's novel led them to illustrate the novel in distinctive ways in an attempt to gain an advantage in a literary marketplace quickly becoming saturated with editions of Stowe's novel. Commingling different illustrations with Stowe's basic text created dissimilar third texts, which, in turn, created new associations and interpretations. For example, in 1852 the London firm of Ingram, Cooke, and Company released an edition with "six spirited engravings." Quite unlike Jewett's seemingly reli-gious illustrations, the pictures found in the Ingram edition focus on sex, vio-lence, death, and torture, lending a salacious quality to Stowe's novel. One of these engravings shows the whipping of George's bare-breasted sister when she refused to accept the advances of her white master (fig. 2). Since George's sister is not an actual character in Stowe's novel but is simply mentioned by George when he explains his hatred of slavery, the choice to depict this scene not only foregrounds a seemingly minor point in the narrative but also offers readers a titillating portrayal of sex and violence in a culture increasingly con-cerned with the importance of female virtue and the impropriety of showing nudity. Joy Kasson has argued that there existed a strong interest in—and con-cern about—the female nude form in nineteenth-century England and Amer-ica, partly derived from a Western interest in the Middle Eastern harem, and that many Protestants went to considerable effort to portray representations of female nudity as dangerous incentives toward vice (175–80). Ingram, Cooke, and Company chose illustrations that might attract readers by showing them the sexually charged, brutal nature of slavery while at the same time allowing them to enjoy the forbidden titillation of such an evil.

In my teaching, I raise a number of issues surrounding illustrations such as the one found in the Ingram edition. First, it is too easy simply to say that there are salacious overtones found in illustrations of Stowe's text that are not pres-ent in the narrative. I challenge my students to think about whether the illus-trations are taking undue license with the text or whether they are picking up salacious thematic elements already present in Stowe's writing. If such ele-ments are present, how do they interact with the heavily moral tone of the work? Second, while gender and nudity are clear issues in figure 2, so is race. This picture of violent, white domination over a black woman raises important issues concerning how a picture so clear in its ethnic brutality might undercut

GEORGE'S SISTER WHIPPED FOR WISHING TO LIVE A DECENT
CHRISTIAN LIFE.

Fig. 2. Illustration from an 1852 English edition of *Uncle Tom's Cabin* published by Ingram, Cooke, and Company. This publisher changed the subtitle of the book to read: "Pictures of Slavery in the United States."

the antislavery narrative it illustrates. For example, I raise questions about how this and similar illustrations might feed desires of racial domination by presenting the seeming rewards of being a member of a group who can exercise such unrestrained power. Finally, different illustrations foreground different narrative elements. I ask students whether illustrations have the ability to significantly influence one's "reading" of a given text. If so, are the different illustrated editions of *Uncle Tom's Cabin* really the same text?

Because so many different editions of Stowe's novel have been illustrated in the past century and a half, the same scene or character often shows up in contrasting ways. One is able to find various pictorial renditions of Eliza escaping across the ice, slaves being sold on the auction block, Uncle Tom learning to read, and the death of Eva. In my own teaching, I have found it fruitful to concentrate on a scene or a character that appears in several different editions to discuss the influence of these illustrations on the reader's experience and interpretation of Stowe's narrative.[5]

An excellent section of the novel on which to focus is chapter 32, "Dark Places." Beginning with an epigraph from Psalm 74 ("The dark places of the earth are full of the habitations of cruelty"), this chapter recounts Tom's arrival at Simon Legree's plantation. Figure 3 shows an illustration from Jewett's upscale 1853 reprint of *Uncle Tom's Cabin*, which is notable for two reasons. First, Jewett is still using woodblock prints to illustrate this edition, maintaining an associative link to ATS religious illustrations; second, these religious overtones are accented by the illuminated letter that begins each chapter's text. The illuminated "T" of this chapter reinforces the religious and truthful nature of the tale by evoking associations with the Bible, the most prominent volume to boast illuminated letters in the United States in this period. Examining the "T" provides a wonderful opportunity to discuss how type fonts can also influence the meaning of a text. Here, I find using examples from present-day magazine advertising helpful. Advertisers well know that presenting words in certain type fonts can guide their reader's interpretation of their message. Thus, words associated with high technology products such as lasers and computers are often presented in futuristic fonts while products associated with antiquity are presented in Gothic or some similar "historical" type font. Type fonts evoke various emotions and interpretations, and Jewett's upscale edition used letters such as the illuminated "T" to convey to his readers that this book was similar to the Bible not only in the value of its contents but also in the high level of craftsmanship indicative of the expensive family Bibles of his era.

Some sixty years later, the publishing firm of Grossett and Dunlap also chose to illustrate the "Dark Places" chapter, but its illustration is a still taken from a Universal Super-Jewel movie production of the novel. Thus, instead of a woodblock representation, the Grossett and Dunlap edition shows a group of slaves in a wagon (fig. 4). This photographic illustration is provocative for a number of reasons. Its caption—"Haley Taking His Slaves Back to His Plantation"—

CHAPTER XXXII.

DARK PLACES.

" The dark places of the earth are full of the habitations of cruelty."

Fig. 3. Illustration from chapter 32, "Dark Places," in the 1853 Jewett edition of *Uncle Tom's Cabin* (p. 428).

A Universal Super-Jewel Production.   *Uncle Tom's Cabin.*
HALEY TAKING HIS SLAVES BACK TO HIS PLANTATION.

Fig. 4. Illustration from chapter 32, "Dark Places," in the 1920s Grossett and Dunlap edition of *Uncle Tom's Cabin* (p. 366).

shows that the editor had not paid careful attention to the chapter's content since it is Legree's plantation, not Haley's, to which the slaves are being transported. And the inaccuracies continue. While Jewett's 1853 illustration correctly places Legree and the two women in the wagon with Tom with the other slaves trailing behind on foot, the Grossett and Dunlap edition shows two women, four men, and a child in the wagon. Because of such inaccuracies, one must ask why Grossett and Dunlap would choose to use such an illustration. A possible answer might be that movies were an increasingly popular entertainment medium in the early twentieth century, and publishers might have considered it a smart move to capitalize on this innovative and fashionable medium to draw readers to a not-so-new book. Accuracy may have seemed a small price to pay to be able to associate their book with the movies by including vivid, motion picture photographs in their edition.

While the choice of photographs associates the book with the emerging medium of motion pictures, it also offers a radically different reading experience than the one given to those using an edition illustrated with woodblock engravings. As Scott McCloud has argued in *Understanding Comics*, photographs particularize rather than universalize characters and themes (29). Unlike cartoon images—such as a smiley face made of a circle containing three dots and a curved line—that tend to universalize characteristics because they are vague and can be applied to a wide range of individuals, photographs are so particular that they invoke individual connotations. Thus, cartoonish illustrations, as often appear in woodblock engravings, have the ability to encompass a wider range of humanity, and readers are more readily able to associate themselves with the themes evoked by the less specific illustration. Photographs do the opposite. They fix themes and characteristics on tightly defined individuals through the use of minutely detailed representations, and thus fewer readers are able to associate with them.

One way to teach the different reading experiences offered by woodblock and photographic illustrations is to place figures 3 and 4 side by side for students. After juxtaposing these images, I then move from simple observation questions to questions centered on the emotional impact of each illustration. Observation questions might include the following: Which picture appears at a greater distance from the viewer? What are the figures doing in each picture? Where are they looking? What are the animals doing? What kind of foliage is found in the pictures? Does the foliage correspond to Stowe's descriptions in "Dark Places"? I then move to more interpretive questions: Which picture packs more emotional punch? Which draws you more into the narrative? What words would you use to describe the tone of each illustration? With few exceptions, students agree that the photographic illustration more forcefully draws them into the narrative by humanizing the misery of slavery. Even though there is more overt violence in the woodblock illustration (Legree holds his whip in a threatening manner toward his slaves), students more easily feel an association with the human figures and their misery in figure 4. The woodblock may be more violent and darker in tone because of its thick wilderness setting, but it is also seemingly positioned at a greater viewing distance from the reader. Figure 4 offers students a number of individuals who are in closer proximity to them as viewers, and the more detailed faces staring directly at them make students feel the horrors of treating people as property. The notion of slaves as property is underscored in both pictures by the animals drawing the wagons. In both cases, the beasts of burdens echo the action of the slaves. The oxen are at rest like the slaves sitting in the wagon. The horses are moving just as the slaves are in the woodblock illustration, and both slaves and horses are possible targets of Legree's whip.

The firm of Grossett and Dunlap was not the only one to adopt photographic illustrations into its editions of Stowe's novel. In 1904, Fenno and Company also released an edition of the book with photographic illustrations. A telling difference between the Grossett and Dunlap and the Fenno editions is that Fenno used blackface characters to depict African Americans, as figure 5 shows with its black-faced Topsy. If, once again, the textual integrity of Stowe's novel is compromised by an inaccurate illustration, a brunette rather than a blond Eva, much more important are the racial and economic overtones of African Americans being depicted by blackface whites. The Fenno edition does not allow African Americans to represent themselves; instead, whites usurp the right of representation, following a theatrical tradition that reached

Uncle Tom's Cabin.　Byron Photo.　Courtesy of W. A. Brady.

Topsy and Eva.　　　—*Page 301.*

Fig. 5. Illustration from the 1904 Fenno and Company edition of *Uncle Tom's Cabin* (p. 301).

back at least as far as the mid–nineteenth century. Thomas Low Nichols, a British physician who wrote extensively of his travels in the United States, tells the story of a blackface dancer working for P. T. Barnum:

> In New York, some years ago, Mr. P. T. Barnum had a clever [white] boy who brought him lots of money as a dancer of negro breakdowns; made up, of course, as a negro minstrel, with his face well blackened, and a woolly wig. One day master Diamond, thinking he might better himself, danced away into the infinite distance.

Barnum, full of expedients, explored the dance-houses of the Five Points and found a boy who could dance a better breakdown than master Diamond. It was easy to hire him, but he was a genuine negro; and there was not an audience in America that would not have resented, in a very energetic fashion, the insult of being asked to look at the dancing of a real negro. [. . .]

Barnum was equal to the occasion. [. . .] He greased the little 'nigger's' face and rubbed it over with a new blacking of burnt cork, painted his thick lips with vermillion, put on a woolly wig over his tight curled locks, and brought him out as the 'champion nigger-dancer of the world.' Had it been suspected that the seeming counterfeit was the genuine article, the New York Vauxhall would have blazed with indignation.

(qtd. in Lott, "Counterfeit" 227–28)[6]

Creating an atmosphere reminiscent of slavery and the prejudice faced by Barnum in giving his audiences the "dancing of a real negro" to watch, publishers who favored the use of blackface characters in illustrating Stowe's novel robbed African Americans of their personhood by failing to acknowledge their right to stand on an equal footing and represent themselves, to say nothing of how African Americans lost any financial benefits that might accompany representing their race in various forms of public display. The act of denying African Americans the right to represent themselves provides insight into race relations in the early twentieth century, as well as into the illustrative ironies found in a narrative that supposedly stands as one of the great polemics for human dignity.

Choosing illustrations that exclude African Americans from representing themselves raises questions about representation itself. For example, are the African Americans in Stowe's narrative accurate representations of slaves of that time? In fact is Fenno, in denying African Americans the right to represent themselves, but an echo of Stowe, who in writing for African Americans gave her own white voice to nonwhite characters? Also interesting in Nichols's commentary on Barnum is the ambiguous nature of representation. He talks of whites passing as blacks and blacks needing to pass as whites portraying blacks. Here one sees the same kind of ambiguity and complexity of representation that one finds throughout Stowe's novel. For example, the shifting, equivocal nature of representation comes across in the character of George who is able to hide his identity as a slave by the ways he dresses and depicts his color. On a deeper level, George has many "white" characteristics such as ingenuity, thrift, and industry that make him threatening to whites who find it more comforting to deal with slaves who do not exhibit so many tendencies toward "whiteness."

The oppression of African Americans in the United States shows up differently in a 1938 illustrated edition of *Uncle Tom's Cabin*. In an expensive, limited edition of Stowe's novel, Heritage Press produced a wonderfully rich and well-manufactured volume illustrated by the Mexican artist Miguel Covarrubias. Deeply concerned with the rights of all individuals to be proud exponents and perpetuators of their ethnic heritage, Covarrubias gave his representation of "Dark Places" a definite political edge.[7] Choosing to universalize his picture, Covarrubias adopts a more cartoonlike style with a chained African American lying before a large plantation house (fig. 6). Ignoring Stowe's description of the house as having a "ragged, forlorn appearance" covered with "frowsy tangled grass," Covarrubias depicts a well-manicured house framed by a weeping willow tree (298). Even the most cursory glance at the illustration leads the reader to associate the plantation house with the White House, a name eerily appropriate for Covarrubias' overall theme of racial oppression. Using the weeping willow to reinforce a deep sense of sadness, Covarrubias draws an immobile, prostrate and chained African American signaling that the United States as a whole, not just Legree's plantation, is "full of the habitations of cruelty" (296). Thus, Covarrubias points out that four score years after the Civil War, African Americans still await emancipation at the hands of a predominantly white, racially insensitive society. Covarrubias's illustrations raise a number of interesting questions, both historical and literary. I use figure 6 to pursue several avenues of investigation: Had the status of the African American significantly improved by the 1930s? Was Covarrubias justified in making his illustration into a political statement? What was the role of *Uncle Tom's Cabin* in the African American fight for equality in the United States? Was racial equality really a goal for Stowe as she wrote her novel? The numerous critical essays and the historical information found at the end of the Norton Critical Edition of the novel enable students to begin to explore some of these questions.

Stowe had seen her vocation in writing *Uncle Tom's Cabin* as "that of a painter" holding "up in the most lifelike and graphic manner possible Slavery, its reverses, changes, and the negro character" (qtd. in Hedrick, *Stowe* 208). This notion of a visual element in written texts has all but disappeared in an age of televisions, motion pictures, and virtual reality. Yet for this intensely visual generation of students, I have found that the hundreds of illustrations that have accompanied Stowe's text from its first edition onward help them recapture a sense of the novel's highly graphic nature. Studying the illustrations gives them the opportunity to note that one's interpretation of a text is influenced not only by what the writer has written but also by how the text has been packaged and presented to its reader. Illustrations allow students to deepen their discussions of a text by talking about medium as well as message. As we move into an age of multimedia and the Internet, discussions of the various editions of *Uncle Tom's Cabin* can help students reflect on more than just the nature of the printed word. Students can also consider the way information is given to them and the way their own perceptions of that information are not strictly content bound, but also tied to how that information reaches them.

Fig. 6. Miguel Covarrubias's lithograph illustration from chapter 32, "Dark Places," in the 1938 Heritage Press edition of *Uncle Tom's Cabin* (p. 226).

A SELECT LIST OF ILLUSTRATED EDITIONS
OF *UNCLE TOM'S CABIN*

John P. Jewett and Company, Boston, 1852. 1st ed., 2 vols. Seven woodcut engravings.

Ingram, Cooke, and Company, London, 1852. "Embellished with Eight Spirited Engravings."

J. Cassell, London, 1852. Twenty-seven illustrations by George Cruikshank.

Partridge and Oakey, London, 1852. Twelve wood engravings by H. Anelay.

Clarke, London, 1852. "People's Illustrated Ed. with 50 splendid engravings."

George Routledge and Company, London, 1853. Illustrations by Phiz, Gilbert, and Harvey.

John P. Jewett and Company, Boston, 1853. New, upscale illustrated edition by Jewett.

Houghton, Mifflin, and Company, New York, 1892. Illustrated by E. W. Kemble.

George M. Smith and Company, Boston, 1897. Over one hundred original illustrations by celebrated artists.

Dominion Company, Chicago, 1897. "Art Memorial Edition."

McLoughlin Brothers, Inc., Springfield, 1900. Abridged, illustrated children's edition.

Grossett and Dunlap, New York, n.d. Illustrated by Louis Betts.

Grossett and Dunlap, New York, n.d. Illustrated from the Universal Super-Jewel Production.

R. F. Fenno and Company, New York, 1904. Illustrated with photographs and lithographs.

A. and C. Black, Ltd., London, 1922. Illustrated by Simon Harmon Vedder.

Heritage Press, New York, 1938. Sixteen lithographs by Miguel Covarrubias.

World Publishing Company, Cleveland, 1939. Chromolithograph frontispiece.

Coward-McCann, Inc., New York, 1947(?). Illustrated by James Daugherty.

Dodd, Mead, and Company, New York, 1952. Introductory remarks and captions by Langston Hughes.

Penguin Books, New York, 1981. Cover illustration and frontispiece.

NOTES

[1]For accounts of the event itself, see Tebbel 225–27 and Zboray 3–5. Sellers writes concerning the growth in book publishing during this same period: "The estimated value of American book output more than doubled from $2.5 million in 1820 to $5.5 million in 1840, and again to $12.5 million in 1850 (371).

[2] For fuller discussions of the popularity of the novel in the early nineteenth century, see Boynton 139–44; J. Hart; Baym, *Novels* 26–43; Davidson, *Revolution* 38–54.

[3]For an example of this concern with textual purity, see "A Note on the Text" in the Penguin edition (H. Stowe, *Uncle Tom's Cabin*, ed. Douglas, 37). Here, as in other recent editions, there is special mention made that the "volume reprints the first-edition

text," but the original illustrations are not present in this supposedly accurate textual reprint. In contrast, the Norton Critical Edition does include the original illustrations.

[4]For a sampling of ATS frontispieces, see L. Thompson; Nord, *Evangelical Origins* and "Religious Reading"; and Tompkins, *Sensational Designs* 149–60.

[5]See the conclusion of this essay for a short (albeit incomplete) list of various editions of *Uncle Tom's Cabin* that include provocative illustrations, helpful for classroom discussion. Perhaps the best strategy for teachers interested in using the book's constantly evolving illustrations in the classroom is to visit their local libraries and bookstores and page through different editions. Because nineteen English versions are still in print, the diversity of ways the book is packaged is stunning—and useful in one's teaching. Libraries and used bookstores are also wonderful sources for finding previous editions of Stowe's most reprinted book.

[6]A teacher choosing to share this quote with a class can use Nichols's comments to make some observations on the changing nature of language. When Nichols wrote his book, the word *nigger* was in common usage among Northern blacks and whites. In contemporary usage, the term carries heavily negative connotations. One way I have addressed this issue of offensive language is to contextualize the evolution of *nigger* to *Negro* to *black* to *Afro-American* to *African American*. Each of these terms has been used to describe African Americans at different points in our nation's history. By exploring the etymological histories of each of these terms, students come to a fuller appreciation of the way labels can give, or take, dignity from the subject they denominate.

[7]For the most complete biographical treatment of Covarrubias and his particular interest in illustrating *Uncle Tom's Cabin*, see: A. Williams.

CONTROVERSY AND DEBATE

Who Gets to Create the Lasting Images?
The Problem of Black Representation
in *Uncle Tom's Cabin*

Sophia Cantave

For late-twentieth-century teachers, the significance of Harriet Beecher Stowe as a white woman creating a national space for an "empathetic" discourse on the slave experience raises several questions. For instance, why didn't Mary Prince's exposé of slavery in the West Indies, *The History of Mary Prince* (1831), or Harriet Wilson's account of de facto slavery in the American North, *Our Nig* (1859), become the proverbial "shot heard around the world"? What enabled Stowe to write *Uncle Tom's Cabin* and begin a national and international literary exchange on slavery? The novel invented the modern idea of a "best-seller," and many of Stowe's characters became national stock types and icons. Even today, readers cry at the right places and express horror, relief, or disbelief where textually appropriate. Most important, Stowe's text allows whites to talk to other whites about the personal and national issues surrounding the slave experience and establishes the character types usually associated with African Americans. Indeed, throughout the second half of the nineteenth century and then the early twentieth century, Stowe's novel provided the nation with a shared cultural context for its discourse on slavery, offering reductive images, phrases, and symbols that quickly became the accepted norm.

For example, early in the twentieth century *Uncle Tom's Cabin* permitted the nameless narrator of James Weldon Johnson's *The Autobiography of an Ex-Colored Man* (1912) to talk finally to his mother about their racial identity. But what does it mean when two highly miscegenated characters use a white woman's novel as the basis for a discussion of their blackness in the United

States? In contrast, *The History of Mary Prince*, though heavily edited, failed to galvanize the literate community or fill the racial imaginings of Americans. And the suppression of Harriet Wilson's *Our Nig* prevented it from shaping the national conceptions of the slave and nonslave experience.

When we use Stowe's novel in the classroom, I think it is important to ask who gets to make our national symbols and who gets to determine when a particular symbol or icon has outlived its usefulness. Although *Uncle Tom's Cabin* was essential in creating an earlier discourse on the slave experience, what is the usefulness of teaching the novel today? I reexamine that question. At the turn into the twenty-first century, I think modern readers want to bury the discourse Stowe began under the fiction that "we already know about slavery"— yet we do not know. To begin a broader discussion of American women's involvement in the "peculiar institution" as slaves, as slave owners, and as writers, readers need to go beyond the humiliating or embarrassing surface of the text and examine the issues that the existence of the novel raises. In this essay, I focus on Stowe's problematic status and symbols to ask where the United States slave experience, as Stowe writes it, should fit in a modern literary context—a question that should surely precede any teaching of the novel.

At first, a return to *Uncle Tom's Cabin* feels like a return to a crime scene with too many nagging questions left unanswered. Because of these questions, Stowe's novel should regain its place in contemporary classrooms and be taught for what it signifies about United States race relations 150 years after slavery. Few African Americans criticized Stowe's novel at the time of its initial publication. In the mid–nineteenth century, African American emancipation depended on acknowledging and supporting the national and international debate sparked by *Uncle Tom's Cabin*. Where all other writers "failed," Stowe succeeded. The significance of her success, and the instant commercialization of her subject, placed many of the African American abolitionists in an odd position. How does Frederick Douglass criticize a novel he feels beholden to? For the most part, Douglass praised the novel's efficacy and tirelessly referred to *Uncle Tom's Cabin* as the "master book of the nineteenth century" (Donovan 17). Of her text, Stowe said, "My vocation is simply that of a painter, and my object will be to hold up in the most lifelike and graphic manner possible Slavery, its reverses, changes, and the negro character, which I have had ample opportunities for studying. There is no arguing with *pictures*, and everybody is impressed by them, whether they mean to be or not"(Hedrick, *Stowe* 208). The power, efficacy, and timeliness of *Uncle Tom's Cabin* cannot be denied. But the unsettling issues surrounding Stowe's access and her relation to the "objects of her study" should not be denied either. At the turn into the twenty-first century, Stowe's novel continues to evoke uneasiness when readers consider blackness and, more important, slavery as the "canvas" that allowed her to write her most famous novel.

As is well known, Stowe's "sketches of slave life," as she popularly referred to her novel (Hedrick, *Stowe* 208), would eventually influence the development of the modern theater, the development of philanthropy as a business, and the marketing of "Uncle Tom" paraphernalia. Less well known is the fact that a viewing of *Uncle Tom's Cabin* served as the catalyst for Thomas Dixon's literary career. As part of his refutation of Stowe's version of Southern slavery, Dixon wrote *The Clansman* (1905), which later became the basis for D. W. Griffith's classic, racist movie, *The Birth of a Nation* (1915). In other words, the negative influence of Stowe's novel on the development of United States popular culture even in cases such as this, where Stowe's text is being attacked, must be considered. And the readily available "canvas of blackness" that allowed Stowe's sketches to come to life continues to enable the nation to solidify its power not only to relegate black people to the margins but also to regulate the discourses surrounding what constitutes human suffering and degradation. The slave experience, far from being understood, is trapped in multiple hegemonic constructions of power and nation as well as by self-imposed restrictions on language.

Many middle-class African Americans want to forget, or get past, the images of Topsy "just growing," of Sambo and Quimbo, of Sam and Andy, of Chloe and Uncle Tom himself. Members of the African American middle class shun what the black urban masses, largely the working poor, often vilify and reclaim with their popular usage of such terms as *niggers* and *hoes*, *players*, and *freaks* when referring to one another. Which national face should African Americans present as what they understand of their positionality and blackness in America? The slave experience, in the African American psyche, continues metaphorically to grope for the words to explain the silence, including the profusion of reactions to a white woman writing and creating a national discourse on slavery. These anxieties, in part, explain late-twentieth-century returns to the Middle Passage and its aftermath. Questions remain about black speaking subjects even as modern writers like Toni Morrison, Octavia Butler, Gloria Naylor, Charles Johnson, and others travel back in time in attempts to wrest control of black images from benevolent but racist white supporters and their detractors.

Josephine Donovan points out that Stowe, in explaining her construction of *Uncle Tom's Cabin*, said:

> "The writer acknowledges that the book is a very inadequate representation of slavery [because] slavery, in some of its workings, is too dreadful for the purposes of art. A work which should represent it strictly as it is would be a work which could not be read; and all works which ever mean to give pleasure must draw a veil somewhere, or they cannot succeed." In fiction, therefore, one can "find refuge from the hard and the terrible, by inventing scenes and characters of a more pleasing nature."   (62)

In her successful attempt to make slavery readable, Stowe falls back on the comic interactions of blacks with other blacks and of blacks while in the presence of whites. By mixing the tragic and the laughable, *Uncle Tom's Cabin* gives white people and black people a way to read slavery together. This does not mean that African Americans did not then, and do not now, make use of comedy to explain parts of slavery. They had to and often did so for the benefit of their owners. Thus the joking relationship and the various uses of the comic exist as one of the earliest accepted signs of black subordination and one that slaves continuously manipulated. But the comic interactions as Stowe uses them do not so much subvert as reinforce the existing order.

This shared reading almost always insists that slavery, in its entirety, cannot be read and that slavery and the slave experience do not make for "good art." In some ways, this designation of slavery as unreadable and unfit for the purposes of high art continues, almost 150 years after the publication of *Uncle Tom's Cabin*. In assessing her novel, Stowe gives herself the power to decide on the purposes of art and when and where to draw the veil when writing on slavery. Thus, despite even her best intentions, *Uncle Tom's Cabin* betrays her overwhelming race and class privileges and the ways she herself helped to further limit African Americans' access to the dominant language and their own literary portrayal of the slave experience.

To do the necessary research for *Beloved* (1987), Toni Morrison went to Brazil to see various slave restraints like the iron collar and muzzle used to control and torture. The United States sterilized and reduced the slave narratives and slavery into formulaic stories that the nation as a whole felt more comfortable reading. Morrison confronts, in writing, what many of the early United States narratives could not when she writes about the devastating psychological trauma of slavery. She exposes the ease with which an exploding national discourse reduced the grossest human violations into instances of comic relief and shows how sentimental release acts as a potent signifier of white hegemonic control. For example, fearing competition where none existed before, Fuzzy Zoeller made a disparaging comment to an understanding white CNN newscaster about fried chicken littering a once exclusive golf tournament, a remark that immediately undercut the record-breaking achievement of Tiger Woods. Despite black excellence and achievement, such jokes, at key moments, perpetuate age-old images of nonwhite incompetence and buffoonery. In choosing to intersperse the comic alongside the tragic, Stowe inadvertently provided a way for white people, when threatened or challenged, to regulate black achievement, black national mobility, and black cultural expression. Even the relationships that black people form with one another are circumscribed by such strategies of the dominant culture and its definitions of blackness.

One way to illuminate these issues is by teaching *Uncle Tom's Cabin* side by side with Harriet Wilson's *Our Nig*, published just seven years after *Uncle Tom's Cabin*. Harriet Wilson, a severely marginalized black woman, began in her writing to make powerful connections with other black people about their shared economic and color oppression. Her disastrous marriage to a black man claiming to be a former slave goes beyond what Stowe imagines as the motivating force behind black female-male relationships. That is, Wilson's Frado

leaves the best home she has ever known and her only moment of relative independence because she is drawn to a man who she believes shares her experiences. Aside from Frado's dead father and the man her mother runs off with,
her husband makes the third black man to enter her life. Wilson makes a point
of saying that Frado reacts to the bond created by their similar backgrounds.
Ironically, however, Frado's husband lies about his slave experience and quickly
abandons his new bride. Yet Wilson does not dwell on this lie. Instead, she
hints that Frado's husband felt compelled to play the role of a former slave in
order to get Northern abolitionists' sympathy and assistance. My point here has
to do with the complexity of Wilson's perspective. Although Frado's marriage
leads to her further physical deterioration, it shows Frado making choices that
do not depend on white benevolence or white fictions of black desire. Yet
because of her husband's dependence on white Northern sympathy, Frado
indirectly suffers.

Wilson's multiple strategies of reappropriation and renaming help her sub-
versively assert herself as a speaking subject. Even though heavily circumscribed and limited, she directs her appeals to her colored brethren, not the
white masses. She asks her colored brethren to forgive her faulty prose and
purchase her novel or, rather, her "sketches from the life of a free black, in a
two-story white house, North." She says in her preface, "I have purposefully
omitted what would most provoke shame in our good anti-slavery friends at
home"(4). Wilson echoes almost the same sentiments as Stowe—that the worst
of slavery has been omitted—but for different reasons. After her abandonment
first by her mother and then by her husband, Wilson had to depend on the
"good anti-slavery friends at home," the class that Stowe belonged to. Wilson's
disclaimer says that she leaves out what would show Northern white abolitionists to be very much like their Southern white slaveholding counterparts. Wilson assumes much more subjectivity than the nation, in 1859, was prepared to
accept or believe in a black speaker. If Stowe's detractors vehemently refuted
"her blacks" as thinking subjects, *Our Nig*, written by a black woman in the
North, gave white readers even more reason to dismiss Wilson's text altogether.
At least with *Uncle Tom's Cabin*, later dramatic adaptations could exclude the
heavily abolitionist tracts and overplay the comic moments that comfortably
disrupt sections assigning blame or showing black agency since the joke always
has a derogatory black reference that serves as the punch line. Students need
to know that Topsy, on the stage, became an instant hit with the audiences in
part because her reformation into a serious-minded missionary was conveniently left out. In contrast, Frado, far from being the butt of the jokes, insti-
gates them and possesses more self-awareness than Topsy, who is primarily
constructed as the antithesis of Little Eva.

Wilson offers her readers Frado's body both in its linguistic negation and as
the epitome of Northern conceptions of blackness despite her light skin and
white mother. Mrs. Bellmont, her keeper, delights in her complete control of
Frado's body. She keeps on hand special blocks that she forces into the child's

mouth in order to beat her with even greater abandon. Mrs. Bellmont cripples Frado's body without ever losing her status as a respectable member of her community. These spaces in Wilson's text of possible catharsis through the sadistic pleasure of physically or mentally violating black bodies present an unexplored area for students to think about. In contrast, Stowe emphasizes the sadism and ruthlessness of slave violation at the hands of white men, making Marie St. Clare the monstrous exception to the rule, while Mary Prince and Harriet Wilson delve deep into the pleasure white women derive from the physical energy expended in beating bodies even more marginalized than their own.

Harriet Wilson, writing her fictionalized autobiography only a few years after *Uncle Tom's Cabin*, gave considerable thought to her audience. She appealed to a black readership while simultaneously considering how white readers might receive her text. Wilson says in her preface, "I do not pretend to divulge every transaction in my own life, which the unprejudiced would declare unfavorable in comparison with treatment of legal bondmen" (4). Because she lived in the North, Wilson left out the worst of what she experienced as a free black there, lest she alienate abolitionists. She wrote her autobiographical novel in an attempt to earn enough money to support herself and her son, who died before she sold one copy and her entire project slipped into obscurity. Conversely, Stowe as a writer committed to the abolitionist movement but also desiring a modicum of success in her endeavor, made the slave's experience readable, palatable for her expected audience. In Uncle Tom's Cabin: *Evil, Affliction, and Redemptive Love* Josephine Donovan says, "The slave narratives tended to focus on one person's unhappy experiences from that individual's point of view. Stowe realized that no one would read a novel that was relentlessly grim (indeed *Uncle Tom's Cabin* outsold all of the slave narratives and abolition novels put together)" (62). The fact that "*Uncle Tom's Cabin* outsold all of the slave narratives" underscores the significance of Stowe's literary and transgressive access to her potent subject matter that fueled the uninhibited imagination of the country. *Uncle Tom's Cabin* sold more copies than any American novel before or, for a long time, after it because Stowe's position as a white woman from a family of preachers enabled her to write not only with moral conviction but also with the necessary distance to calculate a specific textual effect. While being driven by a moral obligation to write against an institution she saw as diametrically opposed to Christianity, Stowe produced a text that surpassed even her wildest expectations.

But what has been the effect of this book on black people? An experiment lasting over fifteen years conducted by Albion Tourgee, a novelist, judge, and activist who spoke out against racial segregation, provides one answer. Tourgee had former slaves read or listen to readings of *Uncle Tom's Cabin* because he wanted "to determine to what extent [they] thought [*Uncle Tom's Cabin*] was an accurate portrayal of southern slavery" (Gossett, *American Culture* 361). " 'Choosing the most intelligent colored people' available he 'found that most ex-slaves did not think Uncle Tom was too meek as later generations of black activists would. Instead they thought of him as unrealistically critical of his masters. Tom spoke out more frankly than a real slave might have dared to'" (Donovan 17). The few recordings of black responses to *Uncle Tom's Cabin* vacillate between evasive silences and complete acceptance of Stowe's words and reactions, suggesting that her depictions are better than what slaves could have produced. Donovan gives the example of a female former slave perfectly content with Stowe's words standing in for her own. "Sella Martin [. . .] in speaking of her difficulty in describing the horrors of being sold at the auction block, remarked, 'happily this [. . .] task is now unnecessary. Mrs. Stowe [has] thrown sufficient light upon the horrible and inhuman agency of slavery'"(17). Stowe also felt that it was *she* who should represent (and profit from) the telling of slave experiences, as her treatment of Harriet Jacobs's narrative illustrates. Instead of giving Jacobs the literary advice she sought, Stowe offered to include Jacobs's narrative in her *Key to* Uncle Tom's Cabin. The slave experience, with all its violations and humiliations, was the property of Harriet Beecher Stowe.

Yet according to one male former slave in Tourgee's study, Stowe "didn't know what slavery was so left out the worst of it" (Gossett, *American Culture* 361). To give even this cautious yet pointed critique was daring. He provides a reason completely different from the one Stowe gives for leaving out the worst of slavery. Attributing only this line to the speaker, Tourgee does not give any more space for the former slave to describe "the worst of it" beyond saying "the worst of it." Tourgee, though, provides his own analysis of speech and non-speech patterns in slave communities. He says, "Perhaps the most striking feature characteristic of slavery was the secretiveness it imposed upon slave nature. [. . .] To the slave, language became in very truth an instrument for the concealment of thought, rather than its expression" (Donovan 17). Little wonder that language "became an instrument of concealment" in the face of overwhelming racial inequality and racial violence. Tourgee himself says, "Men do not argue with those who have the power of life and death over them" (Gossett, *American Culture* 361). Language itself continues to place black bodies as speaking subjects, then and now, at risk. In Uncle Tom's Cabin *and American Culture*, Thomas F. Gossett also discusses the conflicted responses of black people to Stowe's novel. Stowe wrote her novel at a time when African humanity, intelligence, and subjectivity were still being debated. Gossett says that many white readers criticized Stowe's portrayals of black people as being too complimentary. This sentiment, in combination with little or no access to the text, made it difficult for African American readers of that period to challenge the novel's reductiveness. After the publication of *Uncle Tom's Cabin*, African Americans who wanted to speak about blackness in America and be heard had to do it through Stowe or not at all.

Consequently, James Weldon Johnson's protagonist can begin a serious and thoughtful discussion of race only in the context of *Uncle Tom's Cabin*. Ironically, a man who sees himself as white and eventually decides to pass as white reads Stowe's novel in much the same way that sympathetic white readers read *Uncle Tom's Cabin*. The "thingness" of blacks, despite the richness of a culture little understood and searching for its expression, leads the Ex-Colored Man to live the life of "an ordinarily successful white man who has made a little money" (510). The risk involved in expressing himself as a black person causes him to "[sell his] heritage for a mess of pottage" (511), and the unspeakable act of lynching another human being remains uncontested. Significantly, the lynching occurs at the moment the Ex-Colored Man finishes his documentation of black music and cultural expression in the South and begins contemplating the future publication of his findings. Confronted with such a display of power—the lynching of a black man by a group of respectable citizens—a miscegenated black man chooses whiteness and the suppression of any and all claims to black subjectivity and authorship.

In considering issues of authorship and vocality, the following question also needs to be raised in the classroom: When can black people speak and in what words that do not already replicate in some way the dialectic of past ownership and subordination? Even as modern writers anxiously go back to write and say the things that enslaved or freed blacks could not say, what are the words and images that will not leave them at risk and produce yet again another silencing in the present age? Too little has been done with the contemporary resurgence in pop culture of "niggers," "boys," "players," "freaks," and "hoes," all old images with old origins. The comic, the hypersexualized, and the desexualized remain as the most readily available symbols of African Americans in the United States. In place of words, Stowe and a minstrel tradition older than the one she helped formalize give black expression wholly over to hand gestures, mimicry, stoicism, and other nonspeech acts.

Given this reduction of black expression to the guttural, the comical, and the lewd, the dominating theoretical framework for analyzing black literature and black culture, in the early twentieth century, focused on psychic doubling, veils, tricksterism, and masks. All these approaches centered on black performance and the stifling relation of black bodies to a power structure that did not see itself as oppressive or feel culpable in demanding these performances of race. The current discourse on race allows for too many gaps, too many silences, while whole discussions about race and racial equity continue to take place without the participation or presence of black people. Stowe's discarded subtitle, *The Man That Was a Thing*, accurately describes the role of black people when white people gather to discuss who they will and will not allow entry into their coveted circles. African American struggles to wrest control of our national images, icons, and symbols from the white power structure must continue as part of the fight against objectification and erasure.

African American discourse, even in urban slang, still manages to conceal, evade, and leave much, sometimes too much, unsaid. The silent ironies of early African American discourses, though ensuring African American survival despite physical and psychic violation, need to "call Stowe out of her name." To do this "calling out" (and make Stowe's text useful in the classroom) students must question the novel's runaway success and influence not only in the United States but also around the world. Similarly, students must also question the complex social, cultural, and political context, at this fin de siècle, that keeps Stowe's text from being read by both black and white readers. The resistance to the kinds of remembrances that *Uncle Tom's Cabin* provokes about the nation's slave past provides other ways to discuss issues of African American textual silence, erasure, and the continuing appropriation of black images. In rethinking black people's reaction to this encroachment, what happens when irony is lost on its audience, when silence, double subversions, reversals get buried so deep they become undecipherable and completely disconnected from their original negation? African American literary discourse began with multiple capitulations to a white reading public that made discussing and writing about the worst of slavery unacceptable. In addition to the frayed and moldy bills of sale, the "owners" of the slave experience and its symbols also own and regulate the national discourses on slavery. *Uncle Tom's Cabin* may have wanted to show how slave owners could overcome the reification and reduction of human beings to the status of things but this reduction and reification are precisely what happen in the novel and particularly in the Tom shows it inspired. For teachers today, the novel exists as an uncomfortable but necessary place to begin critical discussions about the racial dynamics of literary access, power, and popular culture.

As the writer who helped shape the national discourse on slavery, Stowe provided the parameters of that discourse, establishing where slavery can and cannot go in the popular imagination and as high literature. These stifling limitations explain, in part, why two subversive black women's texts, Wilson's *Our Nig* and Prince's narrative, received little or no literary attention at the time of their original publication. In many ways, 150 years after Stowe published her novel, African Americans still do not have the words to say what the worst of slavery really was, or rather, African Americans did not create the terms that define the slave experience in the national consciousness. African Americans who step outside the accepted parameters of slavery's discourse risk shutting down discussions, arousing white defensive or apologetic barrages and black desires to acquiesce and make nice in the face of such responses. All these responses take away from speaking honestly and critically about power inequities even in some of the most common social interactions. In acquiescing, in giving up the national discursive space to white culture, unspeakable things remain unspoken, especially in the academy where one's vocality, erudition, and authorship matter. "Being nice," helping to keep one's colleagues comfortable, results in the loss of too much ground. All these issues in one way or another come into play in Stowe's novel. *Uncle Tom's Cabin*, precisely because of its literary success and its continuing, though unadmitted, influence on United States cultural history, needs to reenter current, critical discussions of race to shed light on some of the nagging issues that are still too difficult to name.

Historically, *Uncle Tom's Cabin* provided a framework for the United States and the European nations to discuss the "peculiar institution" and their positions within that institution. Stowe's novel in a late-twentieth-century classroom context should highlight issues of appropriation, privilege, national accountability, and the intricate workings of power in the United States. After the publication of *Uncle Tom's Cabin*, almost all slave narratives by black people became a part of Harriet Beecher Stowe's *Key to* Uncle Tom's Cabin. That is, the telling of the slave experience became a strangely white affair, being told in ways that let white audiences be moved to tears and still find the work enjoyable. Yet the former slaves' responses to the novel seem to tell a different story, one about the absence of their words and what it means to accept someone else's language. Stowe's own admission, that slavery as it existed did not make for good art, supports my belief that what the nation as a collective understands about race relations it does not write or readily discuss except, possibly, in the joking relationship. The national fiction of understanding and knowing slavery exists as a complex cultural production depending on black and white people to play their parts. The very idea of Stowe giving her words to a former slave woman disturbingly points to the issues at stake in questions of authority and ownership. The quote of the nameless male former slave who lamented the absence of "the worst of slavery" in literature represents what remains forever out of reach when black people fail to resist and question master/mistress narratives, even ones that are done with the best intentions.

Denying African Americans the opportunity to tell their story without comic interjections left whole things unsaid. Early on, African Americans, the majority of whom were unable to write freely in their own words about their experiences, did not create the lasting images of the slave experience. Simultaneously, Stowe refused to write the worst of slavery. African Americans, unable to tell the worst of slavery directly, packed multiple meanings in generic evasive responses that lessened the linguistic and physical risks involved in speaking in a repressive society. The unspoken, the unspeakable, became its own signifier. Arguing these points in the classroom does not mean that black people did not imagine themselves in relation to other blacks, other people of color, or that black people were not instrumental in advocating for changes that established legal precedents for other groups to follow. It does mean that African American cultural production and discourses need to move from the margins, where they are easily appropriated and reauthored, to the center.

Locating Stowe in her historical moment and outside it, a century and a half later, provides the setting for a discussion of the politics involved in her discursive access to her black subjects and the continuing use of black bodies as fodder for the nation's intellectual, cultural, economic, and political revisions and reassessments. To read the criticism on Stowe, even that which goes beyond questioning her literary status, is to confront over and over again the "thingness" of the African American slave body. Despite Stowe's own marginalization as a woman in her own period, the "thingness" of African American bodies and the pervasive acceptance of a culture based on human ownership made the figures of Uncle Tom, Topsy, Eliza, Cassy, Dinah, Sam, Andy, Sambo, and Quimbo available to her. These images of African Americans persist in their original and updated forms, as efforts to denounce the persistence of the mammy figure in the late 1980s illustrate. After threatened boycotts, the makers of Aunt Jemima pancakes responded to the criticism of their logo by unveiling a new version of the mammy figure. Since removing the logo was out of the question, the Quaker Oats Company decided to remove Aunt Jemima's head scarf and give her a perm. Thus the new "Aunt Jemima" cut short any and all efforts to denounce continued use of the mammy figure. Silence, shame, embarrassment, and powerless indignation filled the space where anger and continued activism belonged. African Americans, in Stowe's time and now, do not own the images and symbols of African American culture, long wedded to big business and commercial success. Only a perm separates a mammy of the slave era from one in the late twentieth century.

To have this myriad of black bodies at the nation's collective disposal bespeaks a power that white culture rarely admits to owning. In the late twentieth century, Uncle Tom/Sam is Clarence Thomas, Eliza/Chloe/Cassy is Anita Hill, and George Harris is potentially a young O. J. on the rise. These black figures act as catalysts for national debates on racial parity, equity in the justice and law enforcement systems, sexual harassment, spousal abuse, and the responsibilities of government agencies to the working poor. Renewed attacks on affirmative action, white culture's only begrudging capitulation to the intricate and exclusive workings of white privilege, reassert white culture's power to decide what constitutes African American access and redress for past inequities. In these displays of power, white hegemony reasserts its control by limiting not only the extent of black people's access but also their creative and competitive potential.

Without any particular acknowledgment or any sense of appropriation, expression of the slave experience became Stowe's own. It is this ownership, this appropriation of African American images, phrases, and culture by white culture, that continues to threaten the legitimacy of African American literature in the academy and that needs to be interrogated in the classroom. Blackness remains, at the turn into the twenty-first century, one of the few subjects that does not go beyond genteel academic or social discussion. In discussing blackness and making it readable for a predominantly white power structure, Stowe says, the jokes, the moments of comic relief at the expense of black people, are indispensable. Thus, as Toni Morrison argues, unspeakable things do remain unspoken and the worst of the slave experience continues to search for its words ("Unspeakable Things").

Black Slaves and White Readers
Stephen Railton

Harriet Beecher Stowe wrote *Uncle Tom's Cabin* to do something for the slaves in the South, but her book never would have become the best-selling American novel of the nineteenth century if it hadn't also done a lot for readers in the North. It has always been hard to say exactly what the novel did for the slaves. It certainly provoked many Northern whites into caring for the first time about the evil of slavery. However, the antislavery Free Soil Party attracted only about half as many votes in the 1852 presidential election, held eight months after Stowe's book was published, as it had in 1848. And in the twentieth century the idea of "Uncle Tom" has become an index of racial degradation. It is equally hard to be precise about the sources of the novel's incredible appeal to its contemporary readers. When Adolphus M. Hart, for example, went to the National Theatre in 1853 to watch one of the four stage versions of the novel that were concurrently running in New York City, he was struck by the difference between the "shouting and holloing" crowds in "the balconies and pit," who had come "to gratify their love of cruelty, and [. . .] gloat over pictures of human wretchedness and misery," and the "air of sanctity in the upper tiers, which betokened that the work had a powerful influence in awakening the religious feelings of certain classes of the people" (qtd. in Birdoff, 74–75). The story of Stowe's story as a popular fiction is very complex.[1] Eliza crossing the ice, Topsy misbehavin', Eva dying, Tom being beaten to death—such episodes became lasting parts of America's cultural consciousness because of the varied and powerful ways they aroused and satisfied Stowe's audience. In this essay I focus on one aspect of that dynamic—we could call it the excursionary aspect—to ask whether it was possible to help black slaves and please white readers at the same time.

Stowe had, of course, to write for her readers. A protest novel must reach people before it can move them. In her preface she says that her goal is "to awaken sympathy and feeling for the African race, as they exist among us" (xiii). Her first task is to bridge the gap acknowledged here, between "them" and "us." The first slave introduced into the novel is little Harry, not just a child but also one who is white enough to pass; the second is Eliza, also "white," and introduced as "The Mother." By these means Stowe creates bonds between her audience, white and mostly female, and the slave, a figure most novel readers at that time would never have met, either in life or in any other novel. Tom, who first appears in chapter 4, is "a large, broad-chested, powerfully-made man, of a full glossy black" with "truly African features" (18), but Stowe immediately domesticates this potentially threatening figure: for most of the chapter he remains quiet while his wife cooks, his children play, the young son of his master teaches him to write, and the infant daughter on his lap "employ[s] the intervals in pulling Tom's nose" (22); at the chapter's end he leads a prayer meeting in his cabin. By thus representing the racial other inside the identities and spheres her readers already cherished—children, mothers, home, food, education, religion—Stowe encourages them to include the slave inside the circle of their sympathies.

In 1851, when the law defined slaves as property and most white Americans, even in the North, thought of slaves as less than human, this was a radical step to get readers to take. At several points Stowe exhorts them directly to give up the protective illusion that, as a "genteel woman" on the steamboat carrying Tom away from his family argues, "We can't reason from our feelings to those of this class of persons" (106, 107): "For, sir," Stowe writes about Tom's grief, "he was a man,—and you are but another man" (34). In the novel's middle section she confronts her audience's preconceptions still more aggressively. She times Tom's arrival at the St. Clare mansion in New Orleans to coincide with that of Miss Ophelia, who, as a conventional Yankee woman, Christian and conscientious, is the clearest surrogate for Stowe's audience inside the story. The elaboration of "Miss Ophelia's Experience and Opinions" (as two consecutive chapters are entitled) is a move that Stowe's Southern critics would never give her credit for and that her Northern readers could hardly have anticipated. Stowe allows Augustine St. Clare, a male Southern slave owner, to demonstrate to Ophelia, a northern white woman with abolitionist sentiments, that she is as much a part of the problem that America must solve as he is: "You see, Cousin, I want justice done us. [. . .] We are the more *obvious* oppressors of the negro, but the unchristian prejudice of the north is an oppressor almost equally severe." St. Clare winds up laying down a very resonant challenge for his cousin and the northern public she represents: "If we emancipate, are you willing to educate?" (273).

Ophelia passes this test. Shown by Eva how to treat Topsy with a love that is both Christlike and democratic, she admits and renounces her "prejudice against negroes" (246); she adopts Topsy and takes her "home to Vermont," where "the child rapidly grew in grace and in favor with the family and neighborhood" (377). Yet we must also note that Stowe declines to narrate this process, a decision that lets her northern readers almost completely off the hook. Since the narrative does follow Eliza north from Kentucky and, later, Cassy north from Legree's, as those two "pass" through America on their way to Canada, the nonnarrated experiences and opinions of Topsy in the free states are a portentous omission. If she had told that story at all, no matter how briefly, Stowe would have brought the issue of "the African race, as they exist among us"—an issue that, as St. Clare points out, includes the evil of racism as well as the evil of slavery—right home to the world her readers lived in. Making that story popular might have been impossible even for a writer with Stowe's extraordinary gifts.

And in any case, the story of Ophelia and Topsy, which dramatizes how whites must change their preconceptions and what they must be willing to do for blacks, is not the main emphasis of the novel's middle section. Tom's story is still at the center. During his long sojourn in the St. Clare household, how-ever, the novel's message shifts, drastically and even perversely, from the suf-ferings and needs of black slaves to the sufferings and needs of the white bourgeoisie—and to how much blacks can do for whites. We never actually see Tom driving Marie, which was the job St. Clare bought him to do, but Stowe devotes this part of the novel to the far more important way he serves Marie's husband and daughter, as the vehicle by which they are brought to God. Read-ing the Bible and singing hymns with Tom teach Eva to see through this tran-sitory world to the heavenly one adumbrated in Revelation. Tom's abounding grace under pressure, his simple faith in God's love despite all his earthly losses, brings Augustine "HOME, at last!" (276); inspired by Tom's living wit-ness to the Word, Augustine is redeemed from worldly bitterness and intellec-tual doubt.

While the change in Ophelia that Topsy provides the occasion for has clear social implications, the change in Eva and her father that Tom presides over is personal and theological. By this stage in Tom's journey the novel is concerned less with abolishing slavery than with gaining the kingdom. Stowe's drawing out of Eva's dying thematically redirects her readers' attention from this world to the next. Augustine's death following so quickly after underscores this shift. When Tom is moved on to the journey's final stage, the theological almost com-pletely displaces the political. Aesthetically, Simon Legree's dark place in the swamp exists essentially in the same allegorical realm as the sites Christian trav-els through in Bunyan's *Pilgrim's Progress*. As Tom struggles through this long dark night of his soul, tempted to despair by "the atheistic taunts" of the demonic Legree (339), sustained by mystical visions of Eva and then Jesus, the meaning of his character changes: instead of being "a man," with the same right to happiness as "another man," he becomes a soul "going into glory" (34, 362). The conflict being dramatized is an inward one. The issue is no longer the moral conflict between people and the institution of slavery, between people and racial prejudice, or between Tom as an individual and the political, social, and economic circumstances that oppress him. Instead, it is the spiritual con-flict between Tom and his own stubbornly human heart, which finds it hard to let go of the world and to accept his miserable lot as providential. Thus "The Victory," when it comes in the chapter with that title, isn't over oppression and prejudice; it's the victory that Tom wins over himself: "the human will, bent, and bleeding, and struggling long, was now entirely merged in the Divine" (341).

This is the triumph of patient self-abnegation and belief over desire and doubt, passion and pain. By winning it Tom takes his place not just beside the eternal Christ, whose perfect example he is imitating, but also in the company of a great many other figures from the popular literature of Victorian Amer-ica—including Longfellow's Evangeline (1847), Emily Graham from Maria Cummins's *Lamplighter* (1854), and Maria Rocke from E. D. E. N. South-worth's *Hidden Hand* (1859).[2] Probably the most telling analogue is Hiram Powers's *Greek Slave*, the period's best-known work of art, just as *Uncle Tom's*

Cabin was its best-known novel. *The Greek Slave* is a young girl who has been captured by Turks and who, according to the narrative Powers wrote to accompany the sculpture, waits in bondage to be sold into a harem; she has been stripped of everything, including her clothes, but as a Christian she remains spiritually transcendent. When the statue toured America in 1847, visiting the major northern and southern cities, several hundred thousand paying spectators saw it as an allegory of the soul's sovereignty over the body, of the way, as Melville's Starbuck puts it, "faith" can "oust fact" (*Moby-Dick* [1988] 492). But allegory can also co-opt reality. This *Greek Slave* inspired hundreds of reviews, sermons, poems, and appreciations, but even though its itinerary included slave-owning cities like New Orleans and Charleston, only a few of these responses make any reference at all to the fact of American slavery.[3] That almost no one saw any incongruity in using an alabaster slave to symbolize the triumph of the spirit just down the street, as it were, from real slave auctions suggests the danger of Stowe's decision to combine the novel she was writing to protest a social injustice with an allegory of individual salvation. To the extent that her readers could see in Tom's sufferings the image of their own pilgrimage, their engagement with him becomes a form of self-gratulation.

Does *Uncle Tom's Cabin* as a whole challenge or confirm its white audience's preconceptions? The dynamic Stowe sets up between black slaves and the souls of white folks can have either a subversive or a reassuring implication, depending on the point of reference. When Eliza, for instance, "with a keen, scrutinizing glance" (72), notes that Mrs. Bird is in mourning dress, she uses the mother's grief for her dead child to gain sympathy for the extreme and remediable peril she is exposed to as a slave mother trying to keep from losing her son. Here shared feelings lead toward political actions. When Stowe, however, uses Tom's great faith to help St. Clare get over his distress at the death of his child, privilege and deprivation have been redefined. Similarly, when Stowe's narrator insists, as she does several times, that slaves are in a uniquely unjust position, white readers are being prodded to imagine what they can do to help. But when she treats Tom's trials at Legree's as the humanly inevitable "true searching test of what there may be in man or woman" (336), it is Tom who is put in a position to help those readers, by enacting for them "what a thing 't is to be a Christian" (363). At the end of his life Tom gives young George Shelby a message to take back to his family and fellow slaves in Kentucky. "Tell 'em all," he says, "to follow me—follow me!" (363). He doesn't mean, of course, get sold down the river so you can be beaten to death by Simon Legree. Neither he nor Stowe is thinking at all about his literal experience, his fate as a slave. That story has been erased, and in its place the novel has put an allegory of salvation, in which the crucified slave can show others the way.

When I teach *Uncle Tom's Cabin* I want students to appreciate its achievement. As just about the first novel to feature blacks in prominent roles, it is trying with great rhetorical skill and courage to put a human face on the racial other. But I also want them to look closely at the way that, despite its intentions, the novel remains deeply inside the persistent patterns of American racism. In the 1920s, for example, in a social climate shaped by Freud's analysis of civilization and its repressed discontents, many bourgeois white Americans made their way to jazz clubs and speakeasies in Harlem. Most, it is fair to say, were uninterested in the plight of African Americans in the urban north. They were instead involved in their own quest for redemption: they wanted to save their bodies from their souls—or, as they would have put it, from their Victorian superegos. To them the Negro other was the cure for the illness they suffered from. A pilgrimage to Harlem was expected to satisfy what W. E. B. Du Bois called "that prurient demand on the part of white folk for a portrayal in Negroes of that utter licentiousness which conventional civilization holds white folk back from enjoying" (qtd. in Rampersad 197). Stowe and her contemporary readers may have been using Tom in just this self-interested, excursionary way. To be sure, the terms for the other are very different. In the 1920s, Harlem and its nightlife were described as savage and sensuous (see J. Anderson 168–80). Stowe does refer to "the negro mind" as "impassioned and imaginative" (25). But her favorite epithets for the "exotic [. . .] African race" (xiii) are "childlike," "gentle," "simple," "trusting," and so on. In Africa, she writes, the "negro race [. . .] will exhibit the highest form of the peculiarly *Christian life*" (156). While the details of the stereotype change, the process of projection remains the same: whether meekly bearing the cross or wildly dancing to jungle rhythms, the other is being exploited. Tom is not allowed to become a person who might want to live next door but remains a personification of what is missing in the Anglo-Saxon inner life.

Students, if they are reading the novel for the first time, are usually surprised to discover that Uncle Tom is not *an* "Uncle Tom" in any obvious sense. He dies, for example, rather than betray his fellow slaves to "Mas'r." But if I'm right that Stowe and her white readers were finally most interested in how Tom could serve them "in the weary way of life" (336), then the label isn't entirely inappropriate. Tom is being used this way most blatantly in the middle section, when Stowe brings him into the elegant but God-less St. Clare household as the answer to their spiritual needs. What he has suffered as a slave becomes the source of his value to the spiritually impoverished Augustine. Here is how Tom offers his story as the antidote to St. Clare's despair at the death of his daughter: "O, Mas'r, when I was sold away from my old woman and the children, I was just a most broke up. I felt as if there warn't nothin' left; and then the good Lord, he stood by me [. . .] and he brings light and joy into a poor feller's soul,—makes all peace; and I's so happy [. . .]" (262). Tom reprises this role at Legree's, when his fervent faith lights Cassy's way back from bitter despair to joy and peace.

St. Clare suffers chiefly from "the habit of doubting" (262); Cassy, from a lifetime of sexual abuse. But they have in common the loss of their children. The loss of children haunts *Uncle Tom's Cabin*—partly, no doubt, because like Eliza, Stowe recognizes that an effective means of arousing her audience's compassion for slaves is dramatizing slavery's destructive impact on families, but also in part for autobiographical reasons. Less than a year before Stowe began writing the novel, her youngest child, Charley, died of cholera.[4] In the book's many variations on the theme of the lost child, we see how such a blow can drive parents to despair or suicide or madness. It may have been from the depths of Stowe's own emotional need that the impulse arose to transform Tom from the representative victim of white America, and as such an accusation against it, into an exemplary savior, and as such a refreshment and consolation to it. That is certainly what he means to Augustine: "St. Clare felt himself borne, on the tide of [Tom's] faith and feeling, almost to the gates of that heaven [Tom] seemed so vividly to conceive. It seemed to bring him nearer to Eva" (263–64).

"The negro race is confessedly more simple, docile, childlike, and affectionate, than other races; and hence the divine graces of love and faith, when inbreathed by the Holy Spirit, find in their natural temperament a more congenial atmosphere" (Stowe, *Key* 45). This quote is from *The Key to* Uncle Tom's Cabin, the book that Stowe published in 1853 to "verify the truth" of her novel. With this ostensibly empirical rationale, she is proving Tom's "extraordinary piety." That Tom has visions of Jesus in heaven, for example, she attributes to the "curious [. . .] psychology" of the African: "their whole bodily system sympathizes with the movements of their minds" (Stowe, *Key* 45). Stowe didn't invent this racialist ideology. Although *Uncle Tom's Cabin* popularized it, the idea that Africans were "peculiarly susceptible to religious experience," as George Fredrickson paraphrases it, had been around for over a decade (*Black Image* 104). And of course Stowe intends her racist remarks as a compliment. But putting the African nearer to God ducks the question of what place the African *American* is entitled to within the society that Stowe and her audience shared as whites. Still worse, it entitles those whites to see themselves as the disadvantaged race. As I said at the start, I believe readers loved the story Stowe wrote for a wide range of reasons. But just as those church groups Hart observed in the upper tiers went to the National Theatre to have a vicarious religious experience, I think white readers went to *Uncle Tom's Cabin* because of what was in it for them. Discussing both the book Stowe set out to write, where the larger cause is freedom for the slaves, and the one she wound up writing, where the ultimate effect is to make the slave serve her readers, complicates the teacher's task. But perhaps the most important lesson *Uncle Tom's Cabin* can teach us is how racial difference is constructed, how hard it has been for white Americans to see the other inside the dark shadow cast by their desire.

NOTES

[1]A good place to begin exploring this larger story is Gossett's Uncle Tom's Cabin *and American Culture*. In *Authorship and Audience* I look at other aspects of the novel's popularity, especially the role gender played in establishing its relationship with the contemporary reading public (see Railton).

[2]There has been a great deal of analysis recently of Stowe's novel in this context (see esp. Tompkins, *Designs*, "Power"; Ammons, "Heroines"). While the project of these accounts is to recuperate the cultural or subversive power of the sentimental aesthetic, my own argument follows the line of the critics who emphasize what is lost when Tom is subsumed under genteel categories (see esp. Baldwin; Spillers, "Changing").

[3]For accounts of the reception of *The Greek Slave* in Stowe's America, see Hyman and Kasson. In "Hiram Powers's *Greek Slave*: Emblem of Freedom," Vivien Green argues that the work is essentially "an abolitionist statement." She cites the few contemporary commentators who did connect Powers's "ideal" Christian slave to the real slaves in Christian America, but to me the effect of those few references is to italicize the way the great majority of responses simply block out any consciousness of slavery as a fact of the nation's life (36–39).

[4]For a poignant account of Charley's death and a different suggestion about its influence on the novel, see Hedrick, *Stowe* 190–91, 199–201, and 213–14.

The Problem of Sentimental Possession
Gillian Brown

There has never been any question that *Uncle Tom's Cabin* is one of the most powerful literary documents ever written. Since the 1850s, critical accounts of Harriet Beecher Stowe's novel have revolved around the nature and degree of its power: its abolitionist performance, its racist influence, and, most recently, its feminist import. The feminist significance of *Uncle Tom's Cabin* rests on a conception that has now become a commonplace of feminist and Americanist literary and cultural criticism: the principle of sentimental power.

A term coined by Jane Tompkins and collaterally developed by a number of scholars working in nineteenth-century American studies (Tompkins; Ammons, "Stowe's Dream"; Yellin, "Doing It"), *sentimental power* has come to signify a feminine—if not feminist—counter-tradition in literary history, an oppositional mode to the masculinist, capitalist, individualistic, and imperialist values operating in American culture. Against these values, the domestic work of women, in their sentimental literary productions or in their household practices, promotes virtues of maternity, co-operation, sympathy, and charity, constituting an alternative vision of American political economy.

Under this revisionary conception of the sentimental, racism has all but disappeared from the spectrum of effects generated by *Uncle Tom's Cabin*.[1] In what follows, I address the racist features of Stowe's sentimentalism that the notion of sentimental power elides as it elaborates the reformist properties of women. To better understand the novel, its sentimentalism and its racism, readers need to take into account the liberal property relations that structure both the feminist polemic of sentimental power and Stowe's antislavery polemic.

The sentimental power that *Uncle Tom's Cabin* marshals against slavery invokes the liberal tradition of possessive individualism, in which individual rights are grounded in the principle of self-ownership (Locke, MacPherson). Following this tradition of entitlement, Stowe links abolitionism to a particular account of possession and possessions. Her feminized ethic of possession, modeled on sympathetic familial relations, translates the fact of slaves being owned into the conditions of their human entitlement. The movement from slavery to freedom appears in Stowe's vision as the process of reclassifying market articles as familiar objects, followed by another reclassification in which these objects are sorted according to color and finally neatly separated. It is in these refinements of possessive individualism that both the power and the limitations of *Uncle Tom's Cabin* and Stowe's sentimental solution to slavery become most clear.[2]

At the end of *Uncle Tom's Cabin*, Stowe counsels her readers to redress and eliminate the wrongs of slavery; there is one thing "that every individual can do,—they can see to it that *they feel right*" (385). Stowe's domestic politics are linked to a sentimental aesthetics in which the right feeling inheres in a nurturing attitude toward one's possessions and responsibilities, in the exemplary maternity that Stowe emphasizes in her novel. Maternity as a model of a different ethic of possession appears most forcefully in the example of Rachel Halliday whose "motherliness and full-heartedness" offer a home to runaway slaves, whose domestic economy is so filled with "the spirit of love" that "it seemed to put a spirit into the food and drink." Not only slaves but the very household items in Rachel's kitchen seem happily enthralled by her "overflowing kindness" (121–22).

Good motherhood and good housekeeping manifest the proper relation between caretakers and their charges, whether they be households, children, or slaves. Thus, Stowe's abolitionist protest against the trade in human beings that separates and destroys families opposes not so much the proposition that humans are things as the fact that they are treated as transferable things, as commodities. What I want to emphasize here are the love and care of household things with which Stowe imbues *Uncle Tom's Cabin*—her differentiation of motherhood from slaveholding, of maternal possessions from market articles, a differentiation that fortifies and domesticates ownership. Furthermore, I would suggest, it is this preservation and perfection of ownership that accounts for what has remained the troubling effect of *Uncle Tom's Cabin*: its simultaneous advancement of domesticity, feminism, antislavery, and racism.

The freed slaves in *Uncle Tom's Cabin* find their home not in a matriarchal or newly liberalized America but in Africa. The novel's double movement that at once emancipates and segregates blacks needs to be understood as a feature of the logic of sympathetic proprietorship. As much as Stowe's feminization of property relations protests against the patriarchal institution and projects a revision of patriarchally inflected capitalist values, she also continues to define blacks as possessions, albeit protected and properly valued ones. If sentimentalism has operated as a representational tactic of extending human rights to the disenfranchised, as Philip Fisher has argued (87–127), it nevertheless retains the slave (or woman or child) within the inventory of human proprietorship. That is, the case for shared humanity and human rights is made not in terms of equality but in terms of the humanity vested in a subject by virtue of its possession, through an intimacy and identification developed through the history of a proprietorship. For example, Mrs. Shelby's experience of teaching her religion to her slaves is what endears them to her and what makes their sale unacceptable; Eliza and Tom merit Mrs. Shelby's help in securing freedom because they have been part of her family and her values, her treasured possessions. What Fisher has called the romance of the object in sentimentality is also a romance of possession.

In the logic of sentimental possession, to be properly owned—mothered and nurtured and tended—is to be possessed of the mother's attributes (or those of the ideal owner she exemplifies, God), inspirited with love and generosity like the children, utensils, and food in Rachel's kitchen. Stowe's sentimentalism, then, does not reflect and generate the process of making a thing into a man, as Fisher asserts (87–127), but rather the process of making commodities into possessions. It is as properly owned property that slaves in *Uncle Tom's Cabin* become persons, better-placed things.

Possession makes what is owned a different kind of a thing: a personal possession, supplemental and hence special to the owner. Possession might be said also to be a personification or, more precisely, a personalization of things that supplement and transmute the thing's objecthood. Once a thing becomes familiar through the association ownership entails, it seems (more) personal, more self-expressive of its owner.

This extension of the proprietor into his or her valued objects is expressed in sentimentalism's emphasis on objective correlatives for feelings and persons, in sentimental culture's proliferation of portraits, keepsakes, mementos, talismans, and souvenirs. The Victorian paraphernalia of sentiment, with which Ann Douglas has identified *Uncle Tom's Cabin* in *The Feminization of American Culture*, to which the event of the novel in great measure contributed (inspiring dolls, toys, games, songs, poems, plays, and finally even the 1893 Columbian Exposition display of a cabin identified as Tom's),[3] belong to and extend the liberal tradition of possessive individualism. Celebrating and elaborating the powers of proprietorship, sentimental possession follows the liberal ideal of owning oneself. The principle of self-ownership defines the individual as his or her own possession. This fundamental objecthood of personhood is reflected and augmented by a complementary system of self-representation in which individuals are identified with their property and labor, with the things most closely under their proprietorship. What the sentimental power of *Uncle Tom's Cabin* demonstrates is the integral relation between human rights and human possessions in the dual sense I have been describing.

Stowe's ethic of sentimental possession shares the liberal ideal of self-realization in property, but she would secure this ideal by replacing market relations with familial ones. Her sentimental politics therefore seek to purify possessive individualism by imagining the humanistic property relation as transcendent to market relations. Stowe does not abrogate but domesticates property and possessions. She takes what she perceives as the affective life of property and tries to isolate it from the market conditions of property. The antimarket project of her domestic politics also predominates in the household advice literature she wrote after *Uncle Tom's Cabin*, where she elaborates sentimental possession as the antithesis and transcendence of market relations: as the superiority of enduring possessions to fashionable commodities.

In a series of articles on domestic concerns that Stowe wrote during the 1860s for the *Atlantic*,[4] creating the right atmosphere and feelings requires a special mode of consumerism, investments in objects for their independence from and defiance of fashion. The right stuff in a home is distinguished by its use and comfort, which are always the same in Stowe's depiction, in contrast to its market currency. Household furnishings and decorative objects are thus regularly decommodified in her domestic economy. In her insistence on use value, she differentiates household possessions, the stuff of sentimental associations, from the ephemeral objects in the marketplace.

The recurrent theme in Stowe's recommendations for home decorations and furnishings is the "better value" of comfort, its permanence and its good influence. Her parable "The Ravages of a Carpet" illustrates the follies of fashionable redecorating (*House* 1–22). When the women of the Crowfield family decide to install a new parlor carpet, the "homelike and pleasant" (7) character of the room changes. At first the new purchase makes all the old furnishings appear shabby and inadequate. So "in less than a year" (14) these are replaced by "a new sofa and new chairs" (12) and "some dark green blinds" (12) and "great, heavy curtains that kept out all the light that was not already excluded by the green shades" (14). In the process, the "feeling of security, composure, and enjoyment" (10) about the room that made it "good to be there" (7) vanishes, or, as the narrator imagines, "the household fairies had left it,—and when the fairies leave a room, nobody ever feels at home in it" (16). The family and their friends eventually follow the original carpet and familiar furnishings with "the marks and indentations" of "good times and social fellowship" (8) to their new location in the father's study. There the warm atmosphere of their once comfortable parlor is reestablished.

The moral of the story, of course, is the incompatibility of fashion with domesticity. In a related story in this series, Stowe emphasizes this opposition as the difference between housekeeping and homekeeping ("Home-keeping versus House-keeping," *House* 23–47). A well-kept house appears beautiful but no one wants to live in it, and "nobody ever comes in to spend an evening" (28). In this story of housekeeping for the perfect appearance, the orderly, perfectly appointed house is so inhospitable that it ruins the children who grow up in it: one son runs away to sea, another becomes "a perfect Philistine" (32). As Stowe summarizes, "Silks and satins—meaning by them the luxuries of housekeeping— often put out not only the parlor-fire, but that more sacred flame, the fire of domestic love"; such housekeeping finally renders the family "*homeless*" (32).

Fashion and its analogue, a good appearance, become inhospitable, as it were, because of their impracticality and their currency. And these are in effect tautological for Stowe: because new furnishings are unfamiliar, they do not invite use. Fashionable items lie outside the domestic orbit of use value; they can be *only* commodities. In this rather remarkable imagination of fetishism as the purification of the commodity, Stowe defines household possessions not only as useful but also as signs of use value, the cornerstone of an extramarket domestic economy. These things of sentimental value and regular use succeed and supersede domestic consumerism. Even though new objects must be purchased at the commencement of a household, Stowe counsels that these be things made to last: selected for their potential as long-standing possessions, as parts of the family. Purified of their market origins, possessions will be inspirited like the Crowfield family room or Rachel Halliday's kitchen. For Stowe, use signifies an intimacy between persons and their possessions; this is why she refers to furniture as our "servants and witnesses" (*House* 8). The service and notarization familiar things perform make the difference between a house and a home, a commodity and a possession.

It is this transformative capacity of sentimental possession that Stowe employs in her abolitionist renovation of American society. This redemptive power resides in the sentimental possession, the beloved domestic object, which is itself both transformed and transforming. A number of mothers' belongings, attributes, and reminders of maternal love accordingly figure crucially in the escapes of slaves. Eliza finds safety in Rachel Halliday's rocking chair, "motherly and old, whose wide arms breathed hospitable invitation, seconded by the solicitation of its feather cushions,—a real comfortable, persuasive old chair, and worth, in the way of honest, homely enjoyment, a dozen of your plush or brochetelle drawing-room gentry" (116). This chair's sentimental persuasions reverberate with the comforting "creechy crawchy" of the "small flag-bottomed rocking-chair, with a patch-work cushion in it, neatly contrived out of small pieces of different colored woollen goods" on which Rachel sits. "It had a turn for quacking and squeaking,—that chair had,—either from having taken cold in early life, or from some asthmatic affection, or perhaps from nervous derangement" (116–17). Besides having its own medical history, this chair bears witness to a familial history: "for twenty years or more, nothing but loving words, and gentle moralities, and motherly loving kindness, had come from that chair" (117).

Just as "head-aches and heart-aches innumerable had been cured there,—difficulties spiritual and temporal solved there" (117), Stowe imagines that slavery can be overcome through the mobilization of sentimental sympathies and associations. As she wrote to her editor, Gamaliel Bailey, she planned *Uncle Tom's Cabin* as the presentation of pictures of the horrors of slavery, for "there is no arguing with *pictures*, and everybody is impressed by them, whether they mean to be or not" (Letter to Bailey). The marketability of slaves, which Stowe represents as their homelessness, is perhaps most poignantly underscored by the "brilliant scriptural prints" and "portrait of General Washington" adorning Tom's cabin (18), the cabin that despite Stowe's title is not his—the home in which Tom is only a temporary inhabitant. It is against this insecurity of market objects that Stowe dispatches her salvific objects. Thus one significant detail in the emancipation of Eliza and her son Harry is the Byrd family gift of their "poor little Henry's" things: the "little coats of many a form and pattern, piles of aprons, and rows of small stockings" that had been worn by their dead child (75). These "memorials" (76) to use are passed on to be of use again, to help restore and fortify the slave family. Similarly, the memorial lock of hair that Simon Legree's mother left him operates to abet the escape of Cassy and Emmeline and to render him powerless. So powerful is this sentimental possession that the memorial lock's influence survives and strengthens in its disposal. Even though Legree throws the lock of hair away, it seems to reappear when he discovers the lock of Little Eva's hair that Tom keeps as a memento. The superstitious Legree is so frightened by the persistence of the token that he takes refuge in drink and fails to notice Cassy's escape preparations. Thus, in the economy of sentimental possessions and sympathy, the market that the slave trader epitomizes is overwhelmed by the power of objects.

Stowe's sentimental fetishism invests domestic possessions with the attributes more usually assigned to the commodity, particularly the sense of its empathy with prospective owners. As Walter Benjamin writes, "If the soul of the commodity which Marx occasionally mentions in jest existed, it would be the most empathetic ever encountered in the realm of souls, for it would have to see in everyone the buyer in whose hand and house it wants to nestle" (55). What Marx takes as the mystified and false conception of the commodity—its concealment of its origin in labor and its fetishistic function, its seemingly independent life (81–96)—Stowe regards as the commodity's true character and antimarket potential. Indeed, from her domestic perspective, commodities appear, as it were, insufficiently fetishized—because not yet owned. Far from concealing productive human relations in market relations, the fetishism of objects in Stowe's political economy projects the productive labor of housekeeping. That is, the liveliness of household things consists in their domestic functions; they take on a life of their own in their usefulness or service. Could sentimental possessions themselves speak, they would say, pace Marx, what belongs to us as objects is our disposition to usefulness.[5] In Stowe's non-exchange domestic economy, objects outside the market can and do speak. The personification of objects, which for Stowe is a function of their removal from the market, makes them mediums of human history. The more lively the object, such as Rachel's vocal rocking chair, the more likely it is to convey familial material history.

The love of things that Stowe advocates exceeds and even nullifies consumerist desire by imagining a reciprocity between persons and their possessions, by seeing them as contiguous and congruent. Ownership, which takes things out of the market and keeps them in the home, confers this congruence. Fetishism is for Stowe a function of an enduring ownership, and it is this familiarizing spirit of proprietorship that she would marshal against the market.

While the logic of fetishism in sentimental property relations might well suggest that feminine proprietorship and decommodification—the domestic transformation of society and its members—could be accomplished by a concerted consumerism, Stowe remains firm in her market antipathy and pointedly limits spending in her domestic economy, stressing the self-sufficiency of home. The congruence and order of this ideal home free it from the market; sentimental fetishism reflects a culture so thoroughly outside exchange values that even use value is imperceptible. Things like Rachel's rocking chair so correspond to the wills and feelings of their owners that they appear to *be* them rather than to be serving them.

That this portrait of self-sufficiency and radical congruence might recall the myth of harmonious familial economy promulgated by slavery apologists (see, e.g., Fitzhugh, *Cannibals*) certainly occurred to Stowe. In her article called "A Family Talk on Reconstruction," she worries in 1869 that "the essential *animus* of the slave system still exists" (*Household* 285). She recognizes this same "desire to monopolize and to dominate" (284) in the persistence of an aristocratic division of labor and particularly in the prominence of the bourgeois lady who depends on servants for her housekeeping. Reliance on servants threatens Stowe's revisionary economy by obtruding in the intimate relations between a housekeeper and her household. Stowe advocates the "dignity of labor" (89), the dignity of "the lady who does her own work" (86) in order to seal her ideal domestic economy from the trade in labor and humans signified by slaves and servants (*House* 125–47).

In ridding the home of servants and the market relations they embody, just as in ridding the nation of slavery, Stowe imagines the replacement of commodity relations with sentimental relations. The market history of the Irish servant can be superseded when she is assimilated into American culture—and Stowe emphasizes that it is the duty of housekeepers, "whether they like it or not," to educate their servants to "form good wives and mothers for the Republic" ("Servants," *House* 150). The abolitionist duty with which *Uncle Tom's Cabin* charged American women translates here into advocacy of the rights and class mobility of servants. "A servant can never in our country be the mere appendage to another man, to be marked like a sheep with the color of his owner; he must be a fellow-citizen, with an established position of his own, free to make contracts, free to come and go, and having in his sphere titles to consideration and respect just as definite as those of any trade or profession whatever" ("Servants," *House* 151).

But being the same color as one's owner or employer is in fact the condition of class mobility in Stowe's economy of assimilation. While she saves her system from becoming another version of a feudal service economy by locating democratic opportunities in domestic relations, she does not include emancipated slaves among the beneficiaries of sentimental acculturation. Blackness marks the slave as forever unassimilable. The only place for former slaves in Stowe's ideal domestic economy is as temporary furniture and family props, as talismanic figures such as the "glossy black" (18) Uncle Tom becomes, or as salvific figures such as Topsy—"one of the blackest of her race" (206)—becomes. Thus, the metamorphosis of the black slave into treasured servant and witness to the white family, or into Christian missionary or martyr and therefore into both familiarity and invisibility, is, like the vision of repatriation with which *Uncle Tom's Cabin* closes, ultimately a way of making blacks disappear.

Even in "a well-trained domestic establishment" (like the New England home to which Topsy goes, before going to "her people" in Africa), freed slaves never become "our folks" (377). The congruence and intimacy of sentimental possession does not allow for miscegenation. More precisely, it does not allow for the potentiality of black to become white, for the passing as whites by which many of the slaves in Stowe's novel achieve freedom. For blackness, the mark of the market, to be expunged, it must first be identifiable. So in the concluding pages of *Uncle Tom's Cabin*, the quantity of blackness is a key feature of black entitlement. Listing examples of the self-possession of free blacks as proofs for her argument that it is a good investment for Americans to educate blacks for their new life in Africa, Stowe details both their proportion of blackness (significantly either full black or no less than three-fourths) and their financial worth. For example:

> C———. Full black; stolen from Africa; sold in New Orleans; been free fifteen years; paid for himself six hundred dollars; a farmer; owns several farms in Indiana; Presbyterian; probably worth fifteen or twenty thousand dollars, all earned by himself.. (387)

Conjoining market value with color, Stowe's list underscores the identity of blacks with commodities even as her ethic of sentimental possession offers a way of transforming commodities into citizens. In doing away with the taints of the marketplace Stowe's purified domestic economy must ultimately do away with blackness, the mark of incongruity and exogamy. Recalling and removing racial difference (to Africa), Stowe's abolitionist vision of safe property veers into purifying practices of keeping the house divided not only from men and markets but also from blacks and immigrants. The process of sentimental assimilation is forestalled with the image of a nearly endogamous race removed to another continent. By the logic of sentimental possession, color, the market trace, ironically rationalizes segregation as well as black entitlement.

We cannot appreciate the sentimental power of *Uncle Tom's Cabin*, then, without recognizing racism as among the varied and unpredictable affections involved in the affective life of property that sentimental possession sustains. This is not to say that Stowe's sentimentalism or sentimentalism in general is always racist but to point out that sentimentalism works both to alter and to emphasize dividing lines and that in this historical instance sentimentalism has worked to institutionalize racial categories. The white feminist retrieval of Stowe's great sentimental artifact has illuminated women's custodial and reformist role in the liberal tradition. The reconstructive work of disowning racism—divesting selfhood of that possession—remains the yet unclaimed legacy of *Uncle Tom's Cabin*. This is the legacy that the teaching of Stowe's novel must confront.

NOTES

[1] I do not mean to say here that African American literary scholarship ignores the racism in the novel; I *do* mean to point out that the white feminist claims for the revisionary force of the novel have set the terms of discourse about *Uncle Tom's Cabin* in such a way that the attempt to consider the relations between racism, sentimentalism, and the feminine sphere would appear an ungallant if not antifeminist act. Hortense Spillers has called this the "muting of 'race'" ("Changing the Letter"). For other criticism on Stowe's influence on African American literary representations, see Stepto; Yarbrough.

[2]Theories of the democratic state and the rights of individuals secured in such a state date back to the seventeenth century, when they were founded in opposition to divinely sanctioned authority and monarchy (see MacPherson). Since then, this originally white-based and androcentric defense of the individual has been applied to the civil rights of women and blacks. My exploration here of these applications, and of the contradictions within possessive individualism that they bring to light, is excerpted from a longer examination published in chapters 1 and 2 of my *Domestic Individualism: Imagining Self in Nineteenth-Century America*.

[3]Excellent documentation of the culture industry in and of *Uncle Tom's Cabin* can be found in J. Hart; Hirsch; and Kirkham.

[4]Stowe's 1864 series of *Atlantic* articles subsequently were collected and published in her 1865 *House and Home Papers*, under the pseudonym Christopher Crowfield; her essays appearing in the *Atlantic* from January to September 1865 were reprinted in 1868 in *The Chimney Corner* (also by Christopher Crowfield). These two collections were later published in one volume called *Household Papers and Stories*, volume 8 in the Riverside edition of *The Writings of Harriet Beecher Stowe*.

[5]I here revise Marx's famous passage, "Could commodities themselves speak, they would say: Our use-value may be a thing that interests men. It is no part of us as objects. What, however, does belong to us as objects, is our value" (95).

Alive with Contradictions:
Close Reading, Liberal Pluralism, and Nonnarratable Plots in *Uncle Tom's Cabin*

David Leverenz

When I teach *Uncle Tom's Cabin*, I present the beginning and ending along familiar critical lines. The early chapters set up a middle-class gender war in black and white, kitchen versus market, while the final chapters dramatize a double victory of the seemingly powerless. Tom's paradoxically feminized yet fatherly spirit triumphs over Legree's sadism, while Cassy impersonates Legree's dead-undead mother to drive Mrs. Legree's "bullet head" son (289) out of his mind.[1] Cassy's Gothic revenge completes the novel's contradictions about womanhood, since she has already killed one of her children (318). Now, in killing another mother's son, Cassy enacts the rage disowned by self-sacrificing Tom and self-sacrificing white mothers, all of whom "had, to the full, the gentle, domestic heart" (81).[2]

Those contradictions are relatively easy to teach, as is the long-running discussion about whether Tom is an "Uncle Tom." To plunge into close readings can stir up a more unpredictable muddle of responses. If you can give the book two full weeks, or more if you're a high school teacher, all sorts of issues can break loose. Sometimes class discussions also bring out a latent tension between my own ideology of liberal pluralism, encouraged by close readings, and the passionate convictions animating various students' political or religious responses.

First, using Joan Hedrick's fine biography, I briefly sketch Stowe's life and historical contexts, mentioning Stowe's evangelical background, her self-discipline as a writer, and some of the Stowes' domestic stresses.[3] After *Uncle Tom's Cabin* became a resounding success, for instance, Stowe's already large husband gained a hundred pounds—as Robert Levine puts it, a pound for each ten thousand copies sold.[4] I also sketch two political contexts for the book's impact: first, the failure of the 1820–50 territorial compromises to resolve growing sectional differences about slavery, and second, the empowering of middle-class white women as agents for moral reform, along with the rise of female-authored bestsellers. The ability of *Uncle Tom's Cabin* to bring these two contexts together ideologically, I argue, helps explain why it had such a wildfire effect.[5] When John W. DeForest coined the phrase "the great American novel" in 1868, he named *Uncle Tom's Cabin* as the strongest contender to date.[6]

At last comes my basic argument: that convergences of class hierarchy with racial and gender dichotomies create the novel's enabling contradictions as well as its allegorized preaching. First I ask for a hierarchy of white male characters by status, listing each man's characteristics on the board. Those at the top (Senator Bird, then Mr. Shelby) can be at least partially influenced by women, while the men lower down (Haley, Marks, Loker) not only lack gentlemanly manners but also seem comfortable with marketplace cruelties. A gentleman such as Senator Bird can allow his feelings and his wife to override his reason and his political positions, though his wife is "a timid, blushing little woman, of about four feet in height" (68). Here students recurrently wonder, how on earth could she could have had babies? Is she real or a "bird-like" allegory of "the little woman"? That discussion anticipates later tensions between realistic and allegorical characterization, especially for Eva and Uncle Tom.

Then I ask, how do the narrator's descriptions of Senator Bird and Shelby contrast with the descriptions of Haley, Marks, and Loker? For the "lower" characters, the narrator emphasizes their bodies and their slang as well as their lack of manners. By implication, I suggest, the narrator is herself a character in this story, with class and gender biases. The narrator's elitism sometimes makes the narrative sound complacently judgmental—"cheesy," a student in an undergraduate class called it in 1992, launching an hour-long debate about Stowe's style. With Marks, as another pointed out in a 1996 graduate class, the narration also suggests a latent homoerotic tension between his sharp, "thin," cat-like "mouser" qualities and his unmanly "snuffing" and "fidgeting" or his "quiet introductory sniggle" (54–56). This student's essay linked Marks with St. Clare's Adolph, a more explicitly campy version of gay masculine performance (142–44).[7]

On the other side of the gender binary, when we compare Mrs. Bird and Mrs. Shelby with Eliza and Aunt Chloe, the narrator's elitism seems partially overridden by her admiration for shared motherly qualities, though with a clear ascent from dialect, practicality, and darker skin color to standard English and spirituality. We analyze how Eliza's whiteness and good English as well as her maternal protectiveness license her escape. Eliza's flight becomes the novel's first instance of the rebellious independence allowed black women while proscribed for black men and white women.

As almost everyone has noticed—it's hard to miss it—the novel preaches that "the last shall be first." The soft, sensitive humanity of self-subordinating white women and black people, who have more receptivity to evangelical religion and motherly feelings, shall overcome the business values associated with men of "the hard and dominant Anglo-Saxon race" (xiii; see also 376). The heart and the head become allegorical metonyms for gender war. Two generations of feminist critics have made these issues manifest; indeed, Stowe builds them into the plot with didactic insistence. The repeated drama of mothers losing their children because of slavery forces feelings of empathy on any white male who has the latent capacity to be a "gentle man." As one student observed in a 1997 discussion, the bad men are childless. Therefore Haley, Marks, Loker, and Legree have no access to parental feelings.

Yet some intriguing tensions between class and gender dichotomies emerge when we look at sentences closely. Shelby vaguely seems "to fancy that his wife had piety and benevolence enough for two" (9), while Haley says, "We men of the world [. . .] don't quite fancy, when women and ministers come out broad and square, and go beyond us" in moral matters (30). Shelby at least has a receptivity to "fancy," while the trader uses the verb as a sneering intensifier of women's impracticality. Does that mean that the gender war pertains only to the lower classes, since gentlemen can be reformed from within? But gentlemen have constructed the system of slavery, as Stowe stresses in her most impassioned jeremiad against complacent male readers (115). After all, it's Shelby's decision that sets the plot in motion. To compare their views on women and religion makes Haley seem more honest as well as ruthless, while Shelby seems more self-deluded and ineffectual.

A related tension emerges when students consider why Shelby has to sell Tom and little Harry: not because of the heartlessness of slavery per se but because Shelby has "speculated largely and quite loosely" (8). Shelby's hapless speculations are only the first instance of white male managerial incompetence, as a student demonstrated in a graduate essay over a decade ago. Mr. Harris takes George away from inventing things in the bagging factory because George makes him feel inferior (10). When "indolent and careless" St. Clare sees Tom's "soundness of mind and good business capacity," Tom takes over from Adolph "all the marketing and providing" for St. Clare's family (176), though Tom seems to be all "heart" in the earlier chapters. Cassy's former master had to sell her and her children "to clear off his gambling debts" (316). After Legree has beaten Tom, Cassy berates him for disabling a useful worker "right in the most pressing season, just for your devilish temper!" (321). Finally, after Shelby dies, his "little woman" proves to be much better at business than he is (220, 360), though he had declared that it would "degrade" a white lady to work (220). Such womanly strength and male weakness can't quite be explained by the binary opposition between rational, calculating, aggressive Anglo-Saxon male heads and the gentle, domestic hearts of women and blacks. Should the system be destroyed, or could it be run humanely by women? Would Rachel Halliday be off her rocker if she were a CEO?

To put it another way, after Mrs. Bird's "liege lord" does exactly what she wants him to with Eliza, she praises him by "laying her little white hand on his." "Your heart is better than your head, in this case, John [. . .]. Could I ever have loved you, had I not known you better than you know yourself?" (75). By implication, even the gentlest gentleman can't be loved as he knows himself. If white men's minds seem incompetent or detestable except when women bring out men's latent feelings, does that indict marketplace reasoning or suggest a link between white male brutality and ineptitude?

What brings the novel to life beyond its passionate convictions inheres in these incipient contradictions, which surface more blatantly in Stowe's characterizations of black people. Here the novel's power depends in part on its ability to narrate "nonnarratable plots" without quite saying so. I borrow the term from Elizabeth Langland, who argues in *Nobody's Angels* that the Pamela plot, in which a servant girl marries a lord, becomes nonnarratable to Victorian readers.

It was too threatening to middle-class women, whose primary domestic task was to manage the servants as well as to represent the husband's status.[8]

Uncle Tom's Cabin engages and suppresses what to antebellum readers were three nonnarratable plots: black male rebellion, white women's anger at being restricted to the roles of wife and mother, and the mutual sexual desire of black men and white women. Stowe's explicitly racist allegorizing asserts that black men just want to be domestic homebodies, as all true women do. Yet the text's vital energies emerge at the moments when the two most didactically enforced binary oppositions—black versus white, women versus men—collide. At those moments, the nonnarratable plots provide a covert charge to the drama, while the narrator uses elevated language to secure her class distance.

Black Sam, for instance, has that name because he is "about three shades blacker than any other son of ebony on the place" (37). Yet he seems to have little of "the gentle, domestic heart" ascribed to the black race (81). In subverting Haley's pursuit of Eliza, Sam exercises entrepreneurial ingenuity. Moreover, he tricks Haley only for heartless self-advancement. At first Sam is all for catching Eliza to please Master Shelby, not to help Eliza—a fact that a lot of students miss. "See if I don't cotch her, now; Mas'r'll see what Sam can do!" But Andy advises him to "think twice; for Missis don't want her cotched, and she'll be in yer wool" (38). Once Sam has figured out which master to follow, his trickster zeal displays "a strict look-out to his own personal well-being, that would have done credit to any white patriot in Washington" (37). Sam's coal-black skin shelters not a motherly sensibility but a white man's "talent of making capital out of everything that turned up" (64). He is the novel's true Uncle Tom: black on the outside, white on the inside. Yet Sam is also a Sambo trickster figure, whose "air of doleful gravity" (64; see also 50) resembles Topsy's, while his behavior anticipates Topsy's and Cassy's more malicious release of contradictory energies.[9]

A little later in the story, to explain George Harris's anger and enterprise, Stowe invokes a flagrantly racist hierarchy to emphasize George's divided racial heritage. "We remark, *en passant*, that George was, by his father's side, of white descent." From his proud white Kentucky father "he had inherited a set of fine European features, and a high, indomitable spirit. From his mother he had received only a slight mulatto tinge, amply compensated by its accompanying rich, dark eye" (94). This looks like strategic essentialism, since Stowe appeases white readers' fears by attributing George's aggressive spirit to white maleness, removing the threat of a strong black man. A closer reading of this passage exposes some unresolvable contradictions. What does it mean, I ask, that Stowe chooses "inherited " to describe George's white side, and "received" for his black side? The contrast implies white male property and privilege on the one hand, as if his "set" of "European features" were the family silverware, and a grudging taint on the other hand, as if George's spirit remains pure Anglo-Saxon while "only" his body has been tainted with "a slight mulatto tinge." And why say "compensated" with a "rich" though "dark" eye? Despite celebrating mothering throughout the book, here the narrator bases her racist binary on a language of patriarchal property.

Another aspect of this brief passage destabilizes both the narrator's racism and our indictment. Again I read aloud the narrator's strangely flip introductory phrase, "We remark, *en passant*." What kind of "we" would say that? A few students immediately detect Stowe's pun, since George is "passing" as a Spanish gentleman at the time. The phrase positions the narrator's "We" at a patronizing distance, as if trivializing the character's performance of whiteness. Yet using the French phrase for "in passing" uncannily invites a return of Stowe's repressed fascination with racial mixture. While the narrator's allegorical binary licenses George's ability to pass among the narrator's kind as an elegant foreigner, the narrator puts on a similar performance, posing as a cultural cosmopolitan. Linguistically, which one is more mixed? Which one is better at passing?

At various other moments when the narrator descends to "life among the lowly," the narrative voice assumes that note of linguistic superiority. When Stowe first introduces readers to Simon Legree, for instance, she lists his disgustingly dirty and fearfully sexualized body parts. Why, for instance, does Stowe emphasize Legree's "long nails" (289)? Students usually mention dirt, vulgarity, and phallic symbolism. In 1997 a student who was taking a course on antebellum southern history informed the class that long nails also imply violence. Backcountry Southern whites would stage public spectacles where they would fight each other to the death, with only their long nails as weapons, as if mimicking upper-class duels.[10]

Yet Stowe also takes care to control the threat. Legree's hands are "garnished" with these nails, as if the nails were a kitchen spice. Twice in this brief passage readers learn that Legree is "short." Also, after surveying Legree's head, eyes, eyebrows, and hair, the narrator asserts that these "were rather unprepossessing items, it is to be confessed." Most students don't know what "unprepossessing" means, and that's part of the point. It means either "unimpressive" or "not having been previously possessed." Why not just say "unimpressive," then? The close reading leads in contrary directions. Implying possession and property (as "garnished" might too), the narrator also reaffirms an elevated social position for herself and her readers, at the moment we first encounter Legree's vulgarity and physical danger.[11]

Perhaps the most self-conscious sequence of linguistic elevations comes at the start of chapter 4, when the narrator invites readers into Uncle Tom's cabin, which turns out to be Aunt Chloe's kitchen. The tensions loom in the chapter's first sentence: "The cabin of Uncle Tom was a small log building, close adjoining to 'the house,' as the negro *par excellence* designates his master's dwelling" (16). Ironies swiftly proliferate. The cabin doesn't stand separately but adjoins the Shelbys' dwelling, which the slaves refer to as "the house." Tom's home is not a house, even to his peers. In fact, it's not even Tom's; it belongs to Mr. Shelby. Moreover, the cabin disappears after the first few chapters; it's "shut up" halfway through (224), only to pop up at the very end as a "memorial" (380). So why does the book have this title? Students usually argue that the name serves as a metaphor or metonym for the triumph of lowly, homely, cabin-kitchen values. Yet the cabin also signifies enslavement and patriarchal property. The material power relations undercut the transcendent meanings.

Moreover, why does the narrator say, "the negro *par excellence*"? The phrase intimates her elegant aboveness, her assumption that all black people speak alike, and her genteel amusement at the oxymoronic spectacle of coupling a French expression with "the negro." Her presumption parallels Mr. Shelby's ownership of slaves and cabin. While her arch literariness secures the superiority of "us," the incongruous juxtaposition of terms betrays an artificiality of diction, at once patronizing and nervous. After all, Stowe is about to do a new thing in white American literature: bring genteel readers into close contact with black people.

Then comes the entrance of "us" into the realm of "them":

> Let us enter the dwelling. The evening meal at the house is over, and Aunt Chloe, who presided over its preparation as head cook, has left to inferior officers in the kitchen the business of clearing away and washing dishes, and come out into her own snug territories, to "get her ole man's supper;" therefore, doubt not that it is her you see by the fire, presiding with anxious interest over certain frizzling items in a stew-pan, and anon with grave consideration lifting the cover of a bake-kettle, from whence steam forth indubitable intimations of "something good."   (17)

We spend considerable time analyzing this passage. Is the narrator condescending, or admiring, or both? What's the effect of those quotation marks? And why does the narrator seem so suddenly pompous: "therefore, doubt not that it is her [. . .] and anon with grave consideration [. . .] from whence steam forth indubitable intimations [. . .]"? Though quotation marks daintily separate black people's dirty "them" language from the narrator's white-gloves "us" language, some students argue that her excessive pretentiousness satirizes nervous white readers venturing for the first time into a black home. Others see the satire directed at a black cook putting on airs for the young white man in her kitchen.

The good liberal pluralist move, of course, is to say, All of the above. In my own reading, Stowe's narration seems undecidably poised among mockery, admiration, and self-satire. On the one hand, a black woman ridiculously struts about as a general. On the other, Chloe stands forth as Archetypal Woman, in command of her natural turf. If Chloe's first words, "get her ole man's supper," in quotation marks and dialect, prompt the narrator's ornate linguistic recoil, the mockery of pretentiousness goes both ways. The homely nouns of the kitchen—"stew-pan," "bake-kettle"—deflate the narrator's parlor pomposities. Just as Chloe's "round, black, shining face" seems "washed over with white of eggs," so the narration itself reflects her "tinge of self-consciousness" (17) with a white self-consciousness of its own.

The result sends a contradictory message. One reinforces a class hierarchy, with the narrator and reader securely perched on top, watching Chloe and her still more "inferior officers" perform for a white audience. The other message affirms the majesty of women's competence in the kitchen, not only exalting the humble but also affirming that black and white women have a common dignity and pride. Chloe even challenges Mrs. Shelby for preeminence as cook: "I was jist so sarcy, Mas'r George" (21). If she's the boss of the sauce, she is also like Black Sam, pleasing a hierarchy of masters by producing good dinners for the Shelbys and her husband, in that order, while her entrepreneurial spirit mirrors white women's behavior. One message says the last shall be first; the other says the last shall stay last.[12]

Later, however, Chloe becomes genuinely independent, rebelling against both Tom and their master. She upbraids her husband for being exactly what his name has come to imply, an Uncle Tom:

> "Marcies!" said Aunt Chloe; "don't see no marcy in 't! 'tan't right! 'tan't right it should be so! Mas'r never ought ter left it so that ye *could* be took for his debts. Ye've arnt him all he gets for ye, twice over. [. . .] Sich a faithful crittur as ye've been,—and allers sot his business 'fore yer own every way,—and reckoned on him more than yer own wife and chil'en!"
> (81–82)

The narrative's most direct challenge to mastery, white and black, racial and patriarchal, comes in a speech almost unreadably dense with dialect. In calmly responding, Tom empathizes with Master Shelby, declares that "it's natur" for Tom to care for his master while Mr. Shelby doesn't "think so much of poor Tom," and concludes, "Yer ought ter look up to the Lord above" (82). Their respective tones continue the narrative's dichotomy between emotional women and rational men. But this time the woman's feelingful, passionate sensibility loses.

Up to now, men have been judged by their capacity to be transformed by their women. Tom is conspicuously *not* influenced by Chloe. Yet he's the book's hero. Why? Students have offered at least five contradictory reasons, and I supply a sixth. Most obviously, Tom holds the promise of religious transformation, beyond Chloe's concerns for family. In that respect he resembles Christian, the hero of Bunyan's *Pilgrim's Progress*, which as Huck Finn says is "about a man that left his family, it didn't say why" (Twain 104). Or perhaps Tom has internalized a white code of Southern honor that makes him keep his word. Third, as one student put it, it might be a more basic manliness: "It's his career. He's trained like a traditional male to see the bigger picture." Fourth, as several students have argued, Tom sacrifices himself to keep other slaves from being sold. And fifth, since my classes have already considered how slave narratives use chiasmus or reversal to master the masters, Tom might be enacting two kinds of chiasmus. "Wan't he put in my arms a baby?—it's natur I should think a heap of him," Tom tells Chloe. His intimate parenting feelings for the master surpass the master's more impersonal feelings for a servant. Moreover, in keeping his promise Tom also displays greater honor, since Mr. Shelby "owed ye yer free-dom," as Chloe says (82). Sixth, I argue, drawing on Mitchell Duneier's *Slim's Table*, Tom might be demonstrating his dignity in the face of emasculation. It may be white readers who want to see a craven slave or a "bad nigger."[13]

Meanwhile Chloe is left helpless and voiceless: "But dar's no use talkin'; I'll jes wet up de corn-cake, and get ye one good breakfast" (82). Thereafter, like the cabin, Chloe remains inwardly boarded up. She briefly speaks to Mrs. Shelby about leaving her children for "four or five years" to make cakes for a *"perfectioner,"* so that Tom can be purchased (221–23). The narrative approves of a motherly woman abandoning her children, since it's for her husband rather than herself, though Mrs. Shelby and Chloe agree that work would never be appropriate for a white lady. In any case, the money—$208 a year—would be the Shelbys', not hers. At the very end, when Chloe hears of Tom's death, she gives all the money she has earned to Mrs. Shelby and turns away. "My poor, good Chloe!" says Mrs. Shelby (379). When I read that line aloud, I perhaps too sarcastically accentuate the irony of "poor."

To focus on close readings, contradictions, and nonnarratable plots gives stu-dents confidence in the diversity of legitimate responses. When that works, by the novel's midpoint classes often take off in unexpected textual directions. Why is it, for instance, that the narrative demonizes Marie St. Clare while indulging Topsy? In different classes, two different students linked Topsy and Marie as products of the marketplace. Just as Topsy was "raised by a specula-tor" to be sold (209–10), inducing trickster guile and self-hatred, so readers first encounter Marie in subtly commodified fragments, as St. Clare "became the husband of a fine figure, a pair of bright dark eyes, and a hundred thou-sand dollars" (132–33). In one student's essay, "a fine figure" took on a nifty double meaning. No wonder Marie is a "creditor in the exchange of affection" and "exacts love, to the uttermost farthing" (134).

Especially in recent years, many students say their most vivid response to *Uncle Tom's Cabin* is their hatred of Marie, particularly when she calls a doc-tor for herself rather than for Eva and when she sells the slaves in willful dis-regard of Eva's and her husband's wishes. If the narrative draws a straight line from Haley through Marie to Legree as products and agents of an increasingly sadistic marketplace, why should Marie seem more hateful than Legree, while Topsy seems so endearing? In part, I suggest, because unmotherly middle-class white women still threaten our values. A little black girl can get away with mal-ice that becomes bad mothering in a white lady. Unfair, students have responded. Topsy is not really selfish; unlike Marie, she's capable of love.

At least once, in 1994, my advocacy of close readings and liberal pluralism led to anger as well as unresolvable conflict. In an upper-level undergraduate class of forty students, we were considering the scene in which Tom manages to meet little Eva because he is "a very Pan" in inventing whistles, and his pocket still has "miscellaneous articles of attraction, which he had hoarded in days of old for his master's children" (127). I read aloud a passage from Hortense Spillers's "Changing the Letter": "A captive person with his pockets full of toys strikes a perfectly ludicrous image to my mind, [. . .] but if the seductive resonance of 'Pan,' 'cunning,' the 'pockets,' is allowed to do its work, then we come to regard aspects of this persona—'sweet-tempered,' Bible-toting, *Uncle Tom*—as a potentially 'dirty old man,' 'under wraps'" (46).

"Absolutely," one student said, laughing. "I feel robbed," another responded. "That's so typical of English teachers," several students said. "Professors see sex in everything!" One student shouted, "He's a typical white male careerist!"

I wrote on the board, "Hortense Spillers." More shouting.

Finally I shouted back, "*She* is a prominent *black female* critic at Cornell."

But their rage wouldn't go away. "This is why I hate psychoanalytic and sexual criticism," said a student. "It keeps pulling texts down to that level. Tom and Eva are religious soul mates." Some classmates enthusiastically agreed. "But the language is there," a female student pointed out, "even though it undercuts the Christian narrative." Another female student nodded her head at that. Then she simply read aloud a key passage a few pages later with a few deletions:

> "Papa, do buy him! it's no matter what you pay," whispered Eva, softly, getting up on a package, and putting her arm around her father's neck. "You have money enough, I know. I want him."
> "What for, pussy?" [. . .]
> "I want to make him happy." (130)

After that collision of interpretations had died down, other students more quietly observed that the unsettling issue for them had to do with parenting, not sex: Tom has toys in his pocket for his master's children but not for his own kids. "Yeah," said someone else. "And why 'his master's children' and not Mrs. Shelby's?" "Maybe he's calculating a way of getting St. Clare to buy him," said someone else. The contradictions were off and running again. "English majors have to be pluralistic, we have to tolerate many readings," one student summed up. "No way," another replied. "Sometimes close reading violates our basic responses."

Several colleagues to whom I told this story immediately interpreted it as anxiety about interracial sex. In the 1990s as in the 1850s, miscegenation remains a more volatile nonnarratable plot than either black rebellion or angry, independent women.[14] But I don't think it's that simple. For one thing, Spillers's point undermines Tom's and Eva's spirituality. Students can preserve the Christian interpretation or their broader reverence for imagined childhood innocence only by dismissing the passage's ambiguous nuances. Spillers's essay has much more complexity, of course. She suggests that Eva's "I want him" becomes the unspeakable yet spoken vehicle for adult white women's disruptive desire, which must be sacrificed through Eva and Tom to preserve and even "galvanize" a murderously patriarchal Calvinism (39–46).[15] Though I felt a certain sadistic pleasure in quoting Spillers, I shared the students' sense of loss and violation. The discussion illuminated for me the impasse between liberal pluralism, whose tolerance is abetted by close readings, and passionate convictions, which close down ambiguities.

The next time I taught this passage, to a freshman honors class of twenty students, I expected a similar ruckus. Again I read Hortense Spillers's interpretation aloud. "I thought of that," one student said quietly. But none of the other students was very much interested in the issue. "Too much analysis," said one. For another it was "just a side impression." "It's all in the voice you choose for Eva," said yet another—"either little girl, or sultry and sexy." What they wanted to talk about was Eva as an interim Christ, and many knew many more of the biblical allusions than I did, especially for her death-bed scene.

Most recently, when I tried Spillers out in a nonhonors freshman course, students seemed neither surprised nor offended. "I thought of that," one student immediately responded. "She's always sitting in his lap." No, said another, "the critic does that because she's bored." To a third student the real nonnarratable issue here was the fear of an older man molesting a younger girl. Another responded, "That's a 1990s reading. It's shaped by our own preoccupations with child abuse." Several pointed out that a problem of genre is involved. Such interpretations work only when we read Eva and Tom as realistic characters. "Eva has a halo, right from the start," one student said. "Just look at how her hair is described. She's not a real person; she's Tom's guardian angel."

The moral here is obvious to any experienced teacher, I suppose: cherish the crazy bounces. A more profound one may be that a literature is rich in proportion to the contrary voices its culture can tolerate. All the better when those voices inhabit the same text. Yet a vital literature, like a vital culture, has to have room for passionate convictions as well as the play of multiple interpretive possibilities. The cultural power of *Uncle Tom's Cabin* comes from its ability to evoke both kinds of responses. The novel's enduring images—Eliza on the ice, Eva's death, Tom's death, Topsy's trickeries, Cassy's force—linger long after our close readings fade.

A final close reading can illustrate both kinds of responses. Just after Eva's death comes a strange last paragraph. "Farewell, beloved child! The bright, eternal doors have closed after thee; we shall see thy sweet face no more. O, woe for them who watched thy entrance into heaven, when they shall wake and find only the cold gray sky of daily life, and thou gone forever!" (257). Who says this? Why the quotation marks?

Without them, the speaker would obviously be the narrator. With them, it has to be a character in the scene—or does it? Students have suggested a variety of possibilities, from St. Clare to Tom to Ophelia to the doctor. Yet it couldn't be

St. Clare, several students suggest, because Eva's father would be too grief-stricken for such a polished oration. Moreover, one student noted, the passage uses "thee" and "thy" and "thou," as if the speaker were a Quaker, perhaps Rachel Halliday's spirit. Maybe it's a collective voice, a Quaker meeting, someone else said. Yes, another student summed up, "It's like the religious response of a congregation." That includes the readers, I add.

A plurality of possible voices becomes an "all of the above." All of the characters, plus Stowe and the readers, speak as a Greek chorus in a collective and spontaneous flow of upward feeling. Yet our participation in Eva's ascent depends on our religious assent. Students who feel disengaged emphasize the stilted and formulaic quality of that seemingly collective voice. As close readings continue to expose the tensions, *Uncle Tom's Cabin* continues to come alive through its contradictions.

NOTES

[1]Cassy's "madwoman in the attic" revenge is borrowed from *Jane Eyre*. On the "dead-undead mother" as a central dynamic in Gothic fiction, see Kahane, "The Gothic Mirror," revising a 1980 *Centennial Review* essay. Two excellent essays by Halttunen historicize Gothic aspects of *Uncle Tom's Cabin*; see "Gothic Imagination and Social Reform" and "Humanitarianism."

[2]The gender war has been explicated by a rich variety of feminist critics (see, e.g., Ammons, "Heroines"; G. Brown, "Getting"; Douglas; Tompkins, *Designs* 122–46). See also Leverenz 19–21, 190–203.

[3]Despite the demands of child rearing, Hedrick notes, Stowe set up her household "so that she would *regularly* have three hours a day to write" (*Stowe* 240). A few students are surprised to learn that Stowe was white; they tend to presume that only black people would have written about slavery.

[4]For Calvin Stowe's weight gain over that eight-year period, I am indebted to R. Levine (private communication). Calvin's Brattleboro letters recount matter-of-factly to his wife how he solaces some of his sexual needs for her by delighting in men who hug him, kiss him, and hold him in bed. One "total stranger," he reports, fell "desperately in love with me, and he kisses and kisses upon my rough old face, as if I were a most beautiful young lady instead of a musty old man" (Hedrick, *Stowe* 180–81). Sometimes a few male students start fidgeting here. But several classes have talked at length about why physical demonstrativeness between heterosexual men in the United States today has become so much more constrained and homophobic.

[5]The novel sold 305,000 copies in the United States in 1852, making the unparalleled sum of $10,000 for the author in its first three months. Hedrick's account of the Stowes' contractual disputes with the novel's publisher highlights Stowe's ability to use her image of modest womanhood in Franklinesque ways, for community action as well as personal credit (*Stowe* 223–24, 239–40). *Uncle Tom's Cabin* also sold 1.5 million copies in Great Britain during its first year (233).

[6]In *Patriotic Gore*, Edmund Wilson resurrects Stowe's novel as well as DeForest's essay (692–98). By 1948, as Wilson notes, *Uncle Tom's Cabin* had gone out of print (3).

Lincoln allegedly remarked to Stowe in the White House in 1862, "So you're the little woman who wrote the book that started this great war!" (Hedrick, *Stowe* vii).

[7]Adolph in turn could be linked to nonmarketplace modes of masculinity, from "exotic" African "passion" to St. Clare's "gay, airy" temperament (177) as a "poetical voluptuary" (141).

[8]See Langland 1–3, 8–9, 110, and 210–21 on the failed attempt of Hannah Culwick and Arthur Mumby to live such a nonnarratable marriage.

[9]On the black Sambo trickster, see Wyatt-Brown.

[10]The student's teacher, Jeffrey Adler, pointed me to Gorn's "Gouge and Bite."

[11]Several years ago, in a freshman class, two students analyzed the changing color of Legree's eyes, from "light-gray" (289) to "greenish-gray" (293) to "greenish" (309). In another class a student pointed out that *le gré* means "pleasure" or "will."

[12]Stephen Nissenbaum's wonderful essay on the creation of New England as a region analyzes the rest of chapter 4 to argue that Stowe is re-creating an idealized New England village in which everyone knows his or her place (55–58). As he notes, Stowe had never visited the South except for one day trip to northern Kentucky (55). Stowe's conflation of a New England village with a Southern plantation raises larger questions about her conflation of plantation slavery with entrepreneurial capitalism.

[13]In *Slim's Table*, Duneier studies black men who frequented a cafeteria near the University of Chicago. The men cultivated styles of moral respectability, notably self-control, will power, and inner strength. Their dignified civility put them at odds with ghetto flashiness and disrespect (66), assimilated middle-class blacks, and white expectations of black male rebelliousness.

[14]The word *miscegenation* postdates *Uncle Tom's Cabin*. *Amalgamation* was used until 1864, when David Croly wrote a scurrilous pamphlet, first published anonymously, ostensibly arguing that Lincoln should be reelected because the white race needed an infusion of black blood and Lincoln favored racial mixing (Croly and Wakeman). Croly coined the word *miscegenation* from *miscere* (to mix) and *genus* (species). The dirty-tricks hoax didn't work, but the word stuck. Croly was the father of Herbert Croly, author of *The Promise of American Life* (1909).

[15] One MLA reader asked why I don't assign Spillers's essay. For graduate classes I assign critical readings; for undergraduate classes I don't, unless they are seminars. Though many of my younger colleagues use criticism and theory extensively in their undergraduate courses, I emphasize close readings of primary texts, with various critical approaches briefly summarized.

Uncle Tom's Cabin and Incidents in the Life of a Slave Girl: The Issue of Violence

Kristin Herzog

Harriet Beecher Stowe (1811–96) and Harriet A. Jacobs (1813–97) both wrote out of a sense of moral urgency as much as out of the need to earn money.[1] They saw slavery as the most insidious scourge of their time, and they portrayed its most vicious aspects from a woman's point of view: the way it tore up families and made women and children victims of sexual and social abuse. Both considered themselves serious Christians while strongly criticizing the Christian establishment. Both portrayed powerful mother figures who represent hope and strength for those around them, and both struggled with the issue of violence and its representation. On this point, however, there are striking differences between their works.

The issue of violence was especially on both authors' minds because of the Fugitive Slave Act of 1850, which required the forcible return of escaped slaves to their masters. Stowe wrote *Uncle Tom's Cabin* in 1851–52, and Jacobs started writing *Incidents* in 1853 (Yellin, Introduction xix; Foster 101). Personally, Harriet Jacobs as a black slave had experienced violence throughout her life. She could be beaten or otherwise physically tortured at any time; she was repeatedly threatened with rape by the white master; she could be sold away from her family at any moment; and she was subjected to psychological and emotional abuse against which she had no recourse. In contrast, Stowe, as a middle-class, free white woman, faced no such sanctioned system of violence, although the extent to which some white middle-class women lived with sexual and social violation can be seen in popular novels such as *The Wide, Wide World* (1850), by Susan Warner, a work that Jane Tompkins has described as "a chronicle of violence" (Afterword 599). While Stowe's thoughts on the violence of war were ambiguous or negative in her later years, she did not hesitate to end *Uncle Tom's Cabin* eleven years before the war with an emotional warning that "injustice and cruelty shall bring on nations the wrath of Almighty God" (388); and in *Men of Our Times*, published in 1868 but written earlier, she assumes that the war has been God's punishment for the national sin of slavery (114–15). She was aware that the violence of slavery had an explicitly sexual side, which she described in *Uncle Tom's Cabin* in the figures of Cassy and Emmeline and the slave Prue who is abused as a "breeder" and later whipped to death (188–91). However, as a white middle-class woman who romanticized the "African race," she would, in contrast to Harriet Jacobs, emphasize the victimization of black people more than their active resistance to violence.

Concentrating in the teaching of *Uncle Tom's Cabin* on a comparison of the treatment of violence in Stowe's novel and Jacobs's *Incidents*, we need to address the question of what these writers could and could not do if they wanted to get their works published. What was the influence of genre conventions on both Stowe and Jacobs, and how did their religious thoughts as well as those of their readers affect their work?

Teachers might assign two student reports on the subject of genre, one on the sentimental novel, focusing on Susan Warner's *The Wide, Wide World*, the other on the male slave narrative, centering on Frederick Douglass's *Narrative* (1845). Fanny Fern's *Ruth Hall* (1855) could also be considered beside Warner's work (Yellin, Introduction 254). An additional choice for a slave narrative might be the one by Henry Bibb, which was one of Stowe's sources.

The Wide, Wide World has been interpreted by Tompkins as portraying an issue of power: "Ellen's predicament—subjugation to a series of authorities over which she has no control—springs from hierarchies of power that still structure most people's experience" (Afterword 597–98). The novel's emphasis on duty, humility, submission, and self-sacrifice and its ending of suffering relieved and virtue rewarded represent the most typical traits of popular Victorian fiction. Both Stowe and Jacobs use conventions of this genre, like the threat of a master's aggression, the virtue of female resistance, and the recurrence of pursuits, escapes, cunning disguises, and madwoman-in-the-attic retreats to appeal to their readers' fears and desires. But for Jacobs these "incidents" take on a unique intensity, because the genre of the slave narrative, which is interwoven with the romance structure, turns her story into a powerful autobiography, whereas for Stowe the genre simply provides material. *Incidents* in fact transgresses all boundaries of genre, because the sexual and social violence Jacobs experienced could not be adequately expressed in any autobiographical narrative by a slave woman.

In Jacobs's narrative the relentless persecution of Linda starts with Dr. Flint harassing the fourteen-year-old with "stinging, scorching words; words that scathed ear and brain like fire" (18). This violation by words can be recorded in proper diction, but its brutality is veiled by the demands of genre and custom. When she expresses her wish to marry a free black man, she declares, "[Flint] sprang upon me like a tiger and gave me a stunning blow" (39). Later, she remarks, "A master may treat you as rudely as he pleases, and you dare not speak" (55). This actual silencing continues because of the demands of respectable writing. After one of Flint's "fits of passion" in which he struck her and pitched her down the stairs, she states, "I was subjected to such insults as no pen can describe" (77). The restriction in life and in writing creates such an intense conflict between form and content, voice and body, that one might even wonder—like Mrs. Flint (56)—whether the doctor actually raped Linda or preferred the titillation of psychological harassment and frequent blows (Foreman 83–84). In any case, his violence has physical implications: refusing to be victimized, Linda chooses another white man to father her children, thereby again becoming involved in something that could not be "told" in a straightforward way but had to take the form of a confession of sin. Lydia Maria Child, in her introduction to *Incidents*, states that she will with this book present slavery "with the veil withdrawn," but actually Jacobs herself has to manage the unveiling (4). She can do so only by signifying the pervasiveness of Dr. Flint's violence: he continually pursues and threatens her, trying to force her to become his mistress. The persecution extends to her family, especially her children; it complicates her relationship to her brother and her grandmother and forces the separation of her aunt and uncle (Jacobs 80–83; Fleischner 68–69). In his erotic lust to maintain power, Flint not only practices a kind of revenge against a slave family but also causes his jealous wife to haunt Linda's bed like a nightly phantom: "She whispered in my ear, as though it was her husband who was speaking to me" (34). Here Linda has to "earwitness" another virtual seduction that in Jacobs's narrative has to be "displaced into language" for "delicate" ears (Garfield and Zafar 108; Foreman 83; Child 4). Even so, the author has to plead with her readers: "But, O, ye happy women, whose purity has been sheltered from childhood, who have been free to choose the objects of your affection, whose homes are protected by law, do not judge the poor desolate slave girl too severely" (54).

Although as far as we know Stowe did not have to deal in a personal way with the problem of sexual violence, she depicts its devastation in Legree's relationship to Cassy and Emmeline. When Cassy is introduced to the reader, she is confronting Legree "with a haughty, negligent air," while he looks into her eyes with "a sneering yet inquiring glance." His "face became perfectly demoniacal in its expression," and "he half raised his hand, as if to strike" (308). The image of a "demoniacal" master is similar to Linda Brent's portrait of her master's "restless, craving, vicious nature [that] roved about day and night, seeking whom to devour" (18)—apparently an allusion to the biblical devil who "prowls around like a roaring lion, seeking someone to devour" (1 Pet. 5.8). "I hate him as I do the devil," asserts Cassy (312). "[He will be] sucking your blood, bleeding away your life, drop by drop" (330). Legree epitomizes violence against women: his mother, Cassy, Emmeline, and the "feminine" Tom. To overcome this demonic violence, Cassy does not mind using violence herself, considering suicide (326), encouraging Tom to kill Legree, and being willing to do it herself (344). Years earlier she had even killed her own child to save it from slavery. To outwit her devilish master, she now plays on his superstitions: "Be careful, for I've got the devil in me," she hisses at him (321). She then proceeds to arouse his fears and the painful memories of his pious mother, terrorizing him to the point where she can play a ghost and flee with Emmeline.

Linda Brent, a trickster of a different order, does not harbor any illusion of a possible change in Dr. Flint, but she realizes that his craving for power and total control is tied up with the idea of commercial property: "Women are considered of no value, unless they continually increase their owner's stock. They are put on a par with animals" (49). She shrewdly figures therefore that only children by another father can escape his grasp, but since Flint loved power even more than money (122), Linda's lover, Mr. Sands, is unable to buy freedom for her and her children. Her withdrawal into the garret, however, eventually brings freedom for her children and herself, at the price of seven years of self-imprisonment. Through her ingenuity and daring—finding care for her children, observing her enemy from a crack in the garret, dressing like a sailor, or faking letters from New York—she finally overcomes violence in a nonviolent way, without any sentimental conversion in either the demonic master or herself. She accomplishes this feat not as an individual—as often occurs in the male slave narrative—but with the help of a number of black and white friends. Whereas Cassy has to be converted away from violence and godlessness by Christian mothers and by the motherly Tom to be fully acceptable to Stowe and to the demands of the genre, Linda is from the beginning a shrewd, nonviolent agent of her own liberation from demonic power, emulating her strong-willed father and rebellious brother as much as she emulates the mother figures in her life (Fleischner 58; Garfield 120). "The war of my life had begun," she asserts, "and though one of God's most powerless creatures, I resolved never to be conquered" (19). This is not the voice of a victim.

The metaphor of "war" for Linda's struggle against Flint's sexual persecution leads us to consider the social violence presented here that seems to have demanded genre-related caution for both Stowe and Jacobs. When in *Uncle Tom's Cabin* Augustine St. Clare's brother Alfred suggests that the "canaille" ought to be kept down and uneducated to prevent uprisings, St. Clare responds with references to the French Revolution and the rebellion in San Domingo as proof that "the masses are to rise" (234). Here Stowe seems to emphasize that revolutionary violence is likely to erupt and will not be prevented by suppression. When George Harris makes his defiant "declaration of independence," the author indirectly tells her readers that his readiness for violence is no more threatening or in need of censure than commonly praised heroism: "When despairing Hungarian fugitives make their way, against all the search-warrants and authorities of their lawful government, to America, press and political cabinet ring with applause and welcome. When despairing African fugitives do the same thing,—it is—what *is* it?" (172). Stowe was making her point carefully and shrewdly, because it went against racial stereotypes and Southern white pride while at the same time evoking images of heroism common to popular domestic novels.

Linda Brent likewise knows how the patriarchal menace of sexual violation goes hand in hand with social violence that cannot be expressed without genre-related caution. In the chapter "Fear of Insurrection" she describes the indiscriminate robberies and insults inflicted by white soldiers on black citizens in the wake of the Nat Turner insurrection (63–67). Lydia Maria Child had encouraged Jacobs to provide concrete examples of such "outrages" in this chapter. Jacobs had also added at the end of her manuscript a chapter concerning John Brown's raid on Harper's Ferry, doubtless to make the book more immediately relevant by reference to this violent event of 1859. Child, however, asked her to omit the chapter, since it did not fit "naturally" into the story, and to end the work with the death of Linda's much-loved grandmother (Yellin,

Introduction 244). Just like Stowe, Child wanted to emphasize motherliness in a narrative appealing to Northern white readers, whereas Jacobs's original intent indicates her conviction that the violence directed toward her person reverberates on the social level (MacKethan 31, Fleischner 92). In fact, when the mob invading Linda's grandmother's house found a personal letter with a poem directed to Linda, the captain "swore" and "raved," because the literacy of black slaves increased the fear and rage of the illiterate invaders (65).

The utter cruelty of slavery is described in the chapter "Sketches of Neighboring Slaveholders." Although this part of the book was edited by Lydia Maria Child and is perhaps not accurate in all its details, many of the atrocities have been substantiated by court records (Yellin, Introduction 267). Extended bloody tortures as punishment for a hungry slave's petty theft of food, blood hounds tearing flesh from runaway slaves, and flogging that leads to an agonizingly slow death—all these incidents are hushed up: "Nothing was said" (47). Even the very few "humane slaveholders" (50) cannot avoid the "all-pervading corruption" and cruelty of which "no pen can give an adequate description" (51). Here again the genre cannot unveil the whole truth.

While the conventions of the sentimental novel and the slave narrative put certain constraints on Stowe's and Jacobs's treatment of sexual and social violence, we must also consider the influence of religious genres and traditions in trying to understand the treatment of violence in their texts. To introduce this topic into the class discussion, students might consult Joan Hedrick's biography of Stowe, Gayle Kimball's *The Religious Ideas of Harriet Beecher Stowe*, or the work of Horace Bushnell, whose thoughts on Christian nurture were similar to those of Stowe. For Jacobs, the class might discuss her epigraph of Jeremiah 32.9 which—in its context—indicates that she sees her work as being like that of a Hebrew prophet predicting devastation of the country if injustice prevails. Throughout the narrative, she points out discrepancies between Christian teaching and practice. As Frederick Douglass put it in the appendix to his *Narrative*, "Revivals of religion and revivals in the slave-trade go hand-in-hand together" (154). In contrast, Jacobs describes the deep faith of her beloved grandmother and her aunt, which she and especially her brother cannot always emulate. The failure of traditional religion to deal with violence becomes clear in Linda's attempt to gain her grandmother's forgiveness for bearing a child out of wedlock. "I had rather see you dead than to see you as you now are," exclaims the grandmother while banishing her from the house (56–57). She finally extends pity but not forgiveness. The slave matriarch, who has never been submissive to whites, is here unwittingly involved in the psychological violence toward Linda and in her silencing. "My lips moved to make a confession, but the words stuck in my throat" (56). When Linda becomes ill and literally loses her speech, she ruminates on why God permits violence:

> Sometimes I thought God was a compassionate father [. . .]. At other times it seemed to me there was no justice or mercy in the divine government.

I asked why the curse of slavery was permitted to exist [. . .]. These things took the shape of mystery [. . .].   (123)

Overall, Jacobs's resistance to the violence of slavery is based as much on a humanistic sense of fairness and justice as it is on biblical faith. Her tale is effective, however, exactly because she reveals, like Stowe, the hypocrisy of the slaveholders' Christianity that hides the violence of domination. The victims of violence are shown to be truly God's people. For Jacobs, religion is an ambiguous, unsettling force. In its traditional form it produces guilt; in its black transformation, however, it releases in her the power of rebellion against slavery that determined the lives of her father, her brother, and her teen-aged uncle. Linda had the urge "to retain, if possible, some sparks of my brother's God-given nature" (19). According to Jennifer Fleischner, "The narrative proposes the radical ideas that a slave's revolt is sacred and that running from slavery is a transcendent act" (89).

To understand how religion shapes the treatment of violence in Stowe, we might examine her novel *Dred* (1856), her text *Men of Our Times* (1868, but written earlier for a Baptist magazine), and some of her columns for the *Independent*. In *Dred*, she sympathizes with a slave rebellion without endorsing it. When five years after the publication of *Dred*, however, the Civil War breaks out, Stowe writes in the *Independent*, "This is a cause to die for, and—thanks be to God!—our young men embrace it as a bride and are ready to die" (F. Wilson 467–68). Comparing this eagerness for war with her stance in *Uncle Tom's Cabin*, we might ask why she speaks much more warmly of Tom's Christian humility than of George Harris's readiness for armed fight. Why does she show greater admiration for the piety and humility of Eva and Eliza than for the militancy of Cassy who kills her own baby and tempts Tom to kill Legree? While in *Uncle Tom's Cabin* she prophesies the coming war as the unavoidable *dies irae*, in *Men of Our Times* she even appears to claim divine hindsight in declaring that the war was God's punishment of the nation for the sin of slavery (114–15). Yet *Uncle Tom's Cabin*, written before the war, forces us to ask the same question that the abolitionist William Lloyd Garrison asked publicly in the paper the *Liberator*:

Is there one law of submission and non-resistance for the black man, and another law of rebellion and conflict for the white man? When it is the whites who are trodden in the dust, does Christ justify them in taking up arms to vindicate their rights? And when it is the blacks who are thus treated, does Christ require them to be patient, harmless, long-suffering, and forgiving? And are there two Christs?   (Sundquist, *Essays* 15)

We have to consider that Stowe lived in an atmosphere of strong millenarian beliefs. Some violent apocalyptic catastrophe was about to erupt: "There is a mustering among the masses, the world over; and there is a *dies irae* coming on, sooner or later" (202). There is also a racial element involved in Stowe's ambivalence between pacifism and enthusiasm for war, as Garrison suspected. The "romantic racialism" of her day (Fredrickson, *Black Image* 113–17; Hedrick, *Stowe* 209) strengthened Stowe's belief that the last shall be first on judgment day, and the last were the black slaves: "And this, oh Africa! latest called of nations,—called to the crown of thorns, the scourge, the bloody sweat, the cross of agony,—this is to be *thy* victory; by this shalt thou reign with Christ when his kingdom shall come on earth" (345). These words are spoken by the authorial voice when the nonviolent Tom tries to keep Cassy from gaining freedom by violence. Why, then, could Stowe be so sure that the Civil War was "God's will" and worth any sacrifice? Why was the slave insurrection planned by Dred *not* God's will? Ironically, her blend of racial prejudice, patriotism, and fervor for black emancipation identified peace with a militarily victorious Union free of slavery. While she admired humility—in her mind vaguely identical with nonviolence—in black people, she admired violent power in "the well-known and romantic story of that Great March" of General Sherman, a white man (*Men of Our Times* 442).

Stowe's limitations are obvious. Her incredible success, however, was partly due to her stubborn, limited, simplifying, and mythologizing way of thinking and writing. Her single-mindedness concerning the emancipation of the slaves made a strong contribution to liberation, and her portrayal of peaceful blacks and conscientious whites may have contributed to the cause of nonviolence in spite of the popular belief that President Lincoln greeted Stowe with the words, "So you're the little woman who wrote the book that started this great war!" (Hedrick, *Stowe* vii). As Philip Fisher has argued, the "ordinariness" of writers like Stowe, Cooper, and Dreiser had a transforming power in culture and society that more subtle geniuses like Melville, Dickinson, and James did not have (8). The political content of Stowe's sentimental novel is democratic and nonviolently revolutionary because it touches the reader's emotions concerning human beings who traditionally had been considered nonpersons: slaves, women, and children (Fisher 99). Stowe remained ambiguous about the difference between just and unjust wars or between mob killing and state-sanctioned killing. She simply was convinced that in the kingdom of God power structures would be turned upside down.

Harriet Jacobs does not deal in theological arguments like Stowe. While she realizes that there are kind and Christian whites (105, 201) and unreliable blacks (63, 67), she lives in a world where the violent power of whites over blacks determines all of life. She would have agreed with Stowe that the respectability and humanity of some "good" slaveholders kept the whole system going and therefore made the brutality of the others possible (*Uncle Tom's Cabin* 295). In her chapters "Fear of Insurrection" and "The Church and Slavery" Jacobs implies that mob violence against black people is made possible by a collusion of church and state. She describes the ludicrous irony of a bloody revolt ending with worship: for fear of having blacks plotting rebellion when among themselves, whites demolish the black church. They permit slaves, however, to attend the white church, "a certain portion of the galleries being appropriated to their use" (67). After all the whites have taken communion and the blessing has been pronounced, the minister invites the slaves to come down and take bread and wine, "in commemoration of the meek and lowly Jesus, who said, 'God is your father, and all ye are brethren.'"

In *Uncle Tom's Cabin*, religion as practiced by slaveholders is closely inter-twined with economics and thereby makes violent control possible. As St. Clare puts it in the process of buying the slave Tom, "The country is almost ruined with pious white people." Even the angelic little Eva simply expresses the power of the market: "Papa, do buy him! [. . .] You have money enough, I know. I want him" (130), and Cassy tells Emmeline before fleeing, "Money will do anything, girl" (353). In Jacobs's narrative, Linda Brent is taught God's word by her mistress but is not recognized as a "neighbor" by her, because slaves are simply "God-breathing machines" in the sight of their masters, no more "than the cotton they plant, or the horses they tend"(8). As Flint states it, "These brats will bring me a handsome sum of money one of these days" (80). Both Stowe and Jacobs realize that it is the law that makes violence possible: "over and above the scene there broods a portentous shadow—the shadow of law" (*Uncle Tom's Cabin* 51). "The law allowed [Flint] to be out in the free air, while I, guiltless of crime, was pent up here" (Jacobs 121).

The only way to overcome this violent control, then, is by escape. Jane Tomp-kins writes about Susan Warner's novel, "Women writers of that era, unlike their male counterparts, could not walk out the door and become Mississippi riverboat captains, go off on whaling voyages, or build themselves cabins in the woods. Escape, consequently, is the one thing their novels never offer" (Tompkins, Afterword 593). Escape, however, is exactly what Harriet Jacobs managed and wrote about, even though she had to cope with the triple handicap of being a woman, a black, and a slave. As far as we know from her story and from histori-cal research, she did not kill or physically hurt people in order to become free.[2] Houston A. Baker, Jr., writes, "In a tactically brilliant act of withdrawal, she con-verts the fruit of her womb (rather than the skill of her hand or the capital of a husbanded store) to merchandise. Her retreat culminates in the children's sale to Mr. Sands" ("Archeology" 187). Escape is also the means to overcome violence in *Uncle Tom's Cabin*, although Stowe's "romantic racialism" celebrates the nonescaping Tom more than any other figure in the story. Cassy and Eliza appear to succeed in their escapes on account of their partly white blood and white training. Motherhood, as exemplified by the white Quaker Rachel Halliday, is for Stowe the main model for nonviolent living, caring for and lifting up suffering black mothers who end up as good Christians. If we look only at the end of the story, Stowe's black women seem to lack the agency and strength of their own tra-dition (Fleischner 58–59). When Eliza crosses the river, however, she appears to have "seven devils in her" (53), and Cassy throughout her torturous years has shown incredible strength. Stowe's "racialism" is not without ambiguity.

How does racial location affect authorial attitudes toward violence and non-violence? How are we to determine what violence is or is not? Are whites justified in the violent suppression of "insurrections," whereas blacks are commanded to be nonviolent? Would it have been wrong for Tom or Cassy to kill Legree or for Linda Brent to kill Dr. Flint, whereas governments can authorize massive killing to keep order or to win a war?

At this point we might well come to the conclusion that it all depends on the circumstances and the point of view. In fact, St. Clare in *Uncle Tom's Cabin* sounds a note of cynicism: "What poor, mean trash this whole business of human virtue is! A mere matter, for the most part, of latitude and longitude, and geographical position, acting with natural temperament. The greater part is nothing but an accident!" (198). If violence and nonviolence are mere accidents, they simply depend on the conditions of discourses and contexts. In discussing this perspective, however, the teacher might point out that there are current theorists who do not end up advocating relativism. A good example is Nancy Fraser. She contends that social practices are necessarily norm-governed and that norms not only constrain but also enable us. We need "normative criteria for distinguishing acceptable from unacceptable forms of power" (33). That does not mean we can find traditional objectivist norms to identify violence in order to find a cure for it. We can, however, critically interpret some issues that particular groups consider their "needs"—protection or self-defense, for example—and then ask certain normative questions about the inclusivity or exclusivity of that needs discourse. Does it, when put into practice, disadvantage some groups of society? Does it conform to, rather than challenge, patterns of domination and submission? Does it rationalize inequality? Does it balance social needs and private rights? Is it democratic? (Fraser 182).

Thus students can be challenged to continue the "unveiling" of violence attempted by Stowe and Jacobs and to weigh the evidence: the white fears of slave rebellion against the "original" or structural violence of slavery and its devastating economic, physical, and psychological pressures; abolitionist efforts of encouraging rebellion against the Southern system but discouraging rebellion by blacks; slavery's violence in separating families against Linda Brent's nonviolent "trickster" strategies to maintain black motherhood or George Harris's readiness for violence in defense of his family (*Uncle Tom's Cabin* 170). In spite of all the ambiguities involved, the works of Stowe and Jacobs can help us figure out criteria for what constitutes violence that can never be justified.

The class might conclude with a screening of a film, either *Glory* or *Amistad*, to provide students not only with literary but also with pictorial images of the ambiguity of violence in the struggle for abolition.

NOTES

I would like to thank Jennifer Fleischner for valuable suggestions concerning this essay.
[1]Painter emphasizes that Stowe was never a radical abolitionist and that she wrote

mainly to make money, but Hedrick's biography paints a more complex picture (see Painter 153; Hedrick, *Stowe* 225–35).

[2]Students from the Southeast of the United States might take an excursion to Edenton, North Carolina, to observe how the town is only now beginning to make visitors aware of the historical circumstances that surrounded Harriet Jacobs. The extent to which *Incidents* is a "true" representation of Jacobs's life has been analyzed by Goldsby; Yellin ("Her Brother's Eyes"); and Knott.

Raising a Passionate Voice: Teaching
Uncle Tom's Cabin to Less Experienced Readers

Mary Jane Peterson

Uncle Tom's Cabin is a productive text for engaging less experienced student readers in a dialogue that lays the basis for effective participation as members of a community. Because of the novel's controversial treatment of race, some teachers are reluctant to teach it, especially before the college level, but I have found that my students benefit from the debate it generates. The approach I use asks them to look at the text in the context of its era and to raise issues of gender, race, class, voice, and rhetorical purpose. It prepares them to articulate as well as to challenge social inequities, a practice that Randall R. Freisinger upholds as a chief goal of education (262). This approach centers on a method of reading and response that moves readers from a focus on a text outward to a consideration of community (in this case their particular educational community) through a series of specific reading and writing assignments and class discussion. The unit assumes that students often feel themselves to have marginalized voices because they haven't yet had much success at making themselves heard in their educational communities. It focuses on how voices at the margin can become instruments of change.

To encourage students' success in reading the novel, I begin with another powerful yet marginalized mid-nineteenth-century voice on slavery: that of Frederick Douglass. Students respond enthusiastically to his *Narrative* because it is short, graphic, and gripping. They also read James Olney's essay " 'I Was Born': Slave Narratives, Their Status as Autobiography and as Literature," which explains in accessible language that the narratives, seemingly so artless and self-evident, are in fact a form carefully calculated to affirm the existence of the slave as a literate human being. His dramatic demonstration of the relations among rhetorical purpose, structure, style, and voice is an eye-opener that prepares students to examine the same connections in Stowe's novel as well as to recognize the use she makes of slave narratives.

Several sources help students understand Stowe's position in her society. E. L. Doctorow's review of Joan Hedrick's biography, *Harriet Beecher Stowe: A Life*, provides a lively biographical summary, and Hedrick's chapter 18, "A Rush of Mighty Wind: 1850–1851," powerfully narrates the events surrounding the passage of the Fugitive Slave Law and impelling Stowe to write. Finally, Alfred Kazin's introduction to the Bantam edition of *Uncle Tom's Cabin* is especially good in characterizing the response to the novel in subsequent eras. All these sources help to locate the novel historically. By building on what they have learned from the study of the slave narrative, students are now able to extend their discussion of both marginalized and empowered voices and to speculate on the degree to which Stowe's race, gender, and class would have privileged or limited her in her era. Hedrick is especially useful in the last regard. Students read these sources before they finish the novel.

Once the students have read the novel, I rely on them to raise the critical issues that shape class discussion, and I use two formal journal responses to do that. The first journal assignment asks only that students write an entry of roughly four hundred words about an observation or issue suggested by their reading that they would like to share with the class. Excerpts from some of the journals demonstrate that this approach raises central issues in powerful ways. Here, for instance, is part of the first journal read in one class last year:

> When I began to ponder Stowe's personal opinion [about race], I became puzzled. Could it be that she was against the act of slavery and all its effects, but she believed that blacks were inferior to the white race, and that although they had this innate handicap, they deserved freedom? Or was she truly an advocate for complete equality among the races but superimposing the prevailing attitude of the period into the story to make it more realistic? [. . .] I had trouble separating her opinions of slavery with her opinions of blacks, and perhaps other readers did so too.
>
> —Lauren Mucciolo[1]

For some who have read the novel uncritically and enthusiastically, questioning Stowe's possible racism is a jolt. The questions the student asks in this journal set the terms of the discussion for most of the week.

Much of the value of the journals lies in the writers' struggle to communicate their strong reactions to the novel. The problematic character of Tom often invites discussion. Here is an excerpt from a "pro-Tom" journal. The student has been moved by Uncle Tom's "memorable actions" and "wonderful personality":

> His goodness and unswerving compassion [. . .] inspired in me a feeling of awe and great admiration [. . .]. What I first noticed about Uncle Tom was his close resemblance to Christ with his goodness, humility, compassion, and love for all people, including his persecutors.   —Eugene Choi

This view of Tom is forcefully challenged by a journal like the following:

> Uncle Tom, who is the stereotypical "house nigger" without the light complexion, may have been a very real person in those days, but his depiction is one that still plagues the black community and brings anger and shame. Making him the hero of the story is another way the "good negro" stereotype flourishes in relationships between the races [. . .]. I can see Stowe seeing the horrors of slavery around her and writing about it, but she must have stayed right where she sat because she definitely didn't ask Tom.   —Jennifer McLune

A third journal shows the writer struggling to justify her admiration for Uncle Tom despite what she knows about the modern meaning of the term and what she perceives to be the political objection to his behavior in the novel. In a torrential style full of passion, she concedes:

> Alright, so Uncle Tom didn't jump up and kill the white slave-owner at every chance he could.
> He was no Black Panther. I admit, Uncle Tom might not seem like the most admirable "freedom fighter" of all time, on the outside. He's old, he believes in the white man's religion.   —Dorothy McGivney

She admits that these qualities open him to the charge of being "the most pathetic of all blacks, collaborators, conspirators, and acquiescers." She understands that the author is making a religious argument against slavery through Tom: Stowe, "an old white woman who was totally religious, believed that the right religion would save us all, and so it would be quite proper, and necessary, for Uncle Tom as a heroic central character to be religious. There is no debasitory attempt in the casting of Uncle Tom here." She notes that just as Stowe "makes Tom a true believer," she "tried, in a way, to make the reader the same type of believer." She concludes, "The more I think about Uncle Tom, the more admirable he becomes in my mind." She ends with a disarming but real question about effect on audience: "Am I just another Harriet Beecher Stowe (obviously not in terms of writing!)?"

These journal excerpts demonstrate how productive this method is in raising important issues through the language of inexperienced readers. They identify ambiguities and problems of the novel, and they query the position from which Stowe is writing. They ponder her relationship to her intended audience and to audiences of our day, and they consider the pulls her style creates between our intellect and our emotions. Most of all they engage students in spirited discussion because the passion in their own voices demands response.

As the teacher I see my job as helping students to ask and debate ever more complex questions, not as attempting to "resolve" issues or to assert a point of view. The mix of students in my classes has never yet failed to provoke richly textured discussion, but if important points of view were not represented, providing additional readings from such work as J. C. Furnas's hostile *Goodbye to Uncle Tom* would enliven response.

The second journal assignment, written after the start of the discussion occasioned by the first journals, asks students to reflect on Stowe's prose style: to quote and analyze a specific passage of their choosing to discover how such elements as diction, syntax, imagery, and authorial stance convey racial, cultural, social, political, and historical attitudes. I also ask students to discuss how such a style affects the audience. This assignment helps students discover more complex textual problems and achieve a richer grasp of issues than they yet have. Their previous work on Douglass's writing style helps them to isolate and contrast characteristic elements of Stowe's style. These style journals are especially effective in highlighting issues related to gender and to violence. Students are interested in comparing what they perceive as Douglass's "masculine" style with the style of Stowe. One journal, for instance, contrasted the predominating male imagery of physical violence in Douglass's *Narrative*, with blood as its emblem, with the characteristically more female imagery of emotional violence, with tears as its emblem, in *Uncle Tom's Cabin*. Students are especially acute in comparing the effects of violence that sunders families as a motif in Stowe with the violence that annihilates personhood as a motif in Douglass's work.

These journal discussions on style always increase understanding of the qualities that give Stowe such a passionate voice, which is what my students respond to the most directly in the novel, even when her style offends them. And it often does. Here, for instance, is a student protesting Stowe's lack of subtlety:

> In the spirit of *UTC*, several paragraphs are devoted to describing how everyone in the room begins to cry or displays a heroic effort to prevent his/her sympathy from blossoming into drops of salty emotion. I felt that this overemotional display became tiresome after the first few times.
>
> —Won Chun

The student recognizes the probable reason for this technique—"to pull open the eyes of the citizens, especially the ignorant souls of the north, to the harsh realities of slavery"—and admits Stowe's success by quoting Lincoln's comment on first meeting her ("So you're the little woman who wrote the book that started this great war" [Hedrick, *Stowe* vii]), a remark the student writer regards as delivered "jokingly, but not entirely inaccurately." He makes an insightful comment about the effect of Stowe's style: "She frequently departs from the story [. . .] to address the reader directly [. . .]. The inevitable question, 'Isn't this abhorrent?' or 'How would you feel in this situation?' accompanies nearly every instance where a slave family is broken up. After a while I got confused whether the dialogue continued with the characters or with myself." Students probe this relationship to audience again and again.

Here, for instance, is a different student analyzing the effect of the style on her:

> I thought it was interesting how when we were reading about the lives of others and experiencing their pain, when [Stowe] talked to us in her own voice, we understood the pain and agony of the sufferers even more. [This technique] made it seem more real and even sadder [. . .]. Through her style she was able to cry out to the people and encourage them to end this horrible institution.   —Michelle Choi

A third student, Katherine Hallissy, observes that another technique that "personalizes her voice is directly appealing to mothers and Christians. As the author made it evident that she fell into both of these categories, any reader who shares these characteristics feels a kinship with the author." Another student, Mark Vignola, asserts that a goal of Stowe's style is to "prove the slaves' humanity before she can prove the inhumanity of slavery."

Whatever directions the discussions of style take, they lead back inevitably to reinvigorated debate over how to read the novel in its historical context and how to read it in ours. My goal is not to reach agreement on any one reading but to understand the issues raised by Stowe in the novel as well as those created by the effect that the novel had in its era and continues to have in ours. This sort of discussion achieves the "standard of collaboration without consensus" that James Berlin argues is necessary to create a healthy educational "climate that allows for dissent." (x).

In response to the two types of journals I have described, students have raised their own voices to identify and debate concerns raised by the novel. I have found, however, that Stowe's voice issues such a strong personal challenge to them that they often want to reply directly to her. A productive exercise, entitled "This Mask Speaks to Harriet Beecher Stowe," asks the student to choose a work of visual art (painting or sculpture—lucky for us we live near the Metropolitan Museum of Art) that would have something to say to Stowe and to address the author in the persona suggested by the art. As Peter Elbow observes, "One of the best ways to find authority or achieve assertiveness of voice is to role-play and write in the voice of some 'invented character' who is strikingly different from ourselves" (15).

These student writings, bold and strong, provide yet another way to examine central issues of the novel. Here for instance, is the voice of a student who has been enraged by Stowe's condescending depiction of blacks. In this opening section she is speaking through Romare Bearden's six-paneled painting of an urban street scene, *The Block* (1971). She is "one of the angels floating to the sky from the second panel featuring a funeral scene." She jeers:

> Harriet!
> Yeah honey, up here!
> No, you're not dreaming.
> I'm the angel that you've tried to bleach out of existence.
> Black as night is black. Pure
> as coal is pure.
> My hair is the halo of coarse verses
> that brings Miss. Ann to her lily white knees.
> Behold the darkness of my being!
> Behold the wildness of my wings
> as they cut the delicate patterns of the solar system!
> —Jennifer McClune

Her entire response of more than fifty lines creates a remarkable poem criticizing the legacy of Stowe's racially denigrating characterization. The student wrote that she chose *The Block* because "just like its canvas was screaming I wanted to yell at Harriet Beecher Stowe [. . .]. I brought up all my anger at this ignorant, hypocritical woman and started off with 'Harriet! Yeah honey, up here!' Soon other verses were tumbling out like they had always been there and I had my poem."

Other students wrote equally compelling addresses to Stowe. Through the voice of an ancient Aztec terra-cotta censer, William Gerba created "an austere prophetic character" whose "penetrating" but "enigmatic" speech commends Stowe for a voice that "has traveled through the Ages" to recognize "what is unjust" but cautions her "to see past [her] sheltered life" to recognize that "the world that you created / Pales in comparison to the world that created you." Through their assumed voices, students probe the strengths and limitations of Stowe's vision. The technique is valuable because it encourages imaginative, insightful critical responses that students might find hard to articulate in their own voices.

Despite widely divergent responses to *Uncle Tom's Cabin*, the students I teach believe that it is a worthwhile reading experience. The final project in this unit asks students working collaboratively (groups of three or four are productive) to argue the novel's worth by designing a curriculum unit with *Uncle Tom's Cabin* as the centerpiece. They must develop a rationale not only for why but also for how to teach the work. The task forces students to negotiate differences among themselves, debating among other things the values intrinsic to Stowe's novel, productive pairings with other texts, and the differing views of education they hold. Some groups predictably define a unit with a historical focus. Other proposals value other outcomes. One group, intrigued by Stowe's powerful voice and commitment to her cause, designed a unit organized around four American literary texts with propagandistic agendas. The final activity in their proposed unit asked each student to write an original piece of "literary" propaganda in support of a social position important to the writer. Another group designed a unit examining sources of present-day racial images in the United States. In addition to Stowe's novel, another key text for them was Patricia A. Turner's *Ceramic Uncles and Celluloid Mammies*.

When groups present their proposals to the larger class, debate about who is privileged and who is marginalized by the proposed curricula intensifies. It becomes passionate and real when individuals or groups in the class feel themselves disenfranchised by curriculum design. One group of students, animated by convictions about experiential education as well as the then-current debate about the proposed historical theme park, Disney's America, included plans for a total-immersion weekend slave "camp." The shocked reaction of classmates to this naive but sincere proposal provided a moment when student voices gained real passion in debating issues central to their well-being as individuals and as citizens in a multicultural society—issues of race, of class, of gender, and of unequal access to the institutions of power.

Because this method of engaging students generates intense personal responses, it is potentially painful for class members. Students risk damage to the vulnerable selves they are struggling to create through words. This approach works only if students believe that each has an important voice—however inexperienced or halting—in a community where expressing a sincere point of view is the ticket to membership. Thus, long before I use this method in teaching *Uncle Tom's Cabin*, students have listened to personal voices in the academy debating similar issues. My approach has been shaped by Gerald Graff's powerful arguments for teaching controversy in *Beyond the Culture Wars*. He points out that "knowledge of what is and is not considered potentially or legitimately controversial cannot be learned a priori [. . .]. Such knowledge comes only through interaction with a community" (110).

If that interaction is honest, it is bound sometimes to be painful. When the "slave camp" controversy erupted, for instance, some students indignantly challenged the sincerity of one group member's leadership of our school's Anti-Bias Committee. In a moving letter to the class, the student accepted responsibility for a poor decision but defended his moral integrity and commitment to combating prejudice. If he had not taken this initiative, I would have asked other students to write about the issue or I would have written myself. This movement from personal reaction to public self by staking a claim through writing is painful because it represents knowledge forged from controversy. I constantly affirm the worth of the particular voice and model the value of sustained discourse in creating the civic self. I also discuss with students the pain inherent in honest exploration of differences but insist on the value of understanding and dignifying all voices.

This method demands flexibility as well as extreme tact. I often have to spend more time than I had planned to be sure all voices are heard, that an inexperienced voice is saying clearly what it intends to say, and that others are really understanding. Otherwise students may only reinforce the stereotypical thinking many begin with. The potential for hurtful misunderstanding is great as students struggle to put into words their personal experiences with race, class, gender, and power; issues that are less explosive—and certainly less exhausting—are left unexplored. African American students especially talk about their anger and frustration in making their experience of racism understood. In *Lives on the Boundary* (another book useful for this method), Mike Rose rightfully calls these attempts in an academic setting "conversations that seem foreign and threatening" but necessary because, under the guidance of a sensitive teacher, they help students "center [themselves] in [their] own developing ideas" (48). A controversial text like *Uncle Tom's Cabin* provides a fertile seedbed for these crucial conversations.

In "The Teacher's Authority: Negotiating Difference in the Classroom," Patricia Bizzell argues that we must provide students with "course material that centers around some moment in American history when different groups were contending for the right to interpret what was going on" so that they can learn from these texts how to negotiate the differences inherent in our own multicultural democracy (199). *Uncle Tom's Cabin* is an excellent text to help inexperienced readers envision this task. Introduced through this series of reading, writing, and discussion activities, it helps students identify and then practice a voice that permits resistance and encourages dissent.

NOTE

[1] I am indebted to my eleventh grade students at Manhasset High School for all they have shared in writing about *Uncle Tom's Cabin* and especially to those students who have permitted me to quote from their journals in this article.

Masochistic Eroticism in *Uncle Tom's Cabin*: Feminist and Reader-Response Approaches

Marianne K. Noble

In 1857, the English doctor William Acton observed, "The majority of women (happily for society) are not very much troubled with sexual feeling of any kind." He qualified his broad observation by conceding that sexual passion might be found in "low and vulgar women," but he insisted, "Many of the best mothers, wives, and managers of households know little of or are careless about sexual indulgences. Love of home, of children, and of domestic duties are the only passion they feel" (qtd. in Haller and Haller 98). Acton's descriptions of "the best" women offer familiar and vivid examples of what Nancy Cott has identified as a widespread ideal of female passionlessness characterizing genteel nineteenth-century discourse ("Passionlessness").[1] The "true woman," also known as the "proper lady" and mythologized as the "angel in the house," was held to be passionless by nature: just as the ovum passively and indifferently awaited the active penetration of the lusty sperm, it was argued, women felt little active sexual desire but naturally submitted to male desire.[2]

Acton's description of female nature exemplifies the way attitudes toward sexual desire can be used repressively by a dominant group seeking to control a "marginal" social group. His parenthetical remark ("happily for society") demonstrates, after all, that female passionlessness was not a matter of indifference to the dominant culture; rather, it was seen as crucial for social stability. He also indicates that race and class are implicated in constructions of sexuality, for women who betray sexual desire will be thought of as "low and vulgar" and unworthy of the respect and protection accorded genteel women. Only white women of a certain socioeconomic background were eligible for the status of "the best mothers [and] wives," and one of the prices they had to pay for that privilege was the renunciation of their sexual desire.

However, many of these white middle-class women in fact did experience sexual passion, but, because they wanted to *be* those very same "best wives and mothers," they were constrained to conceive and articulate that passion in terms different from those Acton might have used. Writing about a longing for a loving transcendence achieved through suffering was one way that women's desires for intimacy, for physical expressions of love, and for an expansive euphoria became thinkable and expressible. As I show in this essay, this particular kind of masochistic discourse characterizes some of the climactic scenes of *Uncle Tom's Cabin*. Because Stowe is so steeped in the culture of evangelical Calvinism, which interprets affliction as a sign of God's love, her descriptions of Tom's martyrdom make torture sound like an experience of loving, physical intimacy bordering on ecstasy. It is possible, though ultimately unprovable, that in this masochistic religious language, Stowe was writing obliquely about an erotic desire that pronouncements like Acton's made otherwise unthinkable for her and other women of her socioeconomic class. Furthermore, as analysis of reader responses to *Uncle Tom's Cabin* demonstrates, identification with tortured fictional characters may have enabled middle-class white female readers to experience a similar taboo physical passion.

After showing how masochistic discourses such as are found in *Uncle Tom's Cabin* make it possible to circumvent prohibitions on middle-class women's sexuality, I describe here the complications in determining an appropriate feminist response to these potential pleasures. Such a question enters into the larger issue of the legitimacy of exploring the erotics of domination, a subject that is hotly debated among current feminist theorists.[3] Some feminists might celebrate the capacity of masochistic fantasies to both screen and generate women's erotic pleasure in *Uncle Tom's Cabin*. Others might emphasize the way that representations of eroticized violence in the novel serve as oppressive agents in the construction of a female attraction to male domination. They might argue that to suggest the possibility that women could take pleasure in fantasies of suffering reinforces the oppressive myth—notoriously pioneered by Sigmund Freud—that all women are masochists by nature.[4] Addressing the erotics of violence in *Uncle Tom's Cabin* enables teachers to bring students into this volatile feminist debate, to engage them in a discussion of the politics of sexual desire and the social construction of sexuality. It also enables teachers to reveal to students the competition between the politics of race and gender in America, for whatever masochistic pleasures there are in reading *Uncle Tom's Cabin* are indulged at the price of the suffering of real African American slaves, who are positioned within the novel as objects of eroticized sympathy rather than as subjects in their own right. The masochistic pleasures of the novel are invariably a double-edged sword of pleasure and oppression.

In a letter Stowe wrote in July 1845 to her husband, Calvin, she expresses the prominent Victorian belief—voiced by Acton—that women are naturally passionless and men are naturally sexually aggressive. Calvin had written his wife a letter agonizing about revelations of sexual depravity among influential members of the clergy. Evidently, he detected with concern a corresponding inclination in his own character. "I try to be spiritually-minded, and find in myself a most exquisite relish, and deadly longing for all kinds of sensual gratification," he privately lamented in a letter a few days later to his father-in-law (qtd. in E. Wilson 23). In her sympathetic but clinical response, Stowe voiced pity and claimed that she herself felt no sexual desire:

> What terrible temptations lie in the way of your sex—till now I never realised it—for tho I did love you with an almost *insane* love before I married you I never knew yet or felt the pulsation which showed me that I could be tempted in that way—there never was a moment when I felt anything by which you could have drawn me astray—for I loved you as I now love God—& I can conceive of no higher love—and as I have no passion—I have no jealousy [. . .]. If your sex would guard the outworks of *thought*, you would never fall.   (qtd. in E. Wilson 22)

Although her premarital love was intense, Stowe insists that she has never felt erotic "pulsations"; rather, her feelings for her husband resemble spiritual love, which her religious tradition defines as free of carnal passion and therefore incapable of "draw[ing]" one "astray" into a worldly attachment. However, the terms Stowe uses to affirm the appropriateness of her marital love suggest an unconscious process of self-censorship on her part. First, by insisting that passion can be prevented through "guard[ing] the outworks of *thought*," she represents passionlessness as a consciously willed stance, an ideal achieved through intentional mental repression, rather than a naturally occurring condition. Second, she demonstrates an instance of such repression on her own part. By calling her premarital love *"insane,"* she suggests that she may well have felt a form of unacceptable (passionate) love, which the label of insanity enables her to disavow as though it were a momentary lapse from her true (passionless) self. The contradictory strands in this passage not only suggest that Stowe in fact did experience passionate desire but also exemplify the way a white Victorian woman constructed for herself a socially desirable identity such as "true woman" through repression: she insisted that dominant narratives like Acton's accurately represented her personal experience, and she carefully ignored or reconfigured whatever impulses she might experience that did not conform to her conception of who she wanted to be.[5]

Stowe implies that her marital love is "higher" than erotic love because it resembles a love for God, which is by definition not carnal. And yet in her fiction she describes religious desire in terms that emphasize physical passion. In a scene in *Uncle Tom's Cabin* in which Tom is about to be whipped to death, for example, Stowe compares the loving words of God to a physical caress. A slave sadistically taunts Tom, but

> the savage words none of them reached that ear!—a higher voice there was saying, "Fear not them that kill the body, and, after that, have no more that they can do." Nerve and bone of that poor man's body vibrated to those words, as if touched by the finger of God; and he felt the strength of a thousand souls in one. [. . .] His soul throbbed,—his home was in sight,—and the hour of release seemed at hand.   (357)

Tom's love for God in the face of torture features precisely those "pulsations" that Stowe denies experiencing with her husband: his body "vibrates" and "throbs" from a combination of fear and desire. In her imagination, his vibrations of fear mingle with and become expressions of his anticipated pleasure of "release" not only from slavery but also from the existential loneliness of life as an individual apart from God. Associated with God's loving touch, these vibrations of terror impart a character of sensuality to this passage.

This passage foregrounds a longing for the ecstasies of a loving, physical touch. In it, Stowe draws upon a blend of religious and sexual language in her effort to express the pleasures she associates with the idea of release from lonely individuality. The use of tropes of violence to express a desire for intimacy and love has ample precedent within the Calvinist tradition that is so central to Stowe's thinking. Calvinist discourses of the Second Great Awakening tend to emphasize those aspects of Christian theology that view affliction as a sign of God's love. "Whom the Lord loveth he chasteneth," Calvinists insist, for affliction reminds people to turn their eyes away from earthly things that separate them from the true source of salvation and pleasure, which is a state of spiritual oneness with God (Heb. 12.6). Stowe expresses a standard Calvinist view of life as a state of painful separation from God when she imagines Tom's last words: "Who,—who,—who shall separate us from the love of Christ?" (363). Because death will eradicate that separation and reunite Tom with Christ, Stowe imagines that Tom joyfully welcomes death as a gateway to the religious bliss of fusion with God. In keeping with that perspective, after being whipped to the brink of death, Tom insists, "[Legree] an't done me no real harm,—only opened the gate of the kingdom for me; that's all!" (363). Wounding in particular can function as a trope for desire, for it offers an array of visual metaphors for piercing isolated individuality and producing vulnerability to God's presence. After Tom is beaten "to the uttermost of physical anguish" (310), for instance, Stowe writes, "He did not know but that the day of his death was dawning in the sky; and his heart throbbed solemn throes of joy and desire, as he thought that the wondrous *all* [. . .] might all break upon his vision before that sun should set again" (329). The idea of death provides Stowe with a metaphor for the ecstasy of a physical union with the *"all,"* an unidentified state of pure desire.[6]

Stowe does not not invariably draw on erotic imagery in her descriptions of martyrdom, however, as the ethereal death of little Eva indicates. In *Uncle Tom's Cabin*, martyrdom fantasies become eroticized when projected onto suffering black bodies. Throughout the book, as Hortense Spillers argues in "Changing the Letter," Stowe expresses covert sexual desire for Tom, most blatantly when Eva urges her father to buy Tom because, as she puts it, "I want him" (130) and when Eva perches on Tom's knee and festoons him with flowers. By sentimentally transforming the black man into a feminized, tortured object of pity, Stowe not only identifies with his torture but also frees herself to love and desire a sexually exciting figure who is otherwise off-limits.[7] Fantasies of sympathetic identification liberate her to express her abiding desire for an expansive union with the "all," while projecting it onto a powerful, sensual black male imparts an erotic air of desire for the physical pleasures typically associated with erotic love—bodily excitation, loving intimacy, and climactic release. This juxtaposition of Calvinist discourses of ecstacic transcendence with sexual language projected onto a sensual black body could have negative implications for black people, though; the oppressive myth of blacks' greater sexual potency has historically justified both sexual abuse of black women and violent restraint of black men on the grounds of the supposedly grave threat they pose to the purity of "true" white women.[8]

Racially coded, masochistic fantasies may have provided Stowe with a language in which to articulate her own disavowed passion; they may also have enabled her readers to experience through fantasized identification some of the ecstatic pleasures she associates with suffering. Stowe specifically directs her readers to feel slaves' suffering, claiming that feeling for slaves constitutes real and sufficient political action: "There is one thing that every individual can do,—they can see to it that *they feel right*" (385). If she could "make this whole nation feel what an accursed thing slavery is," she vows, she could awaken the consciences of America's emotionally deadened politicians and citizens through "the magic of the real presence of distress" (77).[9] However, while Stowe was notoriously successful at producing emotional and physical anguish among her readers, she could not guarantee that the desired humanitarian relief would ensue.[10] Feeling is not necessarily feeling "right"; as Wendell Phillips observed, "There is many a man who weeps over *Uncle Tom* and swears by the [proslavery New York] *Herald*" (qtd. in Gossett, Uncle Tom's Cabin 168).

In fact, many readers have responded to the racially encoded descriptions of domination and submission in *Uncle Tom's Cabin* with sexual arousal. Freud, for example, notes that books like *Uncle Tom's Cabin* afford "a means for onanistic gratification" for many of his patients: "In my patients' *milieu* it was almost always the same books whose contents gave a new stimulus to the beating-phantasies: those accessible to young people, such as the so-called *"Bibliotheque rose*," *Uncle Tom's Cabin*, etc." (107).[11] Marcia Marcus, in her study of masochistic desire, lists the childhood books that provided materials for her own adolescent masochistic fantasies:

> There were the books about boarding school, in which small boys slaved for the bigger boys [. . .]. There were books about the initiation rites of exotic people. There was *Uncle Tom's Cabin*, and other books about black slaves in America. There were books about armies with iron discipline and military justice and punitive expeditions.   (16)

Likewise, Richard von Krafft-Ebing (the sex researcher who coined the terms *sadism* and *masochism*) quotes an anonymous self-diagnosed masochist who writes:

> Even in my early childhood I loved to revel in ideas about the absolute mastery of one man over others. The thought of slavery had something exciting in it for me, alike whether from the standpoint of master or servant. That one man could possess, sell or whip another, caused me intense excitement; and in reading *Uncle Tom's Cabin* (which I read at about the beginning of puberty) I had erections. Particularly exciting for me was the thought of a man being hitched to a wagon in which another man sat with a whip, driving and whipping him.   (172)

This writer may find *Uncle Tom's Cabin* particularly appropriate for erotic fantasies because he believes that "the aim and end of all masochistic ideas is the unlimited power of life and death, as exercised over slaves and domestic animals" (Krafft-Ebing 178). Scenes such as the martyrdom of Tom, the whipping of Dodo, and the sale of Tom and Emmeline foreground this absolute power—in a sexually encoded racial discourse.

It is not only late-nineteenth-century and twentieth-century readers who experienced the erotics of *Uncle Tom's Cabin*. Even Stowe's contemporaries, particularly Southern reviewers, recognized that the book was erotically charged. For example, an anonymous female reviewer in the New Orleans *Picayune* charged that Stowe "painted from her own libidinous imagination scenes which no modest women could conceive of" (qtd. in Gossett, Uncle Tom's Cabin 191). And in his review, or "critical punishment," as he calls it, George Frederick Holmes exhorted:

> Are scenes of license and impurity, and ideas of loathsome depravity and habitual prohibition to be made the cherished topics of the female pen, and the familiar staple of domestic consideration or promiscuous conversation? Is the mind of woman to be tainted, seduced, contaminated, and her heart disenchanted of all its native purity of sentiment, by the unblushing perusal [. . .] of such thinly veiled pictures of corruption? Can a lady of stainless mind read such works without a blush of confusion, or a man think of their being habitually read by ladies without shame and repugnance?   (qtd. in Gossett 190)

One can only assume that Holmes would feel "shame" if ladies read about "ideas of loathsome depravity" because they would have firsthand knowledge of the extent to which their husbands, brothers, and fathers were regularly "seduced [by] thinly veiled pictures of corruption" in the books reserved for them. Surely, the metaphor William Gilmore Simms constructed to express his loathing for Stowe displays an imagination more libidinous than the one he seeks to condemn: "Mrs. Stowe betrays a malignity so remarkable that the petticoat lifts of itself, and we see the hoof of the beast under the table" (qtd. in Gossett 190). His rather ambiguous image suggests that he sees the book as a pornographic representation of female sexual degradation. Because they are impervious to the idealization of interracial bonding in *Uncle Tom's Cabin*, these commentators are alert to the pornographic aspects of the book and concerned about the transgressive effects of that eroticism on their wives and daughters. It is chilling to realize that these Southern critics object to the undercurrent of sadistic prurience in *Uncle Tom's Cabin* out of concern for the purity of white women who will be aroused or contaminated by such images and not for the black victims of sadistic torture.

Explicitly sexual responses to *Uncle Tom's Cabin* tend to be found in readers who are relatively detached, either politically or temporally; Marcia Marcus, for example, is a contemporary Danish writer. But covertly sexual pleasures can also be detected even in the responses of the most passionate admirers of the text when it was first published.

One of Stowe's most intimate friends, Georgiana May, wrote a letter in which sympathy for tortured slaves appears to have provided subtly erotic pleasures:

> I sat up last night long after one o'clock, reading and finishing "Uncle Tom's Cabin." I *could not* leave it any more than I could have left a dying child; nor could I restrain an almost hysterical sobbing for an hour after I laid my head upon my pillow. I thought I was a thorough-going Abolitionist before, but your book has awakened so strong a feeling of indignation and compassion, that I seem never to have had *any* feeling on this subject till now. But what can we do? Alas! alas! what *can* we do? This storm of feeling has been raging, burning like a very fire in my bones, all the livelong night, and all through my duties this morning it haunts me,—I *cannot* do away with it. Gladly would I have gone out in the midnight storm last night, and, like the martyr of old, have been stoned to death, if that could have rescued these oppressed and afflicted ones.
>
> (qtd. in Gossett 167)

May states that she is in pain, but the letter implies that she enjoys this condition. The letter opens with a metaphor to describe her pain, comparing it to being wrenched from a dying child, an image of agonizing powerlessness. Comparing slavery with the death of a child imparts to the institution an air of inevitability, which is reinforced by May's inarticulate cry, "But what can we do? Alas! alas! what *can* we do?" Her anguished feelings of powerlessness, however, find relief in the fantasy of being stoned to death, which offers a gratifyingly concrete, visualizable image of herself as an effective martyr for the good.

One of the fascinating aspects of May's letter is that she uses the image of a storm twice, both to describe her physical sensation ("storm of feeling") and to imagine her desire for agency ("midnight storm"). Repeating the trope associates the ecstasy of religious transcendence she would experience as a martyr in the midnight storm with the inner storm of feeling raging and burning in the bones. This link between her fantasy of pain and her experience of pain enables May to associate her own painful storm of feeling with the ecstasies of martyrdom, such as Tom experiences in torture. This link between pain and ecstasy is encouraged by Puritan representations of ecstatic martyrdom, which provide the discursive foundation for May's physical experience, enabling her to experience the burning sensations as pleasure. And the involuntary nature of her physical response, a body wracked by convulsions and hysterical sobbing she "*cannot* do away with," enables May to experience these physical pleasures without having to acknowledge that she desires them. Thus, she can remain committed to ideals of passionless "true womanhood" and simultaneously experience taboo "pulsations."

Such experiences could be seen as having an antipatriarchal character for white middle-class women like May and Stowe, restoring to them important aspects of their own existence in a simultaneous transgression and consolidation of ideological fictions of true womanhood. Such experiences also represented an important antislavery gesture, for the thrills of eroticized violence sold the book *and* its abolitionist message. The titillating aspects of the novel paradoxically played an important role in the popularity of the book that President Lincoln believed started the Civil War, which resulted in emancipation of the slaves.[12]

But the eroticism of violence in the novel is not purely liberating for white women or for African Americans, for the potentially feminist and abolitionist aspects of the masochistic fantasies are recontained. After all, by presenting "feeling right" as a form of agency available even for women, Stowe unwittingly and subtly *trains* women to think about agency in terms of virtuous, passive suffering. It is disturbing that in response to her own rhetorical question, "What can we do?" Georgiana May fantasizes about being stoned to death. *Uncle Tom's Cabin*, then, fosters the oppressive patriarchal constructions of female identity that the masochistic fantasies had arisen to subvert in the first place, prompting women to fantasize about suffering and martyrdom as forms of pleasure and power. Furthermore, the considerable new energy that the abolitionist movement derived from the novel's titillating fantasies of bondage and domination was surely undermined by the fact that some readers were deriving covert and overt pleasures from identifying with the sufferings of tortured African Americans. The response of a group of Swiss mountaineers, as recorded by Stowe's brother Charles Beecher, for example, reveals a disturbingly exploitative aspect of their sympathy:

> It was touching to listen to the talk of these secluded mountaineers. The good hostess, even the servant maids, hung about Harriet, expressing such tender interest for the slave. All had read "Uncle Tom"; and it had apparently been an era in their life's monotony, for they said, 'Oh, madam, do write another! Remember, our winter nights here are very long!' (C. Stowe 244)

While these mountaineers are sympathetic to the slaves' plight, Charles Beecher suggests that their preoccupation with their own dismally long winter nights partially undermines their pretensions to humanitarian altruism.[13] They long for another tale about bondage in order to alleviate their boredom, and a successful abolitionist movement would deprive them of their titillating fantasies. Even the humanitarian solidarity that readers consciously felt is at least partly eroded by these pleasures of eroticized sympathy—particularly since the repressive effects of the mythology of black supersexuality continue to be felt today.

Addressing the erotics of domination in *Uncle Tom's Cabin* in the classroom is both exciting and illuminating, for it foregrounds the complexity of people's efforts to resist oppression and to live lives that feel full and authentic. In their efforts to achieve relief from oppressive constructions of female sexuality, white women like Stowe and May may have unintentionally exploited and reinforced racist stereotypes of black sexuality and sexist stereotypes of female masochistic desire. Likewise, in Stowe's effort to promote the abolitionist cause, she unwittingly sponsored sadomasochistic fantasies that have been widely indulged at the ongoing expense of suffering African Americans. The teacher will probably find students receptive to the idea of sadomasochistic pleasure in sympathy and eager to identify perverse pleasures in other forms of sympathy, such as rubbernecking, horror movies, sentimental movies, and Harlequin novels. The teacher will also discover that many male and female students are aware of the gendering of domination and submission and are eager to discuss the origins of this pattern. *Uncle Tom's Cabin* offers a clear example of the way fiction both participates in and resists this gendering, and students might profitably debate the ways the potential pleasures of masochistic identification with suffering fictional characters are double-edged for women and perhaps for men too. Furthermore, the link between sex and violence is familiar to students, and confronting the possibility of guilty pleasures in response to representations of violence in *Uncle Tom's Cabin* enables them to think critically about the ethics of sympathy and the pleasures of sentimental fiction.

NOTES

[1]Degler argues, by contrast, that it was widely believed that women in fact did have sexual desire.

[2]Haller and Haller document many scientific attributions of female stasis to female physiology. In 1879, for example, William K. Brooks, a professor of zoology at Johns Hopkins University, contrasted the inherently dynamic nature of the sperm's "vitalizing" function to the inherently conservative, receptive nature of the ovum (69). These characteristics carried over "naturally" to the two sexes' minds.

[3]Bartky; Rich; Jackson and Scott; and Singer all offer useful surveys of this debate. On the side insisting that whatever pleasures that might inhere in feminine masochism are not worth the price, see Linden et al., *Against Sadomasochism*, and many of the essays in Scott and Jackson's *Feminism and Sexuality*, in Jagger's *Living with Contradictions*, and in Jeffreys's *The Lesbian Heresy*. Among those who argue that the pleasure to be gained is worth whatever price is paid, see Califia, Hollibaugh, and Allison; most of the contributions to Vance's *Pleasure and Danger: Exploring Female Sexuality*; Aury's discussions of her novel *The Story of O* in de St. Jorre's article; many of the essays in Weinberg and Kamel's *SandM: Studies in Sadomasochism*; and L. Hart's "Doing It Anyway."

[4]Freud defines "feminine masochism" in a late essay called "The Economic Problem of Masochism" and alludes to it throughout his career in such essays as "A Child Is Being Beaten" and "The Taboo of Virginity." Among the many feminist challenges to his claim, see Caplan's *The Myth of Female Masochism*. Where women seem to exemplify the Freudian myth, feminist theorists have argued that that attraction is *constructed* by patriarchal representations of female desire—that male-authored myths brainwash women to desire suffering or submission. Among these, see Beauvoir, *The Second Sex*; J. Benjamin, *Bonds of Love*; Massé, *In the Name of Love*. For studies of the construction of masochistic identities in sentimental fiction, see Halttunen, "Humanitarianism"; Brodhead, "Sparing the Rod"; and Noble, "Ecstasies." For psychoanalytic theories of the relation between women and masochism, see Hanly's *Essential Papers on Masochism*; Zanardi's *Essential Papers on the Psychology of Women*; and Montgomery and Greif's *Masochism*. Mansfield's *Masochism* offers a lucid and useful discussion of how masochism can function as a mode of self-empowerment.

[5]Romero demonstrates that power functions not through repression nor even internalized forms of self-repression but through the production of subjectivities invested in power, a production that is effected by the discourses in which people speak and think. This letter demonstrates that Stowe constitutes herself as a "true woman," a subjectivity invested in power, by repudiating sexual desire. It thereby illustrates Butler's claim that power produces compliant subjects through the "production of a domain of abject beings [. . .] who form the constitutive outside to the domain of the subject. The abject designates here precisely those 'unlivable' and 'uninhabitable' zones of social life which are nevertheless densely populated by those who do not enjoy the status of the subject, but whose living under the sign of the 'unlivable' is required to circumscribe the domain of the subject [. . .]. The subject is constituted through the force of exclusion and abjection, one which produces a constitutive outside to the subject, an abjected outside, which is, after all, 'inside' the subject as its own founding repudiation" (3). In Stowe's case, erotic passion is that repudiated zone of dreaded identification, and the constant affirmation of that repudiation constitutes her in her own eyes and in the eyes of others as a "true woman" privileged to enjoy the "status of the subject."

[6]The description of human identity offered by the French psychoanalytic theorist Julia Kristeva suggests how wounding and torture might serve ontologically as tropes for ecstasy. Identity, she says, is born from a painful separation from a state she calls "the chora," in which an infant is wholly integrated with its surroundings (14). Kristeva postulates that to produce the fiction of a coherent, individual self, every person must first undergo a process called abjection, repudiating that which represents the not-me. The specter of this repudiated realm, the abject, is always threatening because merging with it would mean death: hence our primal horror at abjected things such as corpses, pus, feces, vomit, and wounds (3). However, the abject also entices, for it represents lost parts of oneself. Reunion with the abject would imply a restoration of a lost wholeness and a transcendence of the limited fiction of coherent subjectivity. Kristeva speculates that disgusting or violent images can stimulate a joyful sensation of transgressing the boundaries of identity. The ecstatic merging they evoke so closely resembles that of orgasmic pleasure that she uses the same word—*jouissance*—to describe the delights of horror.

[7]In "Heroines in *Uncle Tom's Cabin*," Ammons demonstrates that Tom is characterized as "a stereotypical Victorian heroine," a characterization that facilitates women's sympathetic identification (159).

[8]Eldridge Cleaver claims that white women desire black men in America because of a "gulf between the Mind and Body [that] will be seen to coincide with the gulf between the two races" (174). He contrasts the black male "Supermasculine Menial"—associated with tropical heat, fire, blood, and strength—with the white male "Omnipotent Administrator"—associated with frailty, cowardice, impotence, and abstraction. Likewise, he contrasts the black female "Subfeminine Amazon" with the white female "Ultrafeminine," whose "basic fear is frigidity." He claims that the white woman desires black men because she feels a "psychic lust for the flame, for the heat of the fire: the Body" in proportion to her fear of her own frigidity (170). Among literary representations of the myth of black supersexuality and white women's corresponding desire for black men, see Wright's *Native Son*, Baldwin's "Going to Meet the Man," and Faulkner's *Light in August*. See also Lerner.

[9]Hedrick notes that Stowe's sister-in-law, Isabella Beecher, wrote: "Now, Hattie, if I could use a pen as you can, I would write something that would make this whole nation feel what an accursed thing slavery is." Hedrick continues, "One of the Stowe children remembered that when this letter was read aloud in the parlor, Harriet 'rose up from her chair' and declared 'I will write something. I will if I live'" (*Stowe* 207).

[10]Baldwin ("Everybody's Protest Novel") and Fisher both illuminate why the sentimental pathos of *Uncle Tom's Cabin* did not necessarily produce the desired political transformation. As Fisher argues, inevitability and powerlessness lie at the heart of Stowe's sentimental pathos, which associates slave separation with the death of a family member. He writes: "Death cannot be abolished or even mitigated [. . .]. Therefore, where death is used as the analogy for social, remediable suffering, our general helplessness, like the helplessness of the child [. . .] is underlined and the will to act is weakened if not denied. The feeling of suffering becomes more important than the action against suffering. Tears become more important than escapes or rescues" (110). Baldwin also observes that private experience remains in the forefront for readers of *Uncle Tom's Cabin*. They extend sympathy to slaves only to the extent that they see themselves in the slave, who must therefore be stripped of his blackness and the full range of his personality. Because the sentimental reader extends sympathy only to the whiteness in

the slave, that sympathetic self-extension applies only to textual African Americans and is withheld from their real, nonwhite counterparts.

[11]Freud believes that such sadomasochistic impulses are common: "It is surprising how frequently people who come to be analysed for hysteria or an obsessional neurosis confess to having indulged in the phantasy: 'A child is being beaten.'" Even mentally healthy people indulge the fantasy, he notes: "Very probably it occurs even more often with other people who have not been obliged to come to this decision by manifest illness" (106).

[12]Hedrick writes that when Stowe "met Abraham Lincoln at the White House in 1862, the lanky, angular president is said to have greeted Stowe, who stood less than five feet high, with the words, 'So you're the little woman who wrote the book that started this great war!'" (*Stowe* vii).

[13]David Reynolds classifies *Uncle Tom's Cabin* with other sadomasochistic stories thinly veiled by narratives of social reform. He attributes the popularity of *Uncle Tom's Cabin* to its ability simultaneously to gratify readers' sensational desires and to fulfill all the cultural codes of what he calls the "conventional" (74–77). Bersani likewise suggests that all sympathetic pleasures contain a trace of sadistic exploitation that partially undermines the solidarity the sympathizer is conscious of experiencing. He also hypothesizes that the pleasures of sympathy, which would seem sadistic, are actually masochistic (145–50).

Africana Constellations: African American Studies and *Uncle Tom's Cabin*

Sharon Carson

In *There Is a River: The Black Struggle for Freedom in America*, the theologian and historian Vincent Harding paints the 1853 National Black Convention with a broad critical brush stroke, suggesting that the delegates—Frederick Douglass, Martin Delaney, and over one hundred other committed black abolitionists—faltered along the road to a radical challenge of white America. Harding places the convention squarely within intellectual crosscurrents in the African American community over the issues of nationalism and coalition politics with white abolitionists. He also cites Douglass's "accommodating" posture toward Harriet Beecher Stowe as a key factor in the meeting:

> There was another specific and far more troubling background to the gathering. In 1852 Harriet Beecher Stowe, daughter of one of the major Protestant leaders in white America, published her antislavery novel *Uncle Tom's Cabin*. It was an immediate literary and political sensation, selling more than 300,000 copies in its first year. In February 1853 Mrs. Stowe invited Frederick Douglass to her house in Maine. There she indicated that she would soon travel to England and the European continent, and wanted to help raise money overseas for a major project which would "permanently contribute to the improvement and elevation of the free colored people in the United States." She had not decided precisely what sort of project would be appropriate, so after their conversation Mrs. Stowe asked Douglass to send her a letter, proposing what the project ought to be. In March 1853 Douglass wrote to Harriet Stowe, suggesting that a "manual labor college"—in effect, a trade school—be established for black people, preferably in his city of Rochester.
>
> While the details of the proposal were not of great importance, the tone of Douglass's letter was. For it was a letter that Booker T. Washington might have written forty or fifty years later to any similar white benefactor. Denigrating black capacities and praising white power and civilization, at times it came frighteningly close to fawning and groveling—a strange position for a man of Douglass's stature and prestige. [In the letter] the contrast was sharply drawn between free blacks as sadly dependent and unreliable, and whites as all powerful. In this context Douglass awaited Mrs. Stowe's beneficence, and organized the [1853] Rochester convention in anticipation of it. Thus the call which announced the conference emphasized that "there will come before the convention matters touching the disposition of such funds as our friends abroad, through Mrs. Harriet Beecher Stowe, may appropriate to the cause of our progress and improvement." (179–80)

In Harding's analysis, the Rochester convention failed to create autonomous, self-defined political (nationalist or otherwise) momentum for the African American abolitionist movement, instead grasping toward an inherently debilitating conciliatory handshake with white abolitionists. After acknowledging some effort by the convention delegates to develop "radical and self-reliant" black institutions, Harding fine-tunes his political critique:

> Nevertheless, by their indecisive position, the black abolitionists tended to enfeeble their own resolve, and to block and compromise the surge toward black solidarity, self-reliance, and a healthy sense of African nationality. Instead, they closed the convention eagerly expressing their "undying affection" to Garrison and his fellow abolitionists, and announcing that *Uncle Tom's Cabin* was "a work plainly marked by the finger of God" on behalf of black people. The Great Tradition of Black Protest, with all its magnificent representatives whose lives bore undeniable witness to many hard and valiant struggles in the past, could speak no word of clear direction for the present. Their faces were turned too fully to the white community, and what it might think and do. Their own minds were unsettled, their wills unhoned. So they directed the black community neither to open resistance and rebellion, nor to massive civil disobedience or emigration. If they heard trumpets, the sound was uncertain. If they were depending on Mrs. Stowe's promised financial assistance, like so many other promises from the white world, it was not kept.   (182–83)

Notice that in just this short section of Harding's complex book, several key issues in African American history function as the central or "framing" ideas, with Stowe and *Uncle Tom's Cabin* then placed in analytical relation. Critically speaking, the approach here is structured by the dynamics within African American culture, with primary attention toward the ideological tensions within the free black abolitionist community. An example of one of many political issues here is that Harding's analysis, as he is the first to acknowledge, obviously reflects his own intellectual and political commitment to emancipatory African American nationalism. His nationalistic vision, in turn, occupies only one position in the always shifting constellation of American black nationalism. These community differences over the issue of nationalism invite comparative approaches to antebellum black activism in particular and African American and American history generally. *Uncle Tom's Cabin* and Harriet Beecher Stowe are interesting but peripheral players in the narrative, acting more as representative symbols of white undependability than as agents of progressive social change.

Many Americans remain unaware of the extent and range of political activism in antebellum African American communities. During the antebellum years African American writers and orators such as David Walker, Maria Stewart, Richard Allen, Daniel Payne, Harriet Tubman, William Wells Brown,

Frances Harper, Frederick Douglass, Martin Delaney, Robert Young, Sojourner Truth, Henry Highland Garnet, and Harriet Wilson organized, published, protested, lectured, preached, and fought for the freedom denied to them by American law and cultural practice. The black convention movement, of which the 1853 conference was just one meeting, had begun in 1830, giving organized political structure to African American activism that was already widespread. Frederick Douglass's *North Star* (1847) was among the scores of independent black newspapers. Early novels written by African Americans that challenged slavery and/or racism in the North included Harriet Wilson's *Our Nig* (1859), William Wells Brown's *Clotel* (1853), and Martin Delaney's *Blake; or The Huts of America* (1859). In the genres of essay, sermon, poetry, and journalism, African American literary production during the antebellum period alone was expansive, ideologically diverse, and voluminous. Activists holding a wide range of political perspectives engaged in rigorous debate over pressing issues of the day as they were defined from within black communities. Frequent slave revolts crystallized and intensified debates in these same communities over the use of political force as a tactic toward liberation. Independent African American churches emerged as the source for a diverse and dynamic black-defined liberation theology.

Where does *Uncle Tom's Cabin* fit into this picture, conceptually and theoretically? Not at the center, clearly. Instead, readers and critics working in the context of nineteenth-century African American history approach the novel with questions and conceptual frameworks that arise from African American experience.

More important, this context places the reading, teaching, and interpretation of the novel not only in relation to these numerous African American literary works in particular but also within the broader critical perspectives of African American studies as an interdisciplinary academic discipline. Interdisciplinary work, as a critical approach, allows scholars and students to conceptually "break" habits of thinking and questioning in traditionally defined academic disciplines, to think relationally and comparatively among different disciplinary frameworks, and to make an informed and animated critique of the presumptions that generate those frameworks and disciplinary boundaries. From the beginning, African American studies required interdisciplinary analysis and critique for political and philosophical reasons: Given the racial and political history of the Americas, scholarship and teaching in American humanities and social sciences have been embedded in white-defined paradigms and too often structured by implicit and/or explicit presumptions of white supremacy. Interdisciplinary work in African American studies not only critiques those presumptions but also then reinterprets American and world history and culture. This approach requires sustained study of African American social, political, religious, and literary history, all of which are intimately related. For example, to fully engage the rhetorical and tropological complexity of the many nineteenth-century sources listed above, students need to study political theory and social and economic history and do some comparative work in African and African American religion.

Theoretically, an African American studies conceptual framework places Stowe's fictional projection of black experience and antebellum culture in relation to the perspectives of African Americans and African Americanists, with black experience in the so-called subjective or *defining* position. This, philosophically and broadly speaking, is thus an "Afrocentric" critical approach. Afrocentric analysis, as the term implies, places black experience at the center of inquiry. Afrocentrism can perhaps best be understood as the intellectual, inherently political "positioning" of persons of African identity or descent as the "agents of history and culture" (Valade 6).[1] The social critic Molefi Kete Asante has put it this way: "Afrocentricity is the belief in the centrality of Africans in post modern history. It is our history, our mythology, our creative motif, and our ethos exemplifying our creative will" (*Afrocentricity* 6).[2] Asante's reference here to "belief" is quite deliberate; he uses the metaphor of conversion (i.e., new sight) through much of his work. And although Asante and many Afrocentric theorists focus on Afrocentric analysis as a process occurring within black culture(s), they also propose that the Afrocentric interpretive lens can be applied by any thinker committed to make the perceptual shift to "new sight." The implications here, philosophically speaking, are epistemological and ontological: How is knowledge constructed and from what defining perspectives? By whom, for whom? What are the existential (and political) consequences of Afrocentric analytical stances?

African American studies and the philosophical positions we might call Afrocentric are not, however, monolithic. The political spectrum within the field ranges widely, as do perspectives on key methodological and theoretical questions. There is no prescriptive formula for this critical approach. Theories about using "race" as a critical category, for example, can be quite different depending on the writer or scholar; several complicated debates have emerged over the issue of racial or cultural "essentialism." Questions related to African, black, African American, or diasporic identity are complex and rigorously debated. But the common, or shared, underlying presumption in this mode of critical inquiry is that African and/or African American and/or diasporic experience is the filtering lens through which analysis refracts.

Within this context, *Uncle Tom's Cabin* emerges as a novel with nothing to say about black experience or black historical consciousness. But it has much to say about white projection of black experience from the perspective of a Christian evangelical reformer whose theological, political, and racial worldview offers important insight into the ideology that African Americans faced in working with white so-called allies in antislavery politics. As many scholars have noted, Harriet Beecher Stowe's personal experience with the black community was quite limited. Her significant conflicts with not only Douglass but also Harriet Jacobs suggest an inability, shared by many white activists of the time (some would say of the present as well) to work on terms of political and social equality with African American activists.[3] Racism and racial tensions within the abolitionist movement are often neglected issues in contemporary literary study of the novel, which is just one of many interpretive habits disrupted by an Afrocentric approach.

Critiqued from this perspective, *Uncle Tom's Cabin* is at best a complex example of well-intended but failed white liberalism or, from a more condemnatory stance, an example of virulent racism. Tom, as an icon of American literary, social, and religious history, is revealed from this perspective as a "black messiah" objectified and invoked by white America, built to specifications defined by white culture. It is difficult, for example, from the analytical perspectives of African American studies, to infuse Tom with the literary and Christological power sometimes granted to him in other interpretive approaches. James Baldwin, for instance, in 1949 shifted the novel from a redemptive status to one of collaboration with racial violence, arguing that it "is activated by what might be called a theological terror, the terror of damnation; and the spirit that breathes in this book, hot, self-righteous, fearful [. . .] is not different from that terror which activates a lynch mob" (498).[4]

Uncle Tom's Cabin appears in a strikingly culpable light in this particular analysis, with Stowe's failure as an "emancipatory voice" placed in clear relief. The point here is not to offer Baldwin's as the definitive analysis but to propose that this is important terrain to explore, given the still mythic and liberatory status of the novel for many American readers. And contrary to Baldwin's argument, some African American Christian students interpret Tom as a profound black messiah figure; however, they also often come to conclude that his political and theological power, ontological for them in this sense, comes more from their own participation in African American culture than from the rhetorical possibilities of the novel. This realization, offered in dialogue with other students who may claim a more progressive content for the novel and its rhetoric and/or in discussion with students who consign the novel, absolutely, to the body of racist American literature, can be very productively explored within the intellectual frameworks of black studies.

Consider some possible projects: Well into a semester-length seminar on nineteenth-century American literature, one student opens the day's discussion of *Uncle Tom's Cabin* by asking other students and the professor, Do you think Tom (or any other character) reflects an accommodationist and reconciliationist ideology or a self-determinist and nationalist ideology—or both? This student's reading assignment for the night before was Tilden LeMelle's essay "The Status of Black Studies in the Second Decade: The Ideological Imperative," which introduces students to the complexity of these political categories. Another student, assigned a chapter from George Fredrickson's now classic study *The Black Image in the White Mind* critiques *Uncle Tom's Cabin* as an example of nineteenth-century white "romantic racialism"[5] and proposes that David Walker and Martin Delaney (*Condition*) can be read as "countervoices" of emerging black nationalism. A third student has brought copies of James

Baldwin's "Everybody's Protest Novel" and invites the class to debate the claims in the essay. One other student has been off investigating Tom in relation to black theology and the black messiah. She offers the class an overview of the ideas of the political theologians James Cone, Albert Cleage, Jacquelyn Grant, Cornel West, and Wilson Moses[6] and then asks other students to write a short critique of Tom as black messiah.

To take another direction, a class could investigate the widespread success of Tom shows and longer dramatic portrayals based on the novel, conducting this inquiry with a central and comparative focus on the work of African American playwrights in the same period. For example, in 1858 William Wells Brown wrote *The Escape; or, A Leap for Freedom*. He read the play for abolitionist audiences, and it was produced for a short time. But in contrast to the hundreds of Tom shows that toured the country in the later nineteenth and early twentieth centuries, productions loaded with racial stereotyping of black experience and stripped of any shred of antislavery content, Brown's drama fell into obscurity soon after the Civil War, as did other major literary works by African American abolitionists. Comparative study could help students understand the historical displacement of African American "voice" in American literary history, as well as introduce them to the important issue of political expression through the use of literary characters in public performance.

An area of study also clearly suggested within an African American studies context would be the evolution of "Uncle Tom" as an archetype and many-voiced symbol or sign within American black communities, a sign for collaboration with white oppression at worst and self-effacing assimilationism at best. Social critics such as James Baldwin, Richard Wright (by inference) in *Uncle Tom's Children*, J. C. Furnas in *Goodbye to Uncle Tom*, and Wilson Moses in *Black Messiahs and Uncle Toms* have critiqued the myths and meanings of Tom, and numerous African American playwrights have satirized the Tom tradition: Langston Hughes's *Uncle Tommy's Cabin* (1938) and *Little Eva* (1938); Delano Stewart's *Uncle Tom* (1973); Herbert Stokes's *The Uncle Tom's* (1968); and Lionel H. Mitchell's *Uncle Tom's Cabin* (1975), to name just a few. "Tom," working as a literary and political trope here, engages students in questions central to African American cultural history.

All these projects illustrate that teaching *Uncle Tom's Cabin* within the various conceptual frameworks made possible by African American studies requires a sustained intellectual commitment to interdisciplinary work in the field itself, with close critical attention to scholars and writers who focus their analysis through the defining lens of African, African American, or diasporic experience in the fields of history, sociology, literature, philosophy, religion, psychology, political science, music, and art. In turn, these perspectives can be put into dynamic conceptual tension with a range of other critical approaches. In essence and by implication, teaching the novel with Afrocentric "new sight" also requires that teachers engage (and redefine) American literary, political, and social history in all its complexity.

Fortunately, there are many sources now available for scholars and teachers who want to do this work. What follows is a short, though nowhere near exhaustive, bibliographic sketch that I hope will be helpful: first, of critical studies and secondary sources concerning African American Studies, including a couple of specific sources dealing with black history and African American literary study; second, of primary literary sources by African American writers of the early nineteenth century.

An excellent introductory and overview text for the field of African American studies is *Africana Studies: A Survey of Africa and the African Diaspora*, edited by Mario Azevedo. Especially notable for its theoretical and historical detail, this book also provides very useful bibliographies and an introduction to comparative, sometimes conflicting, perspectives on key issues and debates. The focus here is on African, Caribbean, and African American contexts, and Azevedo's diasporan framework continually emphasizes their intricate relations to one another. Like all the introductory texts here, *Africana Studies* also clarifies its interdisciplinary approach for readers. An introductory text that is more "positioned" ideologically is Maulana Karenga's *Introduction to Black Studies*, which offers a more definitively nationalist analysis and a wide interdisciplinary scope, including an extensive bibliography and interpretive sections on political science, history, sociology, religion, psychology, and the arts. Readers interested in focusing on the experience of African American women can begin with *All the Women Are White, All the Blacks Are Men, but Some of Us Are Brave: Black Women's Studies*, edited by Gloria T. Hull, Patricia Bell Scott, and Barbara Smith, a collection notable for its combined theoretical overviews and extensive bibliography. Another good introductory reader is *A Turbulent Voyage*, edited by Floyd W. Hayes III and Arlyne Lazerson, which offers interesting interdisciplinary categories and good historical range. Important for the philosophical foundations of Afrocentric theory are Asante's works *Afrocentricity* and *The Afrocentric Idea*, as are responses to him and debates over other perspectives on Afrocentrist methods that can be found in journals such as the *Black Scholar, Black Studies Journal, Phylon, Sage: A Scholarly Journal of Black Women, Western Journal of Black Studies*, and numerous others. Cornel West, for example, while applauding many of the intellectual contributions of Asante and Afrocentric theory, has cautioned against romanticized and monolithic conceptions of Africa and has questioned the construction of Eurocentrism as a monolithic category as well (*Prophetic Thought* 36). Experienced students will be interested in Kwame Anthony Appiah's dynamic analysis in *In My Father's House: Africa in the Philosphy of Culture*, which engages a wide range of important philosophical issues and includes work with nineteenth-century writers such as Alexander Crummell and W. E. B. Du Bois. Other critics have challenged the racial essentialism they see in Afrocentric thought: Michael Dyson argues against such rigid categorization of race in his essay "Leonard Jeffries and the Struggle for the Black Mind" (*Reflecting Black* 160–63), while he also acknowledges the important intellectual contributions of Afrocentric theory. Students may also be interested in early debates over issues of racial and cultural identity during the formative period of African American studies. If so, they will find several perspectives represented in two collections of essays: Armstead Robinson et al., *Black Studies in the University: A Symposium*, and John Blassingame, *New Perspectives on Black Studies*.

For African American history and literature, there are many texts that provide comparative perspectives and/or wide chronological sweep; there are also numerous studies now available on specific historical subjects, literary movements, or single authors and historical figures. John Hope Franklin's most recent edition of his groundbreaking study, *From Slavery to Freedom: A History of African Americans*, provides detailed historical analysis and an extensive opening section on Africa. Vincent Harding's study *There Is a River*, mentioned at the beginning of this essay, covers African American history through the Civil War and is especially useful in analyzing the antebellum period through the frame of black experiences and perspectives, with Harding presenting a detailed critique of the complex ideological differences among black activists of the period. For theoretical perspectives on African American history as an academic discipline, *The State of Afro-American History: Past, Present, and Future*, edited by Darlene Clark Hine, provides analyses of both specific periods and broader issues and includes essays by many key scholars in the field. A good overview of issues and theory related to the study of African American literature is *Afro-American Literary Study in the 1990s*, edited by Houston A. Baker, Jr., and Patricia Redmond; also Baker's work in *Blues, Ideology, and Afro-American Literature* is very useful for the study of African American antebellum writers from an Afrocentric theoretical stance. For example, in the chapter entitled "Figurations for a New American Literary History: Archaeology, Ideology, and Afro-American Discourse," Baker proposes a reconfiguration, in economic terms, of "tropological thought" regarding American slavery and through this tropological thought, "the alteration of reality itself" (28). His work with slave narrative here might prove provocatively productive for advanced students working with *Uncle Tom's Cabin*. A particularly useful introductory resource is *The Essential Black Literature Guide*, by Roger M. Valade III, published in association with the Schomburg Center for Research in Black Culture. Entries here are short but the range of coverage is extensive; readers will find especially helpful the selections on nineteenth-century African American writers and literary works contemporary with Harriet Beecher Stowe. Another excellent contextual source is *The Oxford Companion to African American Literature*, edited by William L. Andrews, Frances Smith Foster, and Trudier Harris.

Black feminist perspectives constitute the central emphasis of *Reading Black, Reading Feminist: A Critical Anthology*, edited by Henry Louis Gates, Jr., a book that suggests many possible directions for discussion of *Uncle Tom's Cabin*, especially in the context of comparative study with African American writers who represent slavery in fiction. For example, in her essay "The Changing

Same," Deborah McDowell suggests Stowe's influence on Frances Harper, citing Harper's use of *Uncle Tom's Cabin* as a model for her novel *Iola Leroy* (1892). Theoretical essays, especially those in the first section of *Reading Black, Reading Feminist* ("Constructing a Tradition"), will help students ask questions about differences and similarities between Stowe's representations of gender, the economics of slavery, and black experience and literary representations of the same subjects by African American writers such as Harper.

At one time, finding primary texts by nineteenth-century African American writers was extremely difficult. Now, however, excellent sources are widely available in paperbound editions because of projects such as the Schomburg Library of Nineteenth-Century Black Women Writers series: antebellum writers of particular comparative interest with Harriet Beecher Stowe can be found in the volume *Spiritual Narratives*, which contains work by Maria W. Stewart and Jarena Lee, both of whom, like Stowe, use Christian language and imagery in what is also essentially political literature. In the volume *Six Women's Slave Narratives* readers will find, in contrast to the black women characters created by Stowe, the autobiographical perspectives of Mary Prince, Old Elizabeth, Mattie J. Jackson, Lucy A. Delaney, Kate Drumgoold, and Annie L. Burton. Additionally, Harriet Jacob's narrative, *Incidents in the Life of a Slave Girl*, allows students to read an autobiographical account by a woman who had herself been a slave and was also an abolitionist coactivist with Stowe. Possible directions for comparative work with this narrative and *Uncle Tom's Cabin* are suggested by William L. Andrews in *To Tell a Free Story*, where he discusses the response of the black literary community to the novel and addresses important narrative differences between Stowe's fiction and African American self-representation (179–87). Andrews also provides extensive literary analysis of *Incidents in the Life of a Slave Girl*, and his study will help students greatly in their work with autobiographical sources from the nineteenth century.

The oration, fiction, poetry, and nonfiction of writers and orators are especially important in understanding antebellum African American culture and thus are key in understanding *Uncle Tom's Cabin* in an African American studies context. Because the works of Maria Stewart, David Walker, Martin Delaney, Frederick Douglass, Richard Allen, Daniel A. Payne, William Wells Brown, Robert Young, Sojourner Truth, Henry Highland Garnet, Harriet Wilson, Alexander Crummell, and Frances E. W. Harper are now available in a range of places, either as single-text editions or in numerous anthologies, we are easily able to construct courses and reading projects for students in which they can analyze these important literary artists and political philosophers in relation to one another and to Harriet Beecher Stowe. In addition, the published volumes of *The Black Abolitionist Papers*, covering the United States in 1830–46, 1847–58, and 1859–65, edited by C. Peter Ripley, offer readers an invaluable range of perspectives in essays, speeches, letters, and other documents, with very useful introductory and historical information. With this material, students can see key issues addressed across a spectrum of opinion and can more fully understand the intellectual and political diversity among antebellum African American thinkers and activists.

By extension, African American studies as an interdisciplinary academic discipline allows students and teachers to engage the historical complexity of African American experience, to explore the enormous range of philosophical and political thought in black intellectual history, and to open critical questions about American history and literature as they work with *Uncle Tom's Cabin*.

NOTES

[1]This phrasing is from Valade's entry entitled "Afrocentrism." See his reference work for numerous other short but conceptually well-focused entries related to African American studies and literature. It is an excellent initial source for undergraduate students.

[2]Asante's *Afrocentricity* provides students with a strong theoretical introduction to his philosophical stance.

[3]Yellin addresses the problems that Harriet Jacobs faced in working with Stowe in her meticulously documented edition of Jacobs's narrative, *Incidents in the Life of a Slave Girl* (Introduction xviii–xix).

[4]Baldwin's argument here introduces students to important theological tension in *Uncle Tom's Cabin* and also suggests the political complexity of protest literature as a mode of social criticism.

[5]See especially chapter 4, "Uncle Tom and the Anglo-Saxons: Romantic Racialism in the North" (97–129), in which Fredrickson specifically addresses Stowe's creation of Tom as a "natural Christian," and thus a perfectly submissive slave from a white-defined theological perspective. Fredrickson argues that although Stowe and many other white Northerners confronted slavery as a political institution, they also perpetuated a highly idealized and romantic set of racialized, and racist, stereotypes of black persons and experience.

[6]Cone, in *For My People* and *A Black Theology of Liberation*, argues an existential theology that uses "blackness" both literally and metaphorically to create a messianic liberation theology for African Americans and all persons who suffer poverty and oppression. Cleage presents an explicit and exclusive nationalistic theology in both *Black Christian Nationalism* and *The Black Messiah*. In *White Women's Christ and Black Women's Jesus*, Grant constructs a comparative theological critique by proposing African American womanist Christology as a political and spiritual response to racism in white feminist Christian theology. Students will find intriguing possibilities here for working with Stowe in relation to black Christian writers such as Harriet Jacobs, Maria Stewart, and Frances Harper. Moses's *Black Messiahs and Uncle Toms* traces the complexity of the messianic idea through African American history and literature. For work with *Uncle Tom's Cabin*, see especially chapter 4, "The Myth of Uncle Tom and the Messianic Mission of the Black Race." And finally, West fuses critically applied Marxist analysis to prophetic Afro-American Christian thought in *Prophecy Deliverance!*

The Declaration of Independence and *Uncle Tom's Cabin*: A Rhetorical Criticism Approach

Harold K. Bush, Jr.

Audience is a concept that can be difficult for students to grasp. For most secondary and college students, audience simply refers to the instructor who assigns the final grade, a fact signaled by the second-person questions we have all heard: "What is it that *you* want on this paper?" "What do *you* want in the introduction?" "How do *you* think I should conclude this argument?" How might we as teachers hope to advance students beyond such a view of writing and encourage them to think about a potential audience, the majority of which agrees on many primary values, beliefs, and ideological underpinnings?

I believe very strongly in using literary works to show how famous writers have successfully aimed their arguments at certain kinds of readers. Persuasive writers must imagine their audience: they must try to envision what kinds of tropes, metaphors, and argumentative strategies will work best to convince the people who are the targets of their rhetoric. In teaching such fundamental concepts of rhetorical criticism, Harriet Beecher Stowe's *Uncle Tom's Cabin* is an extremely useful and highly readable text. Stowe's underlying strategy is to foster what Kenneth Burke has called "identification," which is promoted when language is employed to overcome the divisions separating people. In brief, Burke describes identification as "the use of language as a symbolic means of inducing cooperation in beings that by nature respond to symbols" (*Grammar* 567). Burkean "identification [. . .] is promoted when language is used to reduce divisiveness and to bring the speaker and listener closer together in their conceptions and perceptions of the world around them" (J. Andrews 55). Identification ultimately culminates in a psychological fusion that Burke calls "consubstantiality" (see Bush 69–70), a fusion similar to what I take to be Stowe's primary aim in writing her novel: to engender a unifying and millennial vision by which the Union might be saved.

One of the attractive features of Stowe's book is that it offers numerous strands of argumentation going well beyond its foundational claim: that slavery is inhumane and should be abolished. These various strands of Stowe's overarching argument are vital to her project because they both reflect on and foster the central myths and ideologies of the culture to which she was making her appeal. An analysis of her argumentative stances, thus, can tell us a great deal about the beliefs and values of the audience Stowe was trying to reach. It reveals, for example, Stowe's allegiance to sentimentalism and to a redemptive form of feminism; it also demonstrates Stowe's passionate belief in a triumphant Christ, an incontrovertible Scripture, and a millennial mission for America. In my teaching, I emphasize another major belief that Stowe assumed her audience shared with her: a belief in American republicanism, primarily as detailed in the Declaration of Independence. My approach is to present the novel's ideological assumptions to students in my undergraduate class, engage them with writing assignments that analyze Stowe's novel as rhetorical discourse, and use writing workshops to foster the concept of audience among undergraduate writers.

Before beginning the book by Stowe, we have prepared by looking closely at one of America's most influential rhetorical documents, the Declaration of Independence of 1776, written mainly by Thomas Jefferson but including the phrases and ideas of many others, including most conspicuously John Adams, Benjamin Franklin, and Richard Henry Lee. The authors' self-proclaimed aim was to "justify [themselves] in the independent stand [they were] compelled to take [to seek] an expression of the American mind" (T. Jefferson, *Writings* 1501). These authors, in their attempt to locate a central "expression of the American mind" and their desire to "justify" the rebellion, admit to the rhetorical nature of the document: it aimed at urging colonial Americans to stand against the tyrannies of the world and declare independence. To justify the stand against the tyrannies imposed by England, the Declaration employs the rhetorical strategy of framing the colonists as slaves to the fiat power of the throne. From this perspective, Edwin Gittleman has analyzed the text as an evangelical document dominated by the metaphor of slavery. For Gittleman, the dramatic myth underlying the Declaration is dependent on the perception of the colonists as slaves (246). In fact, oppression by political powers to the point of slavery was a prominent motif of the Declaration:

> When in the course of human events, it becomes necessary to dissolve the political bands which have connected them with another, and to assume among the powers of the earth, the separate but equal station to which the Laws of Nature and of Nature's God entitle them [. . .] they should declare the causes which impel them to separation.
>
> (T. Jefferson, *Writings* 19)

"Political bands" must be extinguished, and the right to do so, to stand "separate but equal," comes from Nature and God. These opening lines lead logically into a succinct yet overwhelmingly powerful statement of fundamental American moral and political philosophy. The crucial statements are found in the well-known passage expressing the "self-evident" "truths" upon which the American myth would be based: that "all men are created equal" and given "inalienable rights" of "Life, Liberty, and the pursuit of Happiness." These claimed, inherent rights constitute an antithesis to notions of slavery and political oppression. The premise that all men are intrinsically equal, if granted, was perhaps the most powerful and finally the most rhetorically persuasive argument against chattel slavery, and it is a prominent feature of not only *Uncle Tom's Cabin* but also numerous slave narratives, abolitionists' speeches and editorials, and later the crucial, rhetorically brilliant works of Abraham Lincoln.[1]

In addition, it is worth noting that there are two major aspects of the original Declaration. The first, already discussed, is its function as written discourse, as a persuasive written argument. As Jay Fliegelman has argued, however, the story of "America's 'declaring independence'" has hitherto emphasized the drama of the second term at the expense of the drama of the first" (24–25). That is, a full appreciation of the rhetorical work accomplished by the Declaration must consider the fact that complete deliverance from the tyrannies of this world was initially founded on the performative function of the act of declaring. Fliegelman's central focus is "that the Declaration was written to be read aloud." To understand the document fully, one must consider the act of " 'declaring' as performance" and " 'independence' as something that is rhetorically performed" (4). Slaves must enact their independence as well as announce it, and thus the act of protest becomes a fundamental basis of being American, as Roger Lundin has claimed:

> The American conception of the self has stressed the roles of choice and volition to an unprecedented degree. In [Perry] Miller's memorable phrase, "being an American is not something inherited but something to be achieved." [All true Americans] are "protestants" who place the claims of conscience and innovation ahead of established practices or beliefs. [. . .] To be a "protestant" in this sense is to believe in the virtue of a defiant stand against corrupt authority.   (139)

According to Karlyn Kohrs Campbell, such public moves in which "the speaker incarnates the argument" constitute a distinct rhetorical form called "enactment" (435, 444). That is, writers and rhetors lend vast rhetorical power to their arguments when they are willing not only to voice them but also to enact them, to "incarnate" them. Stowe's rendition of the power of enactment is clearly exemplified in the novel. Significantly, such enactment bridges differences of gender by being demonstrated both in male characters, including George Harris, Tom, Simeon Halliday, and Phineas Fletcher, and in female characters such as Eliza, Mrs. Shelby, Rachel Halliday, Cassy, and Little Eva. What Carla Peterson has recently shown to be the burden of numerous antebellum African American women can be expanded to include Stowe: the overpowering desire that all Americans, both male and female, become not just hearers but also "doers of the word" (3). Several of Stowe's characters, including George, the Hallidays, and Little Eva, draw on the liberatory rhetoric of the Declaration in both their speech and their actions.

George Harris's acts of rebellion culminate most obviously in his escape from his master, in the course of which he voices a number of exemplary arguments against slavery in antebellum American culture, including arguments applying republican ideals. As he is disguised and making his way north, George encounters his old supervisor from the factory, Mr. Wilson. Able to "pass" as a white, George draws Wilson aside and lets him in on his secret, but

Wilson, shocked, urges George to return to his master at once. Throughout this scene, Wilson's arguments draw heavily on Scripture, typifying the standard rhetoric used by Christian apologists to support slavery in the antebellum period. George's response signals his (and Stowe's) contempt for Wilson's facile use of Scripture: "Don't quote Bible at me" (95). Even after George's bitter outburst, Wilson proceeds with his exhortation to go back, again quoting the Bible, showing the vast cultural authority accorded to that document by pro-slavery advocates: "Let everyone abide in the condition in which he is called" (a reference to 1 Cor. 7.20). George rejects Wilson's argument by placing Wilson in an equal situation:

> I wonder, Mr. Wilson, if the Indians should come and take you a prisoner away from your wife and children, and want to keep you all your life hoeing corn for them, if you'd think it your duty to abide in the condition in which you were called. (95)

Wilson's counter arguments throughout this dialogue rehearse the rhetoric of those who blindly acquiesce in the status quo. Shocked and dismayed by this encounter with a living and breathing type of the American myth of republican liberty, Wilson appeals to the law of the land: "Why, George, this state of mind is awful; it's getting really desperate, George. I'm concerned. Going to break the laws of your country!" (95). Debunking Wilson's arguments, George neatly demonstrates his cool rationality:

> My country again! Mr. Wilson, *you* have a country, but what country have *I*, or any one like me, born of slave mothers? What laws are there for us? We don't make them,—we don't consent to them,—we have nothing to do with them; all they do for us is crush us, and keep us down. Haven't I heard your Fourth-of-July speeches? Don't you tell us all, once a year, that governments derive their just power from the consent of the governed? (96)

George here implicitly but clearly refers to the Declaration of Independence. One of his primary moves is to distance himself from American society as it was currently constituted through the use of the second person: "*you* have a country, but what country have *I*?" At almost the exact same time, Frederick Douglass often used the same strategy of the second person to distance himself from hypocritical homage to American idealism, perhaps most memorably in his most famous speech, "What to a Slave Is the Fourth of July?" (1852): "This Fourth of July is yours, not mine. You may rejoice, I must mourn [. . .] your celebration is a sham; your boasted liberty, an unholy license; your denunciation of tyrants, brass fronted impudence" (*Life and Writings* 192).[2] The rhetoric of the political hegemony, represented by George as "your Fourth-of-July speeches," is empty and deceptive, constituting a blasphemy of the original principle celebrated on that sacred holiday. Both George and Douglass here invoke the fact that by the 1850s, Fourth of July community celebrations, which featured public readings of the document followed by extensive and highly laudatory orations evoking its patriotic and moral weight as the founding American creed, had become a cultural commonplace. As Rush Welter has put it, these annual performances constituted "religious observance[s], in which the Declaration of Independence (customarily read at the start of the day's festivities) served in lieu of a religious text, and the oration in lieu of the sermon" (396; see also Travers; Martin, esp. 35–48). By lamenting in jeremiadic form the lost ideals of the Declaration, the true meaning of the Fourth of July, and the political notion of popular sovereignty (as the Declaration puts it, "governments derive their just power from the consent of the governed" [Jefferson, *Writings* 19]), George here advances a view of America's rapidly evolving myth, one rooted deeply in the founding vision, including the Constitution and the Declaration. Moreover, George's rebuke indicates that the Declaration had become by the 1850s a central point of contention among rhetors and writers desirous not only of abolishing slavery but also of elevating it to a position as a central symbol of the American myth.

George also relates several critical personal experiences that powerfully seal his declaration of independence from Wilson. The most crucial is the story of his older sister, who was "a pious, good girl," a "member of the Baptist church." George sadly describes how she was unable to live a godly life because of the wickedness of her master and how he would often hear her being attacked: "Sir, I have stood at the door and heard her whipped, when it seemed as if every blow cut into my naked heart, and I couldn't do anything to help her" (96–97). The indelible mark of this memory on George evokes the poignant story told by Frederick Douglass about his Aunt Hester in the beginning of his 1845 *Narrative* (6; ed Baker), again suggestive of the parallel between "real" and fictive rhetors at the time Stowe was writing. Finally, George returns to the republican ideals in what serves as a peroration of his rhetorical appeal to Wilson (and to the reader): "I'll fight for my liberty to the last breath I breathe. You say your fathers did it; if it was right for them, it is right for me!" (97). As Eric Sundquist has argued in detail, slaves explicitly connected their personal rebellion against slaveholding America with the struggle of the revolutionary founders of the nation itself: "In his rhetorical crusade against slavery [. . .] or even in his millennarian uprising against it [. . .] the slave rebel, one could say, became most American" (*To Wake* 36). In consequence, George convinces Wilson that he is justified in his revolutionary act, and as the two men part, Wilson gives George some money as a token of his support. What we see here is Stowe's belief that white Americans like Wilson will ultimately be convinced by the power of enactment as typified by George's personal declaration. The justification has been made for his escape, as in the original Declaration, and thus George, like the Founding Fathers, has not only announced but also begun to act out his independence.

After his meeting with Wilson, George begins to change as a direct result of the practical actions of others. The crucial influence is his encounter with the Quaker household of Simeon and Rachel Halliday, who bring George back together with his wife and son. The peaceful godliness of the Hallidays is symbolized in the opening passage of the chapter by the rocking chair in the shiny and inviting kitchen: it is a "persuasive old chair," we are told, and in it we see "our old friend Eliza," George's wife (116). Throughout this episode, Simeon not only quotes from Psalm 73 and encourages George to seek the Lord, but also testifies to his own convictions through practical action. Meanwhile, Rachel reigns as archetypal "mother-savior" of the perfect Christian household, peppering her gentle speech with the stylistics of the King James Version: "Thee knows thee can stay here. [. . .] Where's thy baby, Ruth? [. . .] Mary, thee'd better fill the kettle, hadn't thee?" (117–18).[3] Rachel, like Jesus, is able to "put a spirit into the food and drink she offered" (122); she "enacts the redeemed form of the Last Supper," and the communal spirit found in Rachel's kitchen "exemplifies the way people will work in the ideal society" (Tompkins, "Sentimental Power" 519). George, for the first time in his life, "sat down on equal terms at [a] white man's table" (122). In contrast to Wilson, Simeon's and Rachel's dependence on Scripture brings about real behavior, resulting in the true power of enactment. Certainly George questions the religion of the Hallidays: "Is God on their side?" (165). But his "doubts" and "despair" "melted away before the light of a living Gospel, breathed in living faces" (122). He responds to the "living" ministry of these "living faces," whose genuine power of enactment finally compels him to concede, "I'll try to feel like a Christian [. . .] and learn to be a good man" (161). George here is clearly being refined by Christian characters whose manifestation of the practical action inherent in Christian love is tangible and real. In short, as Stowe herself explains in an aside referring to Simeon, arguments increase dramatically in rhetorical power when they are wedded to practical action:

> If these words had been spoken by some easy, self-indulgent exhorter, from whose mouth they might have come merely as pious and rhetorical flourish [. . .] perhaps they might not have had much effect; but coming from one who daily and calmly risked fine and imprisonment for the cause of God and man, they had *a weight that could not but be felt*, and both the poor, desolate fugitives found calmness and strength breathing into them from it.   (166; italics mine)

When the time comes for George to continue his journey, Simeon arranges for his friend Phineas Fletcher to escort him and his family to Canada. The climax of the escape comes when the party, led by Phineas, is trapped on top of a ridge of rock by the slave traders Loker and Marks. George, ordered to surrender, "stood out in fair sight, on the top of the rock, as he made his declaration of independence; the glow of dawn gave as a flash to his swarthy cheek

[. . .] and, as appealing from man to the justice of God, he raised his hand to heaven as he spoke" (172). This melodramatic scene invoking the Declaration of 1776 is transformed to mythic significance by being steeped in images of God and the "glow of dawn" and by George's culminating assertion: "We don't own your laws; we don't own your country; we stand here as free, under God's sky, as you are" (171–72). Again, as earlier in his dialogue with Wilson, the key rhetorical feature is the use of the second person, emphasizing the distance and tension between the poles of "we" and "you."

However, the apparent glory of the moment is deflated as Marks cocks his pistol and smirks, "Ye see ye get jist as much for him dead as alive in Kentucky" (172). Phineas, aware of Marks's intentions, sums up the rhetorical value of George's exalted "declaration": "Thee'd better keep out of sight, with thy speechifying [. . .]; they're mean scamps" (172). In the final analysis, such "speechifying" and public enactment by a black man prove to be not only ineffective but also dangerous and perhaps even fatal. Statements only become rhetorically persuasive, that is, insofar as the speaker is able to enact them fully through practical action. Thus, when the slave traders advance on the trapped party on top of the ridge, it is Phineas who steps forward to intercede bodily: "'Friend,' said Phineas, suddenly stepping to the front, and meeting him with a push from his long arms, 'thee isn't wanted here'" (173). Loker is thrown down the chasm, severely injured, but not lost, as again the power of enactment of Christian charity is played out through the healing care of the Quaker women. It is certainly noteworthy that George does fire a shot at Loker—and that the bullet "entered [Loker's] side" (173)—but the upshot of this scene is to show Stowe's ambivalence regarding the ability of any black man to enact fully the Declaration of Independence. George, when he tries to make his "stand," is shot at and almost killed, and even when Tom Loker approaches him, he is unable to finish him off, relying instead on the intervention of Phineas.

This ambivalence exemplifies Stowe's handling of race throughout *Uncle Tom's Cabin*. Later, for instance, the novel further deflates the endorsement of George's revolutionary actions when Stowe insists not only that he be reconciled to Christ the redeemer but also that he relocate himself with his family to Africa. Stowe's call to action, typified in George, is undercut and qualified, reflecting the deep racial biases of which Stowe herself and most of her society were often guilty. Thus, a marked hesitation regarding race must be understood as a fundamental aspect of the rhetorical issues with which I am concerned, since it indicates the limits on Stowe's and many other white Americans' ability finally to envision a black person as enacter of the Declaration of Independence. To put it another way, Stowe simultaneously could envision it and could not envision it.

All of these issues help to explain the most obvious "ambivalence" regarding George as a character: his mixed blood, including that of his black slave mother and his white master father. George's partial whiteness explains for Stowe's antebellum readers his powerful intellect and his passionate desire for freedom. To some degree, his white blood also gives credence to his early rejection of Christian faith, which conflicted with then-popular views of full-blooded Negroes as naturally passive and docile Christians, a view espoused by Alexander Kinmont and later described as the "romantic racialism" of the North.[4] Moreover, the obvious contrast between the revolutionary mulattoes (George, Eliza, Cassy) and the docile, full-blooded Africans (Tom, Chloe, Sam), and more generally Stowe's ever-shifting, antiquated racial politics, has frequently been the topic of some of the most heated and even belligerent criticisms (see, e.g., Baldwin; Yarbrough).

Similar to the confusion surrounding George's racial identity is the problem of his rhetorical position. As one critic suggests, George's "speechifying" signals the inherent contradictions in George as a character who "simultaneously ridicules American ideals and calls for their realization" (O'Connell 26). In a sense, Stowe carries out the same rhetorical strategy, one that is at the heart of many American jeremiads, both past and present. A primary purpose of *Uncle Tom's Cabin* is "to join social criticism to spiritual renewal," making it a classic expression of the jeremiad mode (Bercovitch, *American Jeremiad* xi). It perhaps goes without saying that the major burden of jeremiadic speech, from the seventeenth century to the contemporary public arena, is to foster repentance among listeners and to exhort them toward the complete fulfillment of their individual and collective destinies. One need only read the "Concluding Remarks" (380–88) to understand the earnestness of Stowe's Old Testament-like appeal: as Jane Tompkins has put it, *Uncle Tom's Cabin* "provides the most obvious and compelling instance of the jeremiad since the Great Awakening" ("Sentimental Power" 517).

And yet, as evidence that Stowe is occasionally willing to "ridicule American ideals," she creates the flamboyant slave Sam, whose shenanigans help Eliza escape the slave trader Haley early in the narrative. Sam is probably the most accomplished slave trickster in the book, at least until Cassy makes her appearance near the novel's end. Stowe's descriptions of Sam also demonstrate what had become by the 1850s a rather common social spectacle throughout the States: parodies and burlesques of republican and egalitarian rhetoric, a mode of speaking practiced by many of the nineteenth century's most famous comedic personalities, including John Phoenix, Artemus Ward, Petroleum V. Nasby, Bret Harte, Lucretia P. Hale, Bill Nye, and later, Mark Twain. In these parodies, solemn nationalistic pride becomes "a string of stereotyped, meaningless phrases and misplaced platitudes" (Hurm 244). Thus it is instructive to notice what seems to be a relatively insignificant detail slipped in by Stowe:

> One of Sam's especial delights had been to ride in attendance on his master to all kinds of political gatherings, where [. . .] he would sit watching the orators, with the greatest apparent gusto, and then [. . .] he would edify and delight [other slaves] with the most ludicrous burlesques and imitations [. . .] it not infrequently happened that [the slaves listening]

were fringed pretty deeply with those of a fairer complexion, who listened, laughing and winking, to Sam's great self-congratulation. In fact,
Sam considered oratory as his vocation, and never let slip an opportunity
of magnifying his office.   (64)

Here Sam's function is to highlight and mock the hypocrisies of much public
rhetoric. Importantly, the ring of listeners at his feet includes not just slaves but
also whites, who (like the readers) laugh and wink at his justifiable ridicule of
the earnest orators of the antebellum South. Sam, who in contrast to George is
a full-blooded African slave ("Black Sam, as he was commonly called, [was]
three shades blacker than any other son of ebony on the place" [37]), has his
mockery of the Declaration undercut somewhat by Stowe. His attack on the
Declaration is restrained and jovial compared with George's, and his own personal acts of revolution are all meant as humorous vignettes, such as placing a
"sharp little nut" under the saddle of Haley's horse (39).

   With Sam's oratorical "office" in mind, we can consider the cultural work of
the Declaration later in the novel. The most consequential debate regarding
the Declaration is undoubtedly the lengthy exchange between Augustine St.
Clare and his twin brother Alfred, which is preceded by one of the more hor-
rifying episodes of the novel: the violent beating of the slave Dodo by Henrique, Alfred's spoiled twelve-year-old son. The logical result of slaveholding
philosophy and parenting, Henrique functions as a startling contrast to his
cousin and Augustine's daughter, the messianic Little Eva, whose deathbed
appeal to her listeners, saturated with pathos and selfless Christian love, would
become one of the century's most enduring literary moments:

   I want to speak to you about your souls. [. . .] You are thinking only about
   this world. [. . .] there is a beautiful world, where Jesus is. [. . .] But, if
   you want to go there, you must not live idle, careless, thoughtless lives.
   You must be Christians. [. . .] If you want to be Christians, Jesus will help
   you.   (251)

Eva's deathbed motivations, in touching her auditors and resulting in the salvation of the seemingly reprobate Topsy, illustrate Stowe's version of true
Christian enactment, the liberatory "doing" that Stowe believed might save the
Union. Eva's dying words, "O! love,—joy,—peace" (257), are suggestive of
Christian sanctification, in that they are the first listed "fruit of the spirit,"
according to Galatians 5.22. The rest of the passage from Galatians is worthy
of quotation: "Now those who belong to Christ Jesus have crucified the flesh
with its passions and desires. If we live by the Spirit, let us also walk by the
Spirit" (Gal. 5.24–25). Thus, in their scriptural context, Eva's last words point
directly to a fullness of sanctification among believers. The fruits of the spirit
are so-called because they are the logical issue of true biblical Christianity.

   In all that she said and did, then, lily-white Eva epitomizes the Christian commission to become a "doer of the word." Significantly, the slave who is beaten before the argument with Henrique is given the name "Dodo," a doubling of the verb in question. Thus, throughout this chapter, there are numerous puns that rely on an understanding of Stowe's emphasis on doing. When Eva asks Henrique to love the slave that he has savagely and openly whipped, he replies, "*Love* Dodo?" (237), suggesting that loving equals doing and that true virtue means that we must love to do. Henrique is shocked by this proposition, but Eva tells him that the Bible says we must love everyone. Henrique counters by stating the obvious: "O, the Bible! To be sure, it says a great many such things; but, then, nobody ever thinks of doing them,—you know, Eva, nobody does" (237). The punning reaches its height when Eva first confronts Henrique regarding his cruel actions.

"How could you be so cruel and wicked to poor Dodo?" said Eva.
"Cruel,—wicked!" said the boy, with unaffected surprise. "What do you mean, dear Eva?"
"I don't want you to call me dear Eva, when you do so," said Eva.
"Dear Cousin, you don't know Dodo [. . .]."   (231)

Not only does the doubling of the verb *to do* sound rather funny here but also the very act of violence against "poor Dodo" suggests the deeply ironic humor of an entire culture "doing" violence, literally, to the ideal of "doing" itself. Henrique, the representative child of a fallen culture, remains blind to his own hypocritical acts of violence, not only to Dodo but more generally to both Christian and republican idealism.

This scene is witnessed by the two fathers, and the debate begins with Augustine's chiding remark, "I suppose that's what we may call republican education, Alfred?" Dryly, Augustine suggests Henrique's failure to live up to the "first verse of a republican's catechism, 'All men are born free and equal,'" to which Alfred retorts, "Poh! [. . .] one of Tom Jefferson's pieces of French sentiment and humbug. It's perfectly ridiculous [. . .]. I think half this republican talk sheer humbug. It is the educated, the intelligent, the wealthy, the refined, who ought to have equal rights, and not the canaille" (233). Later, Albert provokes Augustine by asking, "Why didn't you ever take to the stump;—you'd make a famous stump orator! Well, I hope I shall be dead before this millennium of your greasy masses comes on" (234). These twins act as the two sides of the same coin that we have already detected in George's character, his simultaneous idealism and cynicism, demonstrating Stowe's enlistment of and high regard for republican ideals and in particular the moral philosophy of the Declaration, yet showing as well her sense of strong disapproval for those like Augustine St. Clare who are never able to take a stand for their spoken beliefs. Stowe repeatedly employs Jeffersonian egalitarianism as an important subargument supporting her central political and rhetorical agenda: the building of a cultural consensus in favor of abolition and Union. Discrediting the Alfred

St. Clares, she desired to foster a social paradigm by which the Union might perpetuate itself, one that featured the Declaration and its concomitant call to practical action, and in so doing worked to "revive" the founding vision as she conceived it to include abolition and to bring about a consubstantiation by which the United States would be saved. As we have also seen, however, her vision for union and consubstantiation only tangentially included blacks, who are effectively encouraged to clear out and head back to Africa. Despite her yearning to foster equality, Stowe's novel ends up propagating a halting view of the former slaves by promoting to some degree the exclusion of blacks from full citizenship and equality. For these and other reasons, *Uncle Tom's Cabin* continues to be a controversial and complex rhetorical document.

My classroom teaching and discussion connecting the Declaration of Independence and *Uncle Tom's Cabin* lead directly to a writing assignment asking students to evaluate and analyze some aspect of Stowe's rhetorical project. I have found that they respond with enthusiasm and insight into Stowe's strategies, especially when they are given writing topics that are specific and somewhat detailed. For example, here are three questions I have posed to freshmen at the end of a unit in which we have read and discussed the Declaration, Douglass's *Narrative*, and *Uncle Tom's Cabin*:

1. Martin Luther King, Jr., claimed that religion and the Bible were cited and distorted to support the status quo of the slave system. Would Douglass and Stowe agree? Discuss Douglass's "Appendix" and Stowe's "Concluding Remarks" and consider how these ending chapters either support or dispute King's claim.
2. Discuss Stowe's depiction of African Americans in *Uncle Tom's Cabin* and consider how it affects the novel's moral message. What can a close reading of this book tell us about the way Americans thought about race and racism in the 1840s and 1850s?
3. Discuss how both Stowe and Douglass use the motifs of the Declaration of Independence and the Fourth of July in their books. How and why do these writers draw on the traditions of the Declaration in their arguments?

I leave at least one open date before the assignment is due for a writing workshop. In this setting, I ask students to bring two or more copies of a draft version of their paper. I try to group students according to which question they chose, and they are asked to read, edit, mark questions, and then discuss with one another their writing. Usually, the act of reading and responding to one another's work adds to a student's ideas about a topic. Producing a draft version several days before the due date also gets the class to think about the topic, and discussing the questions (often with gusto) pushes ideas and forces students to defend their arguments or come up with better evidence. Finally, and perhaps most important in the context of this essay's general aim, workshops demonstrate to students that they do, in fact, have an "audience" that will hold them accountable, and it is not merely their individual teacher (me!). Student response in virtually every class in which I have used this method has indicated very strongly that students themselves find the writing workshops valuable and positive.

NOTES

[1]The major studies that have given much attention to the cultural work performed specifically by the Declaration in antebellum America are the following: Martin, Wills, Fliegelman, Gustafson, Maier, Goetsch and Hurm, Foner, Detweiler, Bardes and Gossett, Travers, and Bush. Some mention is made of the Declaration in various more specialized studies: for example, in *To Wake the Nations* Sundquist provides useful analysis of how African Americans utilized the revolutionary motif and the Declaration's idealism within their own rhetorical projects. Similar observations about the Declaration's effect on slaves is rendered in W. Andrews, *To Tell a Free Story*. A thorough analysis of the Declaration myth and its pervasive presence throughout American literature and culture remains to be done.

[2]It is not clear exactly who may have been influencing whom in this particular case; Douglass's 1852 speech obviously came after Stowe wrote this scene, but he regularly used the second-person mode before her book's publication as well. For more information about the strategies of antebellum African American rhetoric with specific reference to the Declaration, see Condit and Lucaites.

[3]For a detailed analysis of the depiction of "mother-savior" as I am referring to it here, see Ammons, "Stowe's Dream."

[4]According to Hedrick, Stowe "was familiar with Kinmont," who lectured while she lived in Cincinnati; Stowe "remarks on his death" in a letter she wrote in December 1838 (Personal correspondence). See also Hedrick, *Stowe* 437n31. For historical background on Kinmont and on romantic racialism, see Frederickson, "Uncle Tom."

Acting the Nigger: Topsy, Shirley Temple, and Toni Morrison's Pecola

Kimberly G. Hébert

> The whitest white is made by adding a drop of black.
> —Albert Murray, *King of Cats*

> 'Acting the nigger' was [. . .] what whites expected blacks to do.
> —Robert Toll, *Blacking Up: The Minstrel Show in Nineteenth-Century America*

When T. D. "Daddy" Rice stepped onto the American stage around 1830 to "jump Jim Crow," he helped set in motion a chain of disturbing yet powerful images of African-descended peoples that, as the nineteenth century came to a close, would make the minstrel show white America's most popular form of entertainment (Lott, *Love* 19).[1] These *black performances* that emerged out of nineteenth-century American popular culture clearly signified the complicated relationship—part fear, part anxiety, part desire—that white Americans had with the ever expanding black population in their midst. By adjusting, controlling, and thereby redefining the "other"(ness) in their midst—leaving the "other" to adjust to this white-defined "blackness"—through various forms of American popular culture, whites were able to contain the anxiety raised by African slavery, the abolition movement, and then emancipation. In America, what 'blackness' was to mean and when and how it would be seen would forever be influenced by this country's early "Ethiopian delineators."[2]

This essay depends mostly (though not exclusively) on a cultural studies analysis of Harriet Beecher Stowe's nineteenth-century characterization of Topsy and, more specifically, of how Stowe passed on this black performance to two twentieth-century cultural products: Shirley Temple, the 1930s child star and America's "littlest minstrel," and Pecola Breedlove, Toni Morrison's main character in *The Bluest Eye* (1970), "a little black girl who wanted to rise up out of the pit of blackness and see the world with blue eyes" (174).

Often we as literary critics and teachers find ourselves standing on the border of one discipline and, at the same time, positioned right in the center of another. Traditional approaches to analyzing and teaching literature cannot help us with these intersections except to demand the omission and often even the erasure of narratives that may be, and often are, central to our critique.[3] My methodological approach rests on the premise that "the traditional distinctions that separate and frame established academic disciplines cannot account for the great diversity of cultural and social phenomena" (Giroux 235). Cultural studies gives us that space "between or among the disciplines without being reducible to any or all of them" (Hitchcock) that is necessary for interdisciplinary cultural work. To do a cultural studies reading of a literary text requires that we, as teachers of literature and its critics, expand our readings, which have traditionally included only analyses of literary subtexts, to include analyses of other cultural products that contextualize and inform those literary texts. At the same time, such an approach allows us to test our previous literary readings, theories, and analyses using a broader, more holistic lens through which to see literature as interdependent on other cultural forms. The cultural studies analysis that centers this essay then demands an interdisciplinary reading of the overlap between narratives of literature and the other narrative forms found in popular culture that make up the representations and images in our postmodern world. Teaching these texts together—*Uncle Tom's Cabin*, Shirley Temple's early films, and *The Bluest Eye*—helps put into practice what Raymond Williams calls a "cultural pedagogy": the "educational force of our whole social and culture experience [that] actively and profoundly teaches" (158). Such an approach to reading *Uncle Tom's Cabin* helps students to identify and trace the residue of many current stereotypes about black people in America's most popular cultural forms, to think about such stereotypes as racial constructions or performances, and to see Stowe's text as a major player in that construction and its significant influence on American popular culture.

First, it is important for students to understand that "blackness," like "nigger" and "Negro," traces its conceptual origins to Europe, to "whiteness." In other words, there are no "niggers" outside of a European-centered paradigm. "Blackness" too is not something originally connected to black people but only an other's interpretation of an African and African-descended reality based on that other's viewpoint—developed to fit a particular set of motives. I am speaking here of what Toni Morrison has called Africanisms: "the denotative and connotative blackness that African peoples have come to signify, as well as the entire range of views, assumptions, readings and misreadings that accompany Eurocentric learning about these people" (*Playing in the Dark* 7). Yet these performances tragically came to define how African-descended peoples saw themselves. The lens of the dominant culture demanded that they see 'blackness' as white Americans did, as abject, and themselves as its signifiers.

As James Baldwin argues in "Everybody's Protest Novel" (1949), Stowe's characterization of the nine-year-old slave girl Topsy still rang clear in America's imagination long after Stowe introduced her to America: Topsy is ugly, untouchable, and uncivilized. Not just a black girl who suffered through the horrors of slavery, Topsy is a black performance by Stowe that masks (and at the same time reveals) her anxieties about unmiscegenated blackness—those nineteenth-century enslaved and free(d) blacks who for many reasons still stood outside Christianity and race mixing. Later, Stowe's performance of Topsy was adopted by minstrel performers, and white Americans came to accept this combination of the original performance and later adaptations as authentic images of black children or "pickaninnies," as they were called, images that influenced film, literature, and other forms of American popular culture.

Harriet Beecher Stowe did not originate this particular black performance. At least as far back as medieval Europe, black children have been represented as imps, devils, and "torturers" of white people, both inside and outside Christian mythology.[4] Stowe, while consciously struggling against certain ideological constructions concerning black people, was still deeply entrenched in the many racialized discourses of her day, which continued along the same trajectory that originated in Europe. Topsy, then, can tell us more about Stowe herself than she can about the lives of enslaved black children. Why does Stowe write her as ugly, ignorant, and comic, as a black performance?

According to Stowe's *A Key to* Uncle Tom's Cabin (1853), Topsy "stands as the representative of a large class of the children who are growing up under the institution of slavery [. . .] *feeling the black skin on them, like the mark of Cain*" (91; Arno ed.; emphasis added). For Stowe, Topsy's black skin signifies something horrible that marks its possessor in some irredeemable and unchangeable way, more so than any of the horrors of slavery. Readers should *feel* for Topsy, should see her as tragic, because of this unchanged signifier of her African origins. By contrast, Stowe documents Cassy's history of abuse, and readers are made to feel pity and horror because of what we learn has happened *to* her. Stowe leaves Topsy's history, however, vague. Instead, through her characterization of the child as both tragic and comic because of her black skin, Stowe focuses the reader's attention on the appearance and manner of the present Topsy and her struggle to be "civilized."

Uncle Tom's Cabin introduces Topsy as something not quite human:

> She was one of the blackest of her race, and her round, shining eyes, glittering as glass beads, moved with quick and restless glances over everything in the room. Her mouth [. . .] displayed a white and brilliant set of teeth. Her woolly hair was braided in sundry little tails, which stuck out in every direction. The expression of her face was an odd mixture of shrewdness and cunning. [. . .] Altogether, there was something odd and goblin-like about her appearance." (206–07)

Later, Marie St. Clare declares, "she's just so ugly, and always will be" (248), clearly voicing what the all-knowing narrator refuses to say. Stowe puts in the mouth of Topsy herself the most damning commentary on blackness: "Couldn't never be nothin' but a nigger, if I was ever so good. [. . .] If I could be skinned, and come white, I'd try then. [. . .] There can't nobody love niggers, and niggers can't do nothin'!" (245). Stowe forces her readers to recognize the limitations placed on Topsy by her black skin and, because of it, her need for redemption. When Topsy is dancing, singing, stealing, or just generally "misbehaving," however, we are then meant to be amused by the antics of this semi-human creature: "Her talent for every species of drollery, grimace, and mimicry,—for dancing, tumbling, climbing, singing, whistling, imitating every sound that hit her fancy,—seemed inexhaustible" (215).

As with all black performances, the performance is never about black people and black culture but rather about constructions of whiteness. Thus, Topsy serves to reinforce Stowe's construction of what is most *not* Topsy—little Eva. As "the perfection of childish beauty," of all that is good, all that is pure, all that is *white*, Eva stands in direct contrast to Topsy:

> There stood the two children, representatives of the two extremes of society. The fair, high-bred child, with her golden head, her deep eyes, her spiritual, noble brow, and prince-like movements; and her black, keen, subtle, cringing yet acute neighbor. They stood the representatives of their races. The Saxon, born of ages of cultivation, command, education, physical and moral eminence; the Afric, born of ages of oppression, submission, ignorance, toil, and vice!   (213)

Topsy as the blackest black throws more clearly into relief Eva as the whitest white. Indeed, Stowe's picture of little Eva would be incomplete without Topsy.[5] She compels her reader to recognize the "Saxon's" superiority through an understanding of the "Afric's" inferiority. Once again, the narrative leads the reader to feel sorry for Topsy, not because she was born a slave but because she was born black.

Topsy's presence in the novel serves to highlight the magnanimity of Eva's Christian nature as well as the potential altruistic nature of all "good" white people through the white child's tolerance for blackness and her ability to 'touch' it. That is, Stowe constructs Eva's claim to her place among the angels and all about her that is good and pure and white on the back of Topsy, a slave, literally reproducing the insidious dehumanization of the institution that Stowe worked to abolish. So, if Eva is "murdered by slavery" (Roberts 45), as Stowe's narrative leads the reader to conclude, what happens to Topsy, herself a slave? Why won't the narrative allow the reader to get close to Topsy, to feel her pain—not for being African but for being enslaved—the way the narrative demands tears at Little Eva's death and even Uncle Tom's? If we accept Stowe's characterization of Topsy as a black performance—she writes her as unhuman, ugly, unable in Stowe's representation to carry the tragedy of slavery to a nineteenth-century audience and therefore unrepresentable, as having her physical "origins" ("Never was born! [. . .] I spect I grow'd" [209–10]) as well as her spiritual origins (her conversion to Christianity) in 'whiteness'—then it is important to uncover its purpose. What anxieties, fears, and desires was Stowe masking through this performance?

As Diane Roberts points out, "The white woman writing about race is necessarily a double agent, both acting as 'mistress' in controlling her characters and her plot, and identifying with them" (19). Stowe's anxiety about the non-Western, African-descended person (whose freedom she was fighting for) is no place more apparent than in the nervous laughter we hear between the lines of her comic representations of Topsy, who reveals the author's disorder and confusion.[6] Ambivalent toward postemancipated blacks and, even more significantly, uncertain and anxious about the place of blacks in larger American society, specifically those non-Westernized Africans who couldn't be or had not been saved by Christianity or white blood, Stowe struck a chord in even the most anti–*Uncle Tom's Cabin* reader, solidifying a powerful performance of "blackness" that many whites found hysterically funny and many blacks found unbearably painful.

As black performance, the minstrel show, America's "dialectical flickering of racial insult and racial envy" (Lott, *Love* 18), was more far-reaching than any medium before it and greatly influenced other producers of American culture— writers like Twain, Stowe, Melville, and Thomas Dixon and early screenwriters and filmmakers like D. W. Griffith and Darryl Zanuck.[7] Born out of the "freak show" popularized by P. T. Barnum, with its array of "giants and midgets [. . .] a 'Feejee mermaid' and a bearded lady" (Toll 19), minstrel performances eventually became the most popular and the most successful freak shows with the performing black man as the main attraction. Minstrel performers presented their white audiences with images of blacks as "harmless curiosities" (Toll 42) with the focus on the black man or woman as nonhuman.[8] The minstrel show as the quintessential, most grotesque nineteenth-century black performance

> emphasized Negroes' "peculiarities" and inferiority. [. . .] Minstrel blacks did not have hair, they had wool; they were "bleating black sheep" and their children were "darky cubs." They had bulging eyeballs, flat, wide noses, gaping mouths with long, dangling lower lips, and gigantic feet with elongated even flapping [. . .] heels. [. . .] Negroes had to have their hair filed, not cut; [and] when blacks got sick and pale, they drank ink to restore their color. (Toll 67)

Many historians and cultural theorists who write about minstrelsy discuss the minstrel performers' adaptations of *Uncle Tom's Cabin*, which over time became known as Tom shows, without discussing the characterizations of blacks in Stowe's novel that lent themselves to those adaptations. Stowe's already dehumanized Topsy entered these black performances and fit perfectly the central image of the minstrel show, as if it were custom made for her—that of "the grinning black mask" (Toll 274).

"Pickaninny dancers," as young black children dancers were called, traveled with and performed in touring companies throughout the United States before the popularity of the Tom shows (Gossett, *American Culture* 440), but it was the black performance of Topsy in the minstrel show that brought the image to the forefront and became the most famous. In an early New York production of *Uncle Tom's Cabin*, Topsy received top billing (Hughes and Meltzer 37), and, in George Howard's 1853 production of George L. Aiken's stage adaptation of the novel, she "was the character in the novel who might most easily be transformed into the stereotype of blacks nearly always found in the popular theater, especially in the minstrel shows. [Aiken] himself yielded to the impulse to make her little more than the butt of ridicule in the play" (Gossett, *American Culture* 266). Repeatedly, Topsy's only purpose on stage was comedic; she portrayed "the most obvious and offensive black stereotypes in the play" (Gossett, *American Culture* 380). This black performance of Topsy coming out of Stowe's novel and the minstrel stage caught fire in the white American imagination, staying a fixed image well into the twentieth century; it was one of the most damaging (and revealing) black performances to emerge out of the nineteenth century.

In the 1920s and 1930s, stage versions of *Uncle Tom's Cabin* were still being performed, with a revival of the play in New York City in 1933 and, in 1935, a ballet version with choreography written by E. E. Cummings (Gossett, *American Culture* 368). In 1931, when *Theatre Arts Monthly* ran an article entitled "Uncle Tom Is Dead," the publication received many letters stating just the contrary. Tom shows were still being performed all over the nation, and along with them, the minstrel show made its way well into the twentieth century (Henderson 455). With Hollywood's first feature length talkie, *The Jazz Singer* (1927), starring the world's most famous imitation black and minstrel performer, Al Jolson, the minstrel show had reached its apogee. Then there came a shift in white America's black performances. While the minstrel show "continually acknowledged and absorbed black culture" (Lott, *Love* 40), it had done so in blackface. All signifiers of "blackness" were still present—the "woolly" wigs, the burnt cork, the large painted mouths—but with the growth of the Hollywood film industry, a new form of minstrelsy, a revised black performance, emerged: the performance of blackness in whiteface.[9] These new performances continued the minstrel tradition with one significant alteration—erasure. Lacking the more concrete signifiers of "blackness," they passed themselves off as original, as having no connection to black people or black culture at all. Blacks "became just the unpaid sources of the material—music, dance, humor—that periodically revitalized American popular culture and made white entertainers famous and rich" (Toll 274). While the earlier tradition in blackface had caricatured, dehumanized, and exaggerated certain aspects of black culture, it had also acknowledged the source of the dancing and singing that accompanied the theatrical travesties. By contrast, the new black performances in whiteface erased the act of imitation completely, leaving the imitator as originator of many black cultural forms, "while blacks themselves were allowed to play the parts of comic buffoons or faithful servants, plantation uncles and broad-bosomed mammies" (Pieterse 146). These whiteface black performances are one example of white America's ability to use black culture to its own advantage.[10]

There is no better example of a white-faced black performance than the 1930s child film star and cultural icon, Shirley Temple, to whom we can trace the nineteenth-century black performance of Topsy, from both Stowe's *Uncle Tom's Cabin* and the minstrel stage. Shirley Temple's film performances, from even a superficial analysis, reveal Topsy at every turn, pout, and dance step and show not only how white America's black performances can be accommodated into mainstream white American culture sans burnt cork but also how such performances are necessary underpinnings of its success. If we look closely at her films from the 1930s and the commodification of her image that surrounded them, we can clearly see that there would not have been a Shirley Temple—not one dance step, not one curl—if there had not been a Topsy.

During the decade of the 1930s—when blacks made up less than ten percent of the American population, the Scottsboro boys were on trial for rape, and 119 blacks were lynched (Bergman and Bergman 447–86)—Shirley Temple was the number one box-office attraction for Twentieth Century Fox. In the six years between 1934 and 1940, she made twenty-four feature films and over $25 million for her studio. In 1935, she headed the list of the top ten box-office stars (Basinger 79). At the age of six, she had become a national icon and commodity. Her image was everywhere. There were Shirley Temple dresses, Shirley Temple dolls, Shirley Temple permanents "guaranteed to turn even the most stubbornly straight little-girl hair into a riotous mass of curls," and the world-famous Shirley Temple drink (Basinger 80). What was it about little Shirley that so captured the American imagination? She gave white American audiences, who still flocked in great numbers to see *Uncle Tom's Cabin*, a white child who performed the antics of Topsy that they found so despicably and detestably funny but whom they could take into their hearts and love and cry over like Little Eva. Simply put, she gave them both. With Topsy audiences got pure comedy and with Eva pure melodrama, but with Shirley Temple they could cry and get to watch a great dance number.[11] Shirley Temple's resemblance to Eva is apparent—the white skin, the blond hair—but Topsy, the cleaned-up Shirley Temple version missing the "great welts and calloused spots" from her "back and shoulders" (209), is, at first glance, harder to see. According to a Temple biographer, Jeanine Basinger, Shirley "miraculously maintained a balance between adorable child and vamping coquette [. . .] a salty little wench full of fun and mischief who seized hold of situations and straightened them out for herself" (13–14). There were many adorable children in the Hollywood of the 1930s; it was the vamping coquette, the 'wench'-like behavior—in essence, her performance of Topsy—that got Shirley Temple noticed and made her famous.[12]

Shirley Temple's films from the 1930s, especially *The Littlest Rebel* (1935), *The Little Colonel* (1935), and *Dimples* (1936), brim with clues to Shirley's hidden or masked identity—that of a "passing" Topsy.[13] Black signifiers are all over the place—minstrel songs, blackface, tap dancing, and black people, both children and adults—leaving even ahistorical viewers to question their relevance. "There was an inside industry joke that a Temple picture was incomplete without at least one darky" (Roberts 62).[14] The story line in many of these films also mirrored Topsy's in *Uncle Tom's Cabin*. Shirley often played the part of an orphan child, like Topsy, who was taken in by someone "rich," usually a man, whose family members try to straighten out her manners through various forms of discipline in the hopes of turning her into a more "socially acceptable" little girl. The efforts are all in vain—for it is Topsy, the wicked "black" child, and not Eva, the angelic white child, who emerges victorious every time, and it was this masked black performance that 1930s audiences flocked to see.

The Little Colonel, set on a plantation, makes the dichotomy of Topsy versus Little Eva most clear. When her grandfather scolds six-year old Lloyd (Shirley Temple) for making mud pies with two black children, she stands up and infuriates him more, for her extremities are literally black (with mud)—her hands, arms, legs, and feet. (She even throws mud at him, revealing her Topsy-esque mischievousness, and blackens his white Mark Twain–like planter's suit.) To become "civilized" she is made to go live with him in the Big (white) House, wear antebellum dresses, hoop skirts and all, and learn to curtsy like any proper Southern belle—a hint of Eva. But outside the plantation house, Lloyd's world remains a completely black one. Becky, her "mammy" (played by Hattie McDaniel), sings her to sleep with Negro spirituals and takes her to a black baptism on the river where Lloyd is the only white person present. May Lily and Henry Clay, called "pickaninnies" by the colonel, are her only playmates. Becky even tells Lloyd at one point in the film, "You looks just like an angel outta heaven. No one would know you'se a natchul little devil." But nowhere is Topsy's presence felt more than in Lloyd's dance scene with Walker, the colonel's "servant" (played by Bill "Bojangles" Robinson). This famous tap dancing sequence on the staircase inside the Big House forced contemporary audiences to see double—not only Eva with Uncle Tom but also an Eva who could dance, in the words of Stowe, like Topsy: "keep[ing] time with her hands and her feet, spinning round, clapping her hands [. . .] in a wild, fantastic sort of time" (207). Set up as pedagogy—Walker teaches her how to tap dance—this scene merely confirms for the viewer the link between the signifiers of "blackness" that frame Shirley Temple and her white-faced performances of blackness in this film and those that would follow.

The Littlest Rebel also harkens back to images from *Uncle Tom's Cabin*. The opening credits roll to strains of "Dixie" and "Swanee River," tunes familiar to 1930s audiences as having originated in the minstrel show. Shirley Temple plays Vergie (short for Virginia), who, along with the "trusted" slave, Uncle Billy (played by Bill Robinson), pleads for her father's life with Abraham Lincoln, who pardons him. Imagine a proslavery Little Eva with "Uncle Billy" as her Uncle Tom. She not only sings minstrel songs like "Dixie" and "Polly Wolly Doodle" and tap dances with Uncle Billy while black children merely watch but also, in this film, blacks up. When the "bad" Yankees come to "pillage and burn," Vergie hides in a secret compartment in the plantation house. She grabs a can of shoe polish that is conveniently lying about, and when the Yankees discover her hiding place, she emerges as a "black" child. She hides her white identity behind a black face as protection against the 'evil' Yankee soldiers. This direct allusion to the minstrel show's black performance contextualizes Vergie's other performances in the film— her dancing and singing—and lest the viewer be mistaken, their connection to blackness.

In *Dimples*, the connection between Shirley Temple and Topsy is most visible. Set in New York City in 1850, *Dimples* chronicles the first production of *Uncle Tom's Cabin*. Shirley Temple plays Dimples, a ragged street urchin who dances and sings for passersby while surrounded by black children either dancing with her or playing instruments. In the movie's opening scene, the group's out-front lead performer is, of course, Dimples, but the first face we see in a close-up shot is that of a young black boy playing a harmonica. The lighting is clearly set to accentuate the size and whites of his eyes. When Dimples begins to tap dance, the camera alternates between shots of her and shots of the black boys in this group, forcing the audience to make the connection between Dimples's performance and that performance's originators. (In a later tap dance number, Dimples is flanked by two black boys from the group who tap dance along with her.) While the production of *Uncle Tom's Cabin* as a play runs throughout the film, a rich "spinster" aunt offers $5,000 to adopt the orphan, Dimples, a direct allusion to the selling of children in the slave trade—only, unlike *Uncle Tom's Cabin*, in this film the children who look white are actually supposed to be white. Dimples's grandfather at one point even says to Aunt Caroline, "You'll give me $5,000 for Dimples?"; Dimples later begs, "Please don't sell me." The film frequently alludes to Dimples's similarity to Topsy, from the very subtle coding of references to race—when Dimples is asked by Aunt Caroline what kind of ice cream she prefers, chocolate or vanilla, she replies, "chocolate and vanilla"—to more direct references to Stowe's Topsy and the minstrel show: When Dimples returns a cuckoo clock to Aunt Caroline that her grandfather had stolen the night before, she covers for him and assumes the role of thief, explaining her tendency to steal in words used to describe Topsy in the novel and stage versions of *Uncle Tom's Cabin*: "It's a funny thing about me. I'm so wicked. Isn't it awful? [. . .] I really don't know what's to become of me I'm so bad. The Professor [her grandfather] says I'm gonna wind up in the pinkatentiary [sic] if not in jail."

Dimples's most revealing black performance in the film occurs on stage after the curtain falls on the one-year run of *Uncle Tom's Cabin*, in which Dimples, of course, plays the part of Eva.[15] The last scene of the film's play, as in the actual play, is Little Eva's death; Tom's death was added when a longer stage play was written. So after, we assume, this scene has wreaked havoc on the audience's emotions—Dimples as Eva plays the death scene verbatim from the novel—a postplay performance is introduced to celebrate the end of a successful first-year run: "Out of the South has come a new form of entertainment. Our company wishes to be the first to present it in New York." The curtain rises to a full-fledged minstrel performance complete with Tambo and Bones, who are black men in blackface (one being the actor Stepin Fetchit), and three dozen hand- and thigh-slapping, tambourine-shaking white men in blackface. Dimples, in whiteface, of course, emerges from their midst as Little Eva (since she died in the play only moments before) resurrected, alive—saved by the minstrel show. She tap dances with two black men, sings about "Luziana," and in the spirit of the performance, even tells a joke (in darky dialect: "Mr. Bones, why do firemen wear red suspenders?"). The filmmakers make clear the connection not only between *Uncle Tom's Cabin* and the minstrel show but also between Shirley Temple and Topsy. For as the film shows, Shirley Temple as Eva dies, but Shirley Temple as Topsy in whiteface—the Topsy who dances and sings and "cuts up" in her blond curls—could live and make 1930s audiences comfortable with her black performance for which she needed no burnt cork.

The era of the 1930s was characterized, not exclusively in films but perhaps easiest to see there, by what James Snead in *White Screens, Black Images* calls "exclusionary emulation [. . .] whereby the power and trappings of black culture are initiated [by white America] while at the same time their black originators are segregated away and kept at a distance." Snead sees this desire as part of white America's "larger cultural need to imitate blacks" (60). We can mark, however, a change in the form that imitation took from the blackface minstrel show of the late nineteenth century to the whiteface performances of Shirley Temple and other white actors and actresses of the 1930s. White American audiences were given a more "desirable" white face and figure to replace a less "desirable," grotesque, black one while keeping the black essence of the performance intact. Black signifiers became unnecessary to white America's black performances, continuing a process of erasure until all the audience remembered was the copy and not the original: T. D. Rice rather than the black man who originally "jumped Jim Crow," Shirley Temple rather than Topsy.[16] And with America's people of African descent the created desire was the same—to copy the original—only the original was now a very diluted copy of a copy of a copy of what was supposed to be a black person and black culture. This desire to copy the copy, along with America's erasure of its desire for black culture is what causes problems for Toni Morrison's black heroine in *The Bluest Eye*.

Centering whiteness, which by definition implies the erasure, the expulsion of "blackness" from that center, continues to be an organizing principle of Western culture and contributes to destructive images of African-descended and other black peoples who share the same space of neighborhood and nation. Pecola Breedlove is simultaneously haunted by the "beauty" of Hollywood's white-faced black performances, like Shirley Temple, and the "ugliness" of literary and stage black-faced black performances, like Topsy. Caught between the two, Pecola tries to control her own reflection by retreating into the safety assured by that 'white' center. She attempts to accomplish what Frantz Fanon, in *Black Skin, White Masks*, articulates: "I will quite simply try to make myself white: that is I will compel the white [wo/]man to acknowledge that I am human" (98). By reconstructing herself in the white image centered in Western culture as human, Pecola performs, in some sense, her own black version of a white-faced black performance. What such a performance, which depends on the erasure of visible signifiers of blackness, requires of an African-descended person, however, is the erasure of oneself.

Rewriting Stowe's narrative to tell Topsy's story and describe the damage incurred by blacks from black performances, Morrison does not use Pecola to mask anxiety or desire, nor does Pecola provide comic or tragic relief, being marginalized where others are centered. Pecola is the anxiety or the desire, the black presence that haunts the margins of America's "masterpieces," made human, centered. The narrator tells us not that the Breedloves, including Pecola, were ugly but that "they believed they were ugly" (38). And she names the source of this belief:

> You looked at them and wondered why they were so ugly; you looked closely and could not find the source. Then you realized that it came from conviction. It was as though some mysterious all-knowing master had given each one a cloak of ugliness to wear and they had each accepted it without question. The master has said, "you are ugly people." They had looked about themselves and saw nothing to contradict the statement: saw, in fact, support for it leaning at them from every bill-board, every movie, every glance. "Yes" they had said. "You are right." And they took the ugliness in their hands, threw it as a mantle over them, and went about the world with it.   (38–39)

Locating the source of the Breedloves' belief in their ugliness smack dab in the center of American popular culture, Morrison shows Pecola, in 1930s Ohio, recognizing very early the contrast between herself—her blackness that was "static and dread [. . .] that create[d] the vacuum edged with distaste in white eyes" (49)—and the 'beauty' of little white girls like Shirley Temple. Morrison explores the effect of these white images on young black girlhood and the resulting obsession with those images: "Frieda brought [Pecola] four graham crackers on a saucer and some milk in a blue-and-white Shirley Temple cup. She was a long-time with the milk and gazed fondly at the silhouette of Shirley Temple's dimpled face. Frieda and she had a loving conversation about how cu-ute Shirley Temple was" (19). Pecola "took every opportunity to drink milk out of [the cup] just to handle and see sweet Shirley's face" (23).[17]

The image of Shirley Temple as America's perfect little girl affects not only the way Pecola sees herself but also the way she is seen by her mother, who, Morrison tells us, learned about physical beauty from "the silver screen" (122). This master's narrative keeps her from seeing the beauty in her own child: "I knowed she was ugly. Head full of pretty hair, but Lord she was ugly" (126). Instead, the little girl of the family she "took care of" fits the image of what little girls are supposed to look like—including being connected to beautiful things:

> When she bathed the little Fisher girl, it was in a porcelain tub with sil-very taps running infinite quantities of hot, clear water. She dried her in

fluffy white towels and put her in cuddly night clothes. Then she brushed the yellow hair, enjoying the roll and slip of it between her fingers. No zinc tub, no buckets of stove-heated water, no flaky, stiff grayish towels washed in a kitchen sink dried in a dusty backyard, no tangled black puffs of rough wool to comb.   (127)

Where can Pecola see herself as something other than ugly if she can't even see it reflected in her own mother's eyes?

Morrison explores Pecola's limited space for self-love in the figure of Claudia, through whom she traces the path from self-love to self-hatred—in other words, she reveals the making of a Topsy or a Pecola—and rewrites a very important question posed by Stowe in *Uncle Tom's Cabin*. Claudia forces readers to ask not How could Miss Ophelia and Eva love Topsy? but How could Topsy love them? We can't forget that they wore the skins of those who had abused and enslaved her. The youngest black girl in Morrison's narrative, Claudia at first doesn't understand why her sister, Frieda, and Pecola make out so over Shirley Temple: "I had not arrived at the turning point in my psyche which would allow me to love [Shirley Temple]. [. . .] I couldn't join them in their adoration because I hated Shirley" (19). Claudia, unlike Pecola, can still see Shirley Temple's white-faced black performance. It hasn't all blended yet into the West's insidious ideology of the universal. Claudia hated Shirley "not because she was cute, but because she danced with Bojangles, who was *my* friend, *my* uncle, *my* daddy and who ought to have been soft-shoeing it and chuckling with me. Instead he was enjoying, sharing, giving a lovely dance thing with one of those white girls whose socks never slid down under their heels" (19). Claudia can still hate the image that does not allow her to be. When she receives as a present a doll that looks like Shirley Temple, she "had only one desire: to dismember it. To see of what it was made, to discover the dearness, to find the beauty, the desirability that had escaped me, but apparently only me. Adults, older girls, shops, magazines, newspapers, window signs—all the world had agreed that a blue-eyed, yellow-haired, pink-skinned doll was what every girl child treasured" (20). But as Morrison recognizes, these are only fleeting moments of consciousness, a flash of self-love in a lifetime of self-hatred: Claudia's life would lead her to "conversion from pristine sadism to fabricated hatred to fraudulent love. It was a small step to Shirley Temple. I learned much later to worship her [. . .] knowing even as I learned, that the change was adjustment without improvement" (23). Like Pecola, Claudia must "surrender completely to the master['s] narrative" ("A Writer's Workshop") because the centering of whiteness and European-centered culture depend on it. "The soil [of white, mainstream American culture] is bad for certain kinds of flowers. Certain seeds it will not nurture, certain fruit it will not bear" (Morrison, *Bluest Eye* 206).

According to Judith Butler in *Bodies That Matter*, to become a subject, to enter into language and culture, we must identify with what has been constructed as human, which necessarily implies a disavowal of what is not (8). To identify with what has been deemed nonhuman, what Butler calls the abject, cannot be done "without threatening psychosis, that is, the dissolution of the subject itself" (243). In Western culture, the "blackness" of the black performance occupies the space of the unhuman, and so it becomes necessary for African-descended and other black peoples, who are the signifiers of 'blackness' in this culture, to identify with what is human, that is, whiteness, while avoiding the abject, which in this culture is always already linked to "blackness," in order to prevent self-fragmentation. Such an analysis would then require that we read Pecola's desire for blue eyes, "Alice- and Jerry-blue-storybook eyes" (46), as sane rather than mad. As Morrison so often does, she forces us to shift vantage points. If Pecola's desire for blue eyes is sane, on the basis of the societal norms she inherited, then it must be American society, with its white-faced and black-faced performances, that is mad—the culture that made "a little black girl yearn for the blue eyes of a little white girl" (204) and despise the physical signifiers of blackness. However, when Pecola hates "blackness," the blackness of Topsy, of the minstrel shows, she is not really hating herself but rather is hating an image created by a society that prescribes madness, read through its lens as sanity, for its black members. That society requires the internalization of its definitions of "blackness" for blacks to see themselves as not human, as *nigger*. As Morrison says in *The Bluest Eye*:

> All of our waste which we dumped on her and which she absorbed. And all of our beauty which was hers first and which she gave to us. All of us— all who knew her—felt so wholesome after we cleaned ourselves on her. We were so beautiful when we stood astride her ugliness [. . .]. And she let us, and thereby deserved our contempt.   (205)

For the person of African descent to escape the (in)sanity required to live in a culture dominated by those of European descent demands the redefinition, the reconstruction of a blackness that exists outside white America's black performances. But most important to redefining blackness is reconstructing new ways for defining the human. To do this, blacks must learn not only "new ways to think about [them]selves," as bell hooks asserts (58), but also new ways to think about new ways to think about themselves that are not dependent on European-centered paradigms for self-analysis. As Fanon asserts, "The black [person] should no longer be confronted by the dilemma, turn white or disappear" (100). Thus begins a process that will afford blacks the means for "counter[ing] the seduction of images that threaten to dehumanize and colonize [. . . a process] which makes possible an integrity of being that can subvert the power of the colonizing image" (hooks 6). Such a process offers resistance to the black performances of Shirley Temple and Topsy, a resistance that acknowledges the history of black people, an African history that long preceded the black performance and did not begin with the European's history of enslavement and colonization—a resistance that can begin to acknowledge blackness as human.

White America's black performances reveal much about its relation to those black people (uncomfortably) living in its midst—its fear, its anxiety, and even its desire for what it came to define as "blackness." In teaching about the black performances of Topsy, Shirley Temple, and Toni Morrison's Pecola, who is haunted by both, we see that while white America clearly has benefited from its accommodations of "blackness," black people have struggled and continue to struggle with the damage resulting from their adjustments—of their lives, of their self-images—to these same black performances. It is an ongoing struggle to reclaim the right of self-definition from representations put forth by both old and new Ethiopian delineators.

NOTES

[1]Thomas Dartmouth Rice popularized the minstrel performance that came to be known as "Jumpin' Jim Crow." Some say that Rice adopted this song and dance from an older black man with a limp while others maintain that the model was a black child. According to one 1845 account, "From the nobility and gentry, down to the lowest chimney sweep in Great Britain, and from the member of Congress, down to the youngest apprentice or school boy in America, it was all: 'Turn about and wheel about, and do just so / And every time I turn about I jump Jim Crow'" (Lott, *Love* 57).

[2]Early minstrel performance troupes called themselves "Ethiopian delineators" in advertisements and song sheets to make sure their white audiences knew that they were not real "Ethiopians" but were merely delineating, or representing, black people in blackface.

[3]For more discussion on pedagogy and cultural studies, see Giroux and Shannon.

[4]According to Pieterse, "St. Teresa of Avila complained of being tormented in her visions by a 'small Negro,'" and the Bishop of Alexandria, Althansius, writing around AD 360, insisted that "one of the forms taken by the devil is that of a black boy" (164).

[5]A Topsy/Eva doll was manufactured sometime in the early twentieth century. The two dolls shared one body: "a pretty, well-dressed, blond-haired white doll [that], when turned upside down, becomes a grotesque, thick-lipped, wide-eyed, sloppily dressed black doll" (Turner 14).

[6]The most likely origin of "Topsy" is *topsy-turvy* and was probably chosen by Stowe to represent the upside-down world of confusion and chaos where children like Topsy lived. Ironically, by including Topsy in her text, Stowe reveals her own upside-down (mis)conceptions and mixed feelings about the black people for whom she advocates.

[7]In 1904, Thomas Edison produced a film short, *Ten Pickaninnies*, a forerunner of the *Our Gang* series of the 1930s. As early as 1893, Edison had photographed groups of "nameless" black children as "interesting side effects" who ran about while being referred to as "coons," "bad chillun," and "cute ebonies" (Bogle 7).

[8]Barnum began his career as a blackface performer, and his first major successful exhibition was of a blind, paralyzed black woman, Joice Heath, whom he had 'purchased' in 1835. He claimed that she was 165 years old and had been George Washington's nurse. Barnum put her on display at New York's Niblo's Gardens and made around $1,500 a week (Lott, *Love* 76). Barnum's "Greatest Show on Earth" also exhibited Jo-Jo the Dogface Boy and Zip the Pin Headed, both black men (Hughes and Meltzer 61).

[9]More recent examples of such performances would include Elvis Presley and Madonna, who wore "Shirley Temple curls" during her 1990s Blonde Ambition tour, perhaps to pay homage to an early originator of the black performances for which she is famous.

[10]A longer, more detailed discussion of the ideas in this essay, specifically white-faced black performances, will appear in my dissertation and, thereafter, in book form.

[11]Shirley Temple, in playing the part of both Topsy and Little Eva, is not unprecedented. The third film version of *Uncle Tom's Cabin*, in 1918, cast the same white girl as both Eva and Topsy (Hughes and Meltzer 300).

[12]It's interesting that Basinger uses *wench* to describe Shirley Temple's on-screen persona, for it was what black "women" (performed by white men in both racial and gender drag) were called on the minstrel stage.

[13]These films also reveal early Hollywood's collusion with anti–*Uncle Tom's Cabin* sentiment.

[14]Even in other films where blacks are not featured prominently, Shirley Temple still plays the little white girl who has been "touched," or tainted, by some "other" culture. In *Stowaway* (1936), set in various cities throughout Asia, Shirley Temple is raised by missionaries (her parents were killed during a "Chinese rebellion"), is given a "Chinese" name, and speaks "fluent Chinese." Similarly, in *The Little Princess* (1939), she is born and raised in India by her father, who is a British officer. Her mother is never mentioned—leaving the viewer to wonder if she might have been Indian. Shirley is also "fluent in Hindustani."

[15]The film's many featured takeoffs on the first production of the play are worth noting. Topsy does appear once and is played by an adult actress. The dialogue is slim. The audience is meant to laugh at how Topsy looks and moves about the stage before Eva appears. There is also a mix-up regarding the identity of Uncle Tom, who is played, of course, as are all the parts for black people in the play, by white actors.

[16]See Julie Dash's film, *Illusions* (1983), for an interesting analysis of early Hollywood's obsession with erasing the physical black presence from the screen while exploiting and centering the essence of black culture, particularly in the example of dubbing black voices onto white female screen performers.

[17]According to Basinger, there was a Shirley Temple mug, "available only by buying a box of Bisquick"—one of the many popular items that successfully marketed Shirley's image around the world (83).

Slaves, Slavery, and the Politics of "Home": An Interdisciplinary Approach to Teaching *Uncle Tom's Cabin*

Jamie Stanesa

As a novel, *Uncle Tom's Cabin* invites interdisciplinary analysis. Theologically, the novel is rooted in the Calvinism of the nation's founding and Stowe's childhood but also in the transformations of Protestant thought in the mid–nineteenth century. As a political tract, it contributed to and even heightened the sectional debates of the 1850s, engaging both proslavery and abolitionist ideology in the process. As a social treatise, it perpetuated but also challenged the prevailing notions of separate spheres. It is a domestic novel as much as it is a polemical one, a popular book about serious issues, an example of the moral and intellectual power of one individual but also a testament to the importance of the publishing industry in shaping public opinion. *Uncle Tom's Cabin* is not about any one of these issues so much as it is about their intersection—it is a work about mid-nineteenth-century American culture itself.

My approach to teaching *Uncle Tom's Cabin* is an intertextual, interdisciplinary one broadly informed by the theories and especially the practice of new historicism over the last two decades. Such practices, however differently executed, generally recognize that "art," like other forms of human expression produced in different disciplines, is embedded in a network of material practices; that critics (or students) are products of the culture in which they reside; and that overly rigid disciplinary distinctions may prevent critics and students from observing similarities across disciplines at a particular historical moment.[1] My aims in translating such critical practice to classroom practice are thus twofold: first, to create a learning environment in which the students themselves discover and create the context of the period through their own examination of a diverse body of primary materials, drawn from many disciplines—literature, visual art, history, politics; and second, to encourage the understanding of slavery and domesticity as economic and social systems of human organization that shaped and were shaped by various rhetorical economies—systems of meaning variously negotiated and contested by writers and readers throughout the nineteenth century.

When I first started using interdisciplinary methods to teach *Uncle Tom's Cabin*, I tried to introduce my students to as many aspects of the book as possible, providing background and context in several minilectures as we progressed through the text. The students, however, were impatient with this approach; because they were so eager to talk about the book, my intrusions seemed artificial and awkward. I was also hesitant to concentrate too much on any one element or theoretical approach for fear of squelching their enthusiasm. As a result, our discussions tended to be unwieldy and unfocused; there is, finally, too much rather than too little to say about *Uncle Tom's Cabin*. Recently, I have been teaching the novel through a larger discussion of the competing arguments about slaves and slavery during the 1850s, especially as those arguments turn on divergent representations of "family" and "home." This approach allows for the latitude and flexibility I want in the classroom while focusing the social, political, and theological issues of the novel on an accessible and concrete set of images.

Most recently, I have taught *Uncle Tom's Cabin* in a course on American Romanticism. In presenting an inclusive view of the period, one that integrates as fully as possible the works of African American, Southern white, and women writers, I organize the course materials and assignments around several intellectual, theological, and political issues instead of focusing specifically on the "classic" writers of the period. I spend a bit of time at the beginning of the course establishing the political and social background, talking about such matters as the Missouri Compromise and the settlement of the Louisiana Purchase, the politics of Jacksonian democracy, and the economics of slavery as social and political matters that irrevocably shaped the writers' lives and their works. In addition, I introduce Romanticism as a vital intellectual, philosophical, and aesthetic movement during the period. This approach allows us—the students and me—to talk about what bound variously positioned American writers as well as what separated them as they formulated their own interpretations of America and constructed their own sense of a national identity. I teach *Moby-Dick* (1851), for instance, on the heels of Emerson's *Nature* (1836) but add Augusta Evans's *Beulah* (1859) as a Southern white woman's response to the issues and problems of Romanticism. I also integrate other materials whenever possible to enrich the students' understanding and interpretation of the readings. Since the boundaries of the continental United States took shape during the period, and because states' rights were so important to the social debates and eventually the sectional crisis of the 1850s, we look at contemporary maps of the country.[2] We study the landscape paintings of the Hudson River School while discussing republican ideology and the meaning of "space" in James Fenimore Cooper, William Cullen Bryant, and Lydia Maria Child. Ultimately, I encourage the students to think about the complex relations between texts and contexts and to see Romanticism as a dynamic system of meaning rather than a static concept.

We finally read *Uncle Tom's Cabin* near the end of the course in a unit on slaves and slavery. As in previous units, we read a variety of texts from a variety of authors: political tracts from white Southerners defending slavery; selections from *Swallow Barn* (1832), the plantation romance by the white Southern writer John Pendleton Kennedy; selections from Frederick Douglass's speeches, followed by the *Narrative of the Life of Frederick Douglass* (1845); Stowe's *Uncle Tom's Cabin*; and finally, a slave woman's view of life in the South with Harriet Jacobs's *Incidents in the Life of a Slave Girl*. Throughout the unit, we discuss slavery as a social and economic system in the nineteenth century but also as a rhetorical economy—a system of meaning variously negotiated by writers and readers throughout the period.

We begin the unit on slaves and slavery by looking at the economics and morality of the proslavery argument, discussing its ideological, social, and theological tenets in brief excerpts from the writings of James Henry Hammond, George Fitzhugh, and Thornton Stringfellow.[3] I encourage students to look at the constructions of home and family derived from Southern white notions of paternalism—the moral component of the ideology of slavery that stressed reciprocal obligation and responsibility among members of the plantation community.[4] When Hammond claimed that "slaveholders are responsible to the world for the humane treatment of the fellow-beings whom God has placed in their hands" (*Two Letters* 193), how was he defining "responsibility"? What was he suggesting about the slaves' and the slaveholders' relation to God? and to each other? How was he defining "family" and "laboring class" when he claimed that "every man in independent circumstances, all the world over, and every government, is to the same extent responsible to the whole human family, for the condition of the poor and laboring classes in their own country" (193)? How did Stringfellow use biblical evidence in his defense of slavery as a moral system? When Fitzhugh claimed that slaves are "infinitely better situated as feudal serfs or slaves than as freemen, or rather as slaves to capital" ("Southern Thought" 286), what was he suggesting about the differences in American life, North and South? Through these selections, we discuss several aspects of proslavery ideology as it developed in the South during the first half of the century. We focus on how the moral, economic, and religious arguments for the continuation of slavery initiated and later grounded a unique sense of the plantation "family"—the master as benevolent father presiding over various members of his family, including his slaves, who, in return for his protection and support, promise him their obedience and submission.

Turning then to fiction, we read selections from Kennedy's *Swallow Barn* and discuss how the ideology of slavery is embedded in many fictional representations of the plantation. We look specifically at the first two chapters of the novel, which describe the splendor and order of the plantation and its benevolent master, Frank Meriwether, as well as at chapter 7, "Traces of the Feudal System," and chapter 46, "The Quarter." I supplement our discussions with photographs, etchings, and paintings depicting plantation life and especially plantation homes of all sorts.[5] We discuss the physical organization of most plantations, with slave quarters located some distance downwind but still within sight of the planter's home. We look at photographs of slave cabins and talk about their construction. If time permits, I also read excerpts from a couple of articles on cabin design and construction published in *DeBow's Review* in the 1840s and 1850s, which assert the planters' sense of paternal responsibility for and control over the shape of the slaves' domestic space.[6] The title page of *Swallow Barn* depicts an aristocratic planter on horseback conversing with his smiling slaves in front of a barn, with the main house situated in the background. Another illustration in the body of the novel depicts Meriwether's wife, Lucretia, providing a moral lesson to her slave children, reinforcing her role as "mother" within the idealized plantation order. Currier and Ives also produced numerous lithographs during the period depicting rural life in the northeast as well as plantation life in the South.[7] A *Cotton Plantation on the Mississippi* (1884) sentimentalizes the laboring conditions and spatial organization of plantation life; slaves or free black laborers work in the fields, with the smoke of a steamship visible in the distance. In *Low Water in the Mississippi* (1867) black laborers dance merrily in front of a cabin in the foreground as steamships pass each other on the Mississippi; a Palladian-style plantation house stands on a hill in the background. Another series of prints entitled *American Country Life* sentimentalizes the social relations of the plantation "home." In *American Country Life: October Afternoon*, for instance, a finely dressed woman with an infant in her arms greets her husband at the gate of their elaborate home as he returns from the hunt.[8] Students are fairly adept at digging into the economic and social content of these illustrations as well as Kennedy's representations of the Big House and the slave quarters in *Swallow Barn*; they are often surprised by what they find, especially in Kennedy's portrayal of Meriwether and his wife as "father" and "mother" to the entire plantation "family."

As we move on to Frederick Douglass, I provide a brief overview of the antislavery movement and the tenor and variety of abolitionist thought from 1820 to 1860[9] as an introduction to the *Narrative of the Life of Frederick Douglass*. After a single class period on one of Douglass's essays, such as "What to the Slave Is the Fourth of July?" (1852), in which we discuss his engagement with the political and social rhetoric of the period, we read the *Narrative* in its entirety. We examine it first within the context of Douglass's oeuvre and the genre of the slave narrative, and then begin to think about the text within the context of the proslavery arguments of the period. We discuss the problems of family and home for Douglass, who did not know when he was born, who was separated from his mother as a child, and who could not secure his own family without the legal right to citizenship and marriage—experiences that, of course, run counter to the idealized picture drawn by many white Southern defenders of the slave system. As we work through the text, we discuss Douglass's inversion of the images of the plantation home and family depicted by Kennedy, as well as his pointed critique of paternalism and slaveholding religion in the appendix. Students inevitably want to talk at length about the "root" and Sandy Jenkins, whom Douglass depicts as an "old advisor" (ch. 10) as well as a comrade in the escape plot; many of them see Sandy as an alternative "father" or "brother" to Douglass, thus subverting the paternalism inherent in the proslavery argument.

We read *Uncle Tom's Cabin* immediately after completing the *Narrative*, and the students immediately pick up on the likeness between Douglass's self-presentation and Stowe's fictional portrait of George Harris. I also provide a brief lecture during the first or second class period, illustrated with slides and overhead transparencies, on domestic architecture and interior design in the mid–nineteenth century. Drawing from the work of architectural historians and material culture specialists, I lead students into a discussion of the physical design and construction of nineteenth-century homes and their interiors.[10] While the students examine the designs of several architects, I talk briefly about their visions of domesticity during the period.[11] The designer and writer Andrew Jackson Downing especially perpetuated the widely held vision of an American landscape dotted with individual family homes. For Downing and others, the pleasant and orderly Gothic cottage embodied the "universal" republican and Christian values associated with rural American life. Turning again to Currier and Ives, we look at prints from two series, *American Farm Scenes* (1853) and *American Homesteads* (1869), which sentimentalize the morality and social ideology of rural New England life. Modest cottages and farmhouses are the subjects of these prints, with white children playing and animals grazing in the foreground or mother and father engaged in the work of the farm—plowing a field, feeding chickens, or picking apples.[12] Inevitably, someone notices the difference between the prints depicting plantation and "country" life and those depicting "farms" and "homesteads," particularly in terms of the differing laboring conditions and familial relations they portray. We then turn to the interior of these homes, examining the organization and specialization of domestic space, even in the tiniest log cabin, and especially the function and decoration of the parlor or drawing room. As Katherine Grier argues in *Culture and Comfort*, the nineteenth-century parlor became a symbol of middle-class success and social attainment—a separate space devoted to social ceremony, a "cultivated facade" of a family's individual taste and gentility (2, 20–58). Last but not least, we look at several illustrations from Catharine Beecher and Harriet Beecher Stowe's *American Woman's Home* (1869) and talk about their vision of "domestic economy."

By the time we start *Uncle Tom's Cabin*, the students have at least a cursory understanding of the character of proslavery and abolitionist thought, as well as a taste of the intense cultural focus on the "home" as a dominant cultural ideology in the nineteenth century. As in our discussions of Kennedy and Douglass, we turn at once to the images of home and family in the novel, and I begin the first discussion by asking several questions about Uncle Tom's cabin. What is peculiar about Stowe's depiction of the cabin in chapter 4? When the narrator takes us into the dwelling, what do we see? Who is there, and what are they doing? What does the construction of the cabin home tell us about Stowe's perspective? Why is the book named for this dwelling? Students are very attentive to the details of the chapter: Chloe's brilliant cookery as she prepares her "ole man's supper" (17); Tom and Chloe's neat and distinguished "*drawing-room*" within the cabin (18); the dinner table set with cups and saucers; the scriptural prints and "colored" portrait of Washington hanging over the fireplace (18); the abundance of food; the rollicking children; the Bible reading. Yet George Shelby is there, interrupting what appears to be an idealized portrait of domestic life and bourgeois family relations. What is he doing there? Why is he eating with Tom's family, and why does Chloe give him the "first griddle full of cakes" (19)? By exploring the domestic organization and social dynamics within Tom and Chloe's cabin, we build on previous discussions of home and family, discussing regional and social variations in the depiction of home as well as the integral relation between the "private" sphere and the larger public issues of the period.

Our discussion usually moves from Tom and Chloe to George and Eliza Harris. Students are quick to recognize that both George and Eliza are idealized types within the gendered dichotomy of separate spheres; George is as industrious and intelligent as Eliza is religious and maternal. But, as with Tom and Chloe, their status as slaves within the economy of slavery precludes their ever fully becoming bourgeois subjects within that dichotomy. We compare Eliza's room in the Shelby house (ch. 5) with the dream she has of an Edenic home while staying in the Quaker settlement (ch. 13). We discuss George's frustration in being, like Douglass, denied compensation for and equal access to work (ch. 2), as well as in being denied the right to claim legally his own wife and child (ch. 11). In telling Mr. Wilson "I haven't any country, any more than I have any father" (97), George explicitly links his white biological father with the entire slaveholding nation and rejects them both, thus upending the Southern ethic of "paternalism" in the process.

At other times, we turn next to the Shelbys and the Birds. How do both couples represent and yet challenge the ideology of separate spheres? How do Mr. and Mrs. Shelby differently conceive of their public and private responsibilities to their slaves? Why is Mrs. Shelby afraid that her religious instruction will go unheeded by slave women like Eliza? I always remind students at this point to pay particular attention to the sentimentalism operating in chapter 9. How and why does Stowe construct a conflict between public reason and private feeling? How do Mr. and Mrs. Bird talk about their respective "duties" at the beginning of the chapter? How do their views change after the fugitive Eliza appears on their doorstep? How and why does Stowe draw such a deep and immediate maternal identity between Mrs. Bird and Eliza, and how is Mr. Bird's behavior then affected by that identity? What does the character of the Birds' marriage suggest about the ideology of separate spheres? about the paternal and moral arguments defending slavery?

Our discussions proceed in this manner from home to home, family to family, as we examine the religious, social, and political values embedded in each portrait: the matrifocal Quaker home of Rachel Halliday, the St. Clare household and its members, Miss Ophelia's ideas about "domestic economy" and her reaction to Dinah's kitchen, Eva's visions of her heavenly "home" and Tom's dream of a crown without thorns, Cassy and Emmeline as "mother" and "daughter," George and Eliza's Canadian and Liberian homes, and finally, the satanic, womanless, decaying plantation of Simon Legree. We continually look back to Douglass and Kennedy in our efforts to understand the novel's intertextuality. What do Stowe's portraits of Marie St. Clare and Simon Legree tell us about the limitations of white Southern "paternalism"? Marie, for instance, gives voice to the biblical argument for slavery when she tells Augustine and Ophelia of a wonderful preacher who, in citing Ecclesiastes, "showed how all the orders and distinctions in society came from God" and "proved distinctly that the Bible was on our side, and supported all our institutions so convincingly" (158). We also look closely at the contrast between Augustine and Alfred St. Clare. If they are "twins," why is one light-skinned and passive while the other is dark and controlling? What do their temperaments tell us about the development of personal identity at "home"—and of the mother's responsibility to that development? What does their debate about the relative merits of Jeffersonian republicanism and natural equality tell us about their political and social views (ch. 23)? How is each brother interpreting the nation's founding principles and to what end?

The students do very well with this kind of comparative or intertextual analysis, especially within *Uncle Tom's Cabin* itself, since Stowe invites us to compare and contrast various pairs of characters: Marie and Ophelia, Eva and Topsy, Eva and her grandmother, Eva and Tom, Tom and Cassy, Legree and Augustine, and so on. By the time we get to Simon Legree, the students do most if not all the talking and demonstrate a good deal of sophistication in their interpretations of the end of the novel. We look closely at Stowe's descriptions of the interior and exterior of Legree's decaying estate, which "had formerly belonged to a gentleman of opulence and taste" but now stands "merely as an implement for money-making" (298), the molding wallpaper in the sitting room now "garnished with chalk memorandums, and long sums footed up" (320). Our discussion from this concrete image of Legree's "home" and its inhabitants is always rich and varied. Some students compare his plantation with St. Clare's, suggesting that his dilapidated estate is another attempt on Stowe's part to show us what happens to the "family" when the business and economy of slavery enter the domestic sphere or when a man wanders too far from his mother's moral instruction. Some compare the relationship between Cassy and Legree with one of the other "marriages" in the novel. Others compare his sitting room with the "parlor" space in Tom's cabin to demonstrate how neither measures up to the ideal of the nineteenth-century parlor.

Since I started teaching *Uncle Tom's Cabin* in this way, using an intertextual, interdisciplinary approach in which the students themselves discover and create the context through their own examination of primary material, I have found them more willing and better able to proceed from the details of the text to higher-level analysis about the novel and its relation to the period. I also assign a reading journal to encourage such attention, intertextual comparison, and critical analysis. Students complete two or three directed journal assignments for each unit. I require them to write for at least an hour outside class for each entry; most produce two or three typed pages each time. I distribute a list of discussion questions for each journal assignment, but students are always free to explore their own interests; ideally, they develop topics for their formal essay in their journal entries. Because I regularly ask students to respond to specific passages in many of the journal questions, most become better readers and interpreters by the end of the semester; their eight- to ten-page essays, due at the end of the term, are better—more analytical and more focused on the language of the text itself rather than on unsupported generalities or bland plot summary—than those I have read in past semesters. What surprises and pleases me most, however, is the originality and creativity many students demonstrate in their comparative analyses of the primary works.

Thus, the chief advantage of this approach is that it allows me to focus the complex interweaving of social, political, and theological issues in *Uncle Tom's Cabin* on a concrete set of images that are accessible and meaningful to students. Those who might have been uninterested in introductory lectures on historical or religious background instead exhibit enthusiasm and confidence while analyzing those issues in relation to the various households in the novel. Some of the broader issues we have discussed in class through this approach include the economics and morality of slavery versus capitalism; Stowe's revisions of Calvinism; race, gender, and class relations as they differ in the North and the South during the antebellum period; the effect of abolitionist and proslavery ideologies on Stowe's novel; and individualism and paternalism as competing modes of personal and social behavior. This approach allows the students and me considerable latitude and flexibility during class, since our discussions are not limited to the extent they might be if we were to focus on a single thematic or social issue. Instead, we are free to explore a combination of issues in the novel, as well as to experiment with several theoretical approaches, such as new historicism, reader-response theory, and feminist criticism. Depending on the interests and sophistication of my students in a given semester, we might, for instance, talk about the relations of power in the historically, racially, and regionally specific domestic relations in *Uncle Tom's Cabin* while reading a bit of Marx or Foucault. Or we might examine the gendered division of labor and explicit heterosexuality of Stowe's vision along with a sampling of feminist criticism or theory.

Finally, this approach allows us to explore such traditionally "literary" matters as the novel's style, structure, and genre. How does Stowe use her depiction of various homes and families to challenge other representations circulating during the period? How does she place those homes in her novel, and how do they enhance its narrative and thematic structure (for instance, Tom's movement south compared with George and Eliza's movement north)? What do those homes tell us finally about Stowe's political agenda, and how is that agenda linked to her narrative strategy? How do we define "sentimentalism" as a narrative mode or device in *Uncle Tom's Cabin*? What is the connection between the "sentimental" and "domestic" in Stowe's work? To what degree is *Uncle Tom's Cabin* as much a domestic novel as it is a polemical one? Ultimately, I want the students to think about the relation between form and content—to think about the book as a work of "fiction" whose domestic settings ground not only its content but also its characterization, plot, and narrative structure.

NOTES

Many heartfelt thanks to the students in English 361, American Romanticism, at Iowa State University (1993–96) for the pleasure of their company as well as their participation in and enthusiasm for this approach to *Uncle Tom's Cabin*.

[1]For general but still useful sources introducing the possibilities and limitations of new historicism as an interdisciplinary practice, see Veeser; Porter.

[2]Important historical sources on the settlement and development of the American South, as well as on the growing sectional crisis during the early nineteenth century, include Morgan, *American Slavery*; Potter; and McCardell. Van Ermen's *The United States in Old Maps and Prints* is an excellent source of early maps; specifically, I use maps of the nation drawn in 1793, 1837, and 1850 to talk about the development of territories into states and an 1859 map of the rail lines to illustrate the growing sectional divisions during the 1850s. *America's History*, a college-level history textbook edited by Henretta et al., also contains many useful maps and graphics; I recommend this text to students who want to catch up on the history of the period. For an overview of the Hudson River School, see Howat; Czestochowski. Rans offers an excellent discussion of Cooper's relation to republican ideology.

[3]I use Hammond's *Two Letters*, Stringfellow's *Brief Examination of Scripture Testimony*, and Fitzhugh's, "Southern Thought." Through their political, religious, and publishing activity, all three men contributed greatly to the development of proslavery thought during the period. Hammond (1807–64) was among South Carolina's leading citizens, gaining prominence first as an attorney and sectionalist newspaper editor and later as a member of the United States House of Representatives, as governor of South Carolina, and as a member of the United States Senate. Stringfellow (1788–1869), the son of a major slaveholder, was a Baptist minister in Virginia for most of his life; he published numerous tracts and sermons, which justified slavery in biblical terms as a moral system ordained by God. Descended from one of Virginia's oldest and most prominent families, Fitzhugh (1804–81) was never prosperous himself, as the agricultural decline in the 1820s forced the sale of the family plantation; he educated himself, eventually entering the practice of law, and later produced a substantial body of work on the social issues of the period, contributing regularly to Southern newspapers and agricultural journals and authoring two of the best-known books on the slavery question, *Cannibals All!* (1857) and *Sociology for the South* (1854). See Faust for selections of the essays cited here, as well as for an introduction to the tenets of the proslavery argument and a bibliography of secondary sources. Important collections published in the nineteenth century include *The Pro-slavery Argument* and Elliott.

[4]Genovese explores the radically different interpretations of paternalism by masters and slaves in *Roll, Jordan, Roll* (25–49), arguing that while paternalism and slavery merged into a single idea for most masters, slaves separated the two and transformed paternalism into a doctrine of protection of their own rights (49). See also W. Jenkins 3–106; Fox-Genovese 100–45. L. Levine's discussion of the surviving elements of West

African culture in the slave quarters in *Black Culture, Black Consciousness* is also important in this context.

[5]I use photographs of plantation homes and slave quarters reprinted in Fox-Genovese; Harris; and G. Wright. Both Fox-Genovese and Harris discuss intraregional variations in housing as well as the range of modest and affluent plantation homes in the Old South. Wright's chapter on the Big House and slave quarters is also useful (41–51).

[6]See, e.g., *DeBow's Review* 3 (1847): 419 and 10 (1851): 623. *DeBow's Review* was founded in 1845 by J. D. B. DeBow, who envisioned a journal focused on the agricultural, economic, and social issues of the South in an effort to encourage the spread and diversification of agriculture throughout the South and West. Although DeBow himself stopped short of endorsing Southern nationalism in the 1850s, *DeBow's Review* regularly published the work of leading Southern defenders of slavery. The journal remains one of the most important sources for historians on various economic and social issues in the South during the sectional period. Many research libraries have a few hardbound copies of *DeBow's* in their manuscript holdings; others, such as Perkins Library at Duke University and Widener Library at Harvard, have extensive holdings. The journal is also available on microfilm in many research libraries.

[7]Sources for Currier and Ives lithographs include *Currier & Ives: A Catalogue Raisonné* and *Currier & Ives Favorites*, a collection of prints from the Museum of the City of New York.

[8]Other prints of interest include *A Home on the Mississippi* (1871) and *Loading Cotton on the Mississippi* (1870). Kuspit, Simmons, and Stewart's *Painting in the South* is also useful, with commentary and reprints of several important paintings depicting Southern and particularly slave life in the nineteenth century.

[9]For summaries of the extensive literature on the abolition of slavery, see J. Stewart; Waters.

[10]On domestic interiors, see especially Grier; Ames. Ames, Ayers, and Garrison have edited *The Material Culture of American Homes*, an excellent twelve-unit collection of slides with taped commentary on American interiors from colonial times to the 1930s. For an overview of the mid-nineteenth-century home in historical context, see Clark, *The American Family Home*, and "Domestic Architecture"; G. Wright.

[11]See, e.g., Vaux; Downing, *Cottage Residences* and *Architecture*. See also G. Wright 73–89 and Handlin 1–88 for background on Downing and his influence during the period.

[12]See also *Home, Sweet Home* (1869) and *Home Sweet Home* (1874).

NOTES ON CONTRIBUTORS

Sylvan Allen is a graduate student at the University of North Carolina, Greensboro, currently on leave to work for Americorps in rural North Carolina. She is the author of articles and reviews in local publications and an undergraduate thesis on the coming millennium's effect on contemporary literature.

Elizabeth Ammons is Harriet H. Fay Professor of Literature at Tufts University, where she teaches courses in American literature. The author of *Conflicting Stories: American Women Writers at the Turn into the Twentieth Century* (1991) and *Edith Wharton's Argument with America* (1980), she is the editor of a number of volumes, including the Norton Critical Edition of *Uncle Tom's Cabin* (1994) and *Short Fiction by Black Women, 1900–1920* (1991). She is the coeditor, with Annette White-Parks, of *Tricksterism in Turn-of-the-Century American Literature: A Multicultural Perspective* (1994) and, with Valerie Roby, of *American Local Color Writing, 1880–1920* (1998). Ammons is currently at work on a book on race theory and various texts in the United States during the early 1880s.

Susan Belasco is associate professor of English and director of the university writing program at the University of Tulsa. The author of articles and reviews on nineteenth-century American women writers and the literary marketplace, she is the editor of *Summer on the Lakes, in 1843*, by Margaret Fuller (1991), and *Ruth Hall*, by Fanny Fern (1996). She is coeditor, with Larry J. Reynolds, of *"These Sad but Glorious Days": Dispatches from Europe, 1846–1850, by Margaret Fuller* (1991) and, with Kenneth M. Price, of *Periodical Literature in Nineteenth-Century America* (1995). Her current project is a study of Toussaint-Louverture in antebellum literature and culture.

Gillian Brown is professor of English at the University of Utah. She is the author of *Domestic Individualism: Imagining the Self in Nineteenth-Century America* (1990) and of essays in *American Quarterly, Representations, Yale Journal of Criticism, American Literary History, Studies in the Novel*, and *Modern Fiction Studies*. Her current project is "The Consent of the Governed," a book on consent theory and eighteenth-century American culture, forthcoming from Harvard UP in 2000.

Harold K. Bush, Jr., is assistant professor of English at Saint Louis University, where he teaches courses in literature and American studies. He is the author of *American Declarations: Rebellion and Repentance in American Cultural History* (1999) and of articles and reviews in *New England Quarterly, American Quarterly, College English, American Literary Realism, American Transcendental Quarterly*, and the *Robert Frost Review*. His current project, tentatively titled "Mark Twain's Pastor," is a book-length study of Twain's friendship with Joe Twitchell and their engagement with Gilded Age religion.

Sophia Cantave is a doctoral candidate in African American literature at Tufts University. She is the author of an essay, "Geography, Language, and Hyphens: Felix Morisseau-Leroy and a Changing Haitian Aesthetic," forthcoming in the *Journal of Haitian Studies*. She has also presented papers at the College Language Association and the Zora Neale Hurston Festival.

Sharon Carson is associate professor in the Department of English and the Department of Philosophy and Religious Studies at the University of North Dakota. A contributor to the *Oxford Companion to African American Literature* (1997), she is the author of articles on *Incidents in the Life of a Slave Girl* and the *Narrative of the Life of Frederick Douglass* in the *Journal of Religious Thought* and *Religion and Literature*. Her teaching and research interests are in African American literature and interdisciplinary black studies and comparative religions and literature.

Paul C. Gutjahr is assistant professor of English and American studies at Indiana University, Bloomington. He is the author of *An American Bible: A History of the Good Book in the United States, 1777–1880* (1999); "Constructing Art and Facts: The Art of Composition, the Facts of (Material) Culture," in *Left Margins: Cultural Studies, Rhetoric, and Composition Theory* (1995); and articles and reviews in *Mosaic, ATQ, American Literature, Church History*, the *Winterthur Portfolio*, and the *Journal of American History*. He is coediting a collection tentatively titled "Illuminating Letters: Essays on Typography and Literary Interpretation." His teaching and research interests include the history of the book in America and American religious history.

Kimberly G. Hébert is a doctoral candidate in American literature and a lecturer at Tufts University. Her publications include an essay on Pauline Hopkins in *Ngũgĩ wa Thiong'o: Texts and Contexts* (1995) and "Who will Lead the Revolution?" in *Skin Deep: Women Writing on Color, Culture, and Identity* (1994). Her teaching and research interests include literature and texts written by and about persons in the African diaspora and uncovering African-based ways of reading and rewriting the dominant culture's representations of black people.

Kristin Herzog is an independent scholar in Durham, North Carolina. She is the author of *Finding Their Voice: Peruvian Women's Testimonies of War* (1993) and *Women, Ethnics, and Exotics: Images of Power in Mid-Nineteenth-Century American Fiction* (1983). Her areas of research are in American literature by women and ethnic minorities, feminist theology, and Peruvian literature and religion. Her current projects are American women's war literature and images of childhood in theology and literature.

David Leverenz is professor of English at the University of Florida. He is the author of *Manhood and the American Renaissance* (1989), *The Language of Puritan Feeling* (1980), and numerous articles on nineteenth-century American literature, most recently on Poe. He also coedited *Mindful Pleasures: Essays on Thomas Pynchon* (1976). His current projects are an essay, " 'Male' Authorship in the Early Republic," for the forthcoming *History of the Book in America*, and a book, "Daddy's Girls, Daddy's Boys: Narrating Upward Mobility in Early Corporate America."

Lisa Logan is assistant professor of English at the University of Central Florida. She has had articles published in *Early American Literature* and *Southern Quarterly*, and she is the author of essays appearing in *Critical Essays on Carson McCullers* (1996), *Safe Space: Violence and Women's Writing* (1998), and *Teaching the Introduction to Women's Studies* (1999). Her teaching and research interests include American women's popular prose before 1865. Her current projects include an essay on Harriet Prescott Spofford's fictions of race, romanticism, and national identity and a study of the relations among gender, authorship, and feminist theory in women's Indian captivity narratives.

Marianne K. Noble is assistant professor at American University. She is the author of *The Masochistic Pleasures of Sentimental Literature* (2000) and numerous articles on nineteenth-century American sentimental literature and poetry. Her article on *Uncle Tom's Cabin* in the *Yale Journal of Criticism* was the subject of a follow-up forum comprising three responses and her response to the responses. Her teaching and research interests are in nineteenth-century American literature, women's literature, and feminist and psychoanalytic theory.

Susan M. Nuernberg is associate professor of English at the University of Wisconsin, Oshkosh. She is the editor of *The Letters of Russ Kingman* (1999) and *The Critical Response to Jack London* (1995). Her teaching and research interests include realism and naturalism, race in popular American fiction, Native American literature, and women writers.

Mary Jane Peterson is an English teacher and trainer of peer writing tutors and director of the writing center at Manhasset High School, Manhasset, New York. She is the coauthor of "Can Anybody Come Here? Sharing the Vision of the Manhasset Writing Center" in the *Pennsylvania Council of Teachers of English Newsletter* (1993). Her current project is conducting research on the effectiveness of peer tutors in high school writing centers. Her peer tutoring program at Manhasset has been recognized by the New York State English Council as a Program of Excellence in Language Arts.

Stephen Railton is professor of English at the University of Virginia, where he teaches courses in nineteenth-century American literature. He is the author of *Authorship and Audience: Literary Performance in the American Renaissance* (1991) and *James Fenimore Cooper: A Study of His Life and Imagination* (1978). His current projects include a book, "Being Somebody: Samuel Clemens's Career as Mark Twain," and the development of two Web sites, *Mark Twain in His Times* and Uncle Tom's Cabin *and American Culture*.

Jamie Stanesa is director of the Professional Studies Division, Graham School of General Studies, at the University of Chicago. She has taught women's studies, American studies, and English courses at Emory University, Wayne State University, and Iowa State University and currently teaches at the continuing education unit at the University of Chicago. Her publications include articles on Caroline Hentz, and she is currently at work on a book on the intersection of political and social ideologies and Protestant Christian theology in the works of American women writers from 1848 to 1867.

Stephen R. Yarbrough is associate professor of English at the University of North Carolina, Greensboro. He is the author of *After Rhetoric: The Study of Discourse Beyond Language and Culture* (1999) and *Deliberate Criticism: Toward a Postmodern Humanism* (1992), as well as coauthor of *Delightful Conviction: Jonathan Edwards and the Rhetoric of Conversion* with John C. Adams (1993) and *Irving Babbitt* with Stephen C. Brennan (1987). His teaching and research interests include rhetorical theory, the history of American rhetoric, critical theory, and pedagogy. His current book project is tentatively titled "The Questions of Teaching: Critical Issues for a Pragmatic Pedagogy."

CONTRIBUTORS AND SURVEY PARTICIPANTS

The following scholars and teachers of Stowe's work contributed essays for this volume, made valuable suggestions, or participated in the survey that preceded and provided materials for the preparation of this book:

Sandra Adickes, *Winona State University*
Sylvan Allen, *University of North Carolina, Greensboro*
Elizabeth Ammons, *Tufts University*
Herman Beavers, *University of Pennsylvania*
Susan Belasco, *University of Tulsa*
Gillian Brown, *University of Utah*
Harold K. Bush, Jr., *Saint Louis University*
Sophia Cantave, *Tufts University*
Sharon Carson, *University of North Dakota*
Kamilla Denman, *Brookline, MA*
Deborah De Rosa, *University of North Carolina, Chapel Hill*
Bill Ellis, *Pennsylvania State University, Hazleton*
Audrey A. Fisch, *Jersey City State College*
Paul C. Gutjahr, *Indiana University, Bloomington*
Kimberly G. Hébert, *Tufts University*
Joan Hedrick, *Trinity University*
Kristin Herzog, *Durham, NC*
Jon Hodge, *Tufts University*
Linck C. Johnson, *Colgate University*
Susan Kurjiaka, *Florida Atlantic University*
Kris Lackey, *University of New Orleans*
Keith Lawrence, *Brigham Young University, UT*
David Leverenz, *University of Florida*
Lisa Logan, *University of Central Florida*
David Miller, *Allegheny College*
Marianne K. Noble, *American University*
Susan M. Nuernberg, *University of Wisconsin, Oshkosh*
David R. Peck, *California State University, Long Beach*
Elizabeth Peter, *Tufts University*
Mary Jane Peterson, *Manhasset High School, Manhasset, NY*
Stephen Railton, *University of Virginia*
Sarah Robbins, *Kennesaw State College*
Ona Russell, *University of California, San Diego*
Robert Sayre, *University of Iowa*
Ann R. Shapiro, *State University of New York, Farmingdale*
Merrill M. Skaggs, *Drew University*
Gail K. Smith, *Marquette University*
Grant T. Smith, *Viterbo College*
Jamie Stanesa, *University of Chicago, IL*

Bhoomika Thakur, *Raipur, India*
Stephen R. Yarbrough, *University of North Carolina, Greensboro*
Sandra Zagarell, *Oberlin College*

WORKS CITED

Editions of *Uncle Tom's Cabin*
(in Chronological Order)

Stowe, Harriet Beecher. *Uncle Tom's Cabin; or, Life among the Lowly*. Boston: Jewett, 1852.

——. *Uncle Tom's Cabin: A Tale of Life among the Lowly; or, Pictures of Slavery in the United States*. 3rd ed. London: Ingram, 1852.

——. *Uncle Tom's Cabin; or, Life among the Lowly*. Boston: Jewett, 1853.

——. *Uncle Tom's Cabin; or, Life among the Lowly*. New York: Fenno, 1904.

——. *Uncle Tom's Cabin; or, Life among the Lowly*. New York: Grossett, n.d.

——. *Uncle Tom's Cabin; or, Life among the Lowly*. Ed. Raymond Weaver. New York: Heritage, 1938.

——. *Uncle Tom's Cabin; or, Life among the Lowly*. Ed. Kenneth S. Lynn. Cambridge: Harvard UP, 1962.

——. *Uncle Tom's Cabin*. New York: Signet-NAL, 1966.

——. *Uncle Tom's Cabin*. Introd. Alfred Kazin. New York: Bantam, 1981.

——. *Uncle Tom's Cabin; or, Life among the Lowly*. Ed. Ann Douglas. New York: Penguin, 1981.

——. *Three Novels:* Uncle Tom's Cabin; The Minister's Wooing; Oldtown Folks. Ed. Kathryn K. Sklar. New York: Lib. of Amer., 1982.

——. *Uncle Tom's Cabin*. Ed. Christopher W. Bigsby. Boston: Everyman's, 1993.

——. *Uncle Tom's Cabin*. Ed. Elizabeth Ammons. New York: Norton, 1994.

Books and Articles

Adams, John R. *Harriet Beecher Stowe*. New York: Twayne, 1989.

Ahlstrom, Sydney E. *A Religious History of the American People*. New Haven: Yale UP, 1972.

Allen, William G. "[About *Uncle Tom's Cabin*]." H. Stowe, *Uncle Tom's Cabin*, ed. Ammons 463–66.

Allison, Dorothy. "Public Silence, Private Terror." Vance 103–14.

Ames, Kenneth L. *Death in the Dining Room and Other Tales of Victorian Culture*. Philadelphia: Temple UP, 1992.

Ames, Kenneth L., William Ayers, and Nancy Garrison, eds. *The Material Culture of American Homes*. Winterthur: Du Pont Winterthur Museum, 1990.

Ammons, Elizabeth, ed. *Critical Essays on Harriet Beecher Stowe*. Boston: Hall, 1980.

——. "Heroines in *Uncle Tom's Cabin*." Ammons, *Critical Essays* 152–65.

——. "Stowe's Dream of the Mother-Savior: *Uncle Tom's Cabin* and American Women Writers before 1920." Sundquist, *New Essays* 155–95.

Anderson, Jervis. *This Was Harlem: A Cultural Portrait, 1900–1950.* New York: Farrar, 1982.

Andrews, James R. *The Practice of Rhetorical Criticism.* 2nd ed. New York: Longman, 1990.

Andrews, William L. *To Tell a Free Story: The First Century of Afro-American Autobiography, 1760–1865.* Urbana: U of Illinois P, 1986.

Andrews, William L., Frances Smith Foster, and Trudier Harris. *The Oxford Companion to African American Literature.* New York: Oxford UP, 1997.

Appiah, Kwame Anthony. *In My Father's House: Africa in the Philosophy of Culture.* New York: Oxford, 1992.

———. Introduction. *Early African-American Classics.* Ed. Appiah. New York: Bantam, 1990. vii–xxiv.

Aptheker, Bettina. *Woman's Legacy: Essays on Race, Sex, and Class in American History.* Amherst: U of Massachusetts P, 1982.

Asante, Molefi Kete. *The Afrocentric Idea.* Philadelphia: Temple, 1987.

———. *Afrocentricity.* Trenton: Africa World, 1988.

Ashton, Jean W. *Harriet Beecher Stowe: A Reference Guide.* Boston: Hall, 1977.

Askeland, Lori. "Remodeling the Model Home in *Uncle Tom's Cabin* and *Beloved.*" *American Literature* 64 (1992): 785–805.

"Authors among Fruits." *New York Daily Times* 28 Sept. 1855: 1.

Azevedo, Mario. *Africana Studies: A Survey of Africa and the African Diaspora.* Durham: Carolina Acad., 1993.

Baker, Houston A., Jr. "Archeology, Ideology, and African-American Discourse." *Redefining American Literary History.* Ed. A. LaVonne Brown Ruoff and Jerry W. Ward, Jr. New York: MLA, 1990. 157–95.

———. *Blues, Ideology, and Afro-American Literature: A Vernacular Theory.* Chicago: U of Chicago P, 1984.

Baker, Houston A., Jr., and Patricia Redmond, eds. *Afro-American Literary Study in the 1990s.* Chicago: U of Chicago P, 1989.

Baldwin, James. "Everybody's Protest Novel." *Partisan Review* 16 (1949): 578–85. Rpt. in H. Stowe, *Uncle Tom's Cabin*, ed. Ammons 495–501.

Banks, Marva. "*Uncle Tom's Cabin* and Antebellum Black Response." *Readers in History: Nineteenth-Century American Literature and the Contexts of Response.* Ed. James L. Machor. Baltimore: Johns Hopkins UP, 1993. 209–27.

Bardes, Barbara, and Suzanne Gossett. *Declarations of Independence: Women and Political Power.* New Brunswick: Rutgers UP, 1990.

Baron, Walter. *Evolutionary Ideas in the Writings of J. F. Blumenbach.* Paris: Hermann, 1962.

Bartky, Sandra Lee. *Femininity and Domination: Studies in the Phenomenology of Oppression.* New York: Routledge, 1990

Basinger, Jeanine. *Shirley Temple.* New York: Pyramid, 1975.

Baym, Nina. *Novels, Readers, and Reviewers: Responses to Fiction in Antebellum America.* Ithaca: Cornell UP, 1984.

———. *Woman's Fiction: A Guide to Novels by and about Women in America, 1820–70.* Ithaca: Cornell UP, 1978.

Baym, Nina, et al., eds. *The Norton Anthology of American Literature*. 5th ed. 2 vols. New York: Norton, 1998.

Beauvoir, Simone de. *The Second Sex*. Trans. H. M. Parshley. New York: Vintage, 1989.

Beecher, Catharine. *A Treatise on Domestic Economy*. Ed. Kathryn Kish Sklar. New York: Schocken, 1977.

Beecher, Catharine, and Harriet Beecher Stowe. *The American Woman's Home; or, Principles of Domestic Science*. New York: Ford, 1869.

Belcher, Max, Svend E. Holsoe, Bernard L. Herman, and Rodger P. Kingston. *A Life and Land Remembered: Americo-Liberia Folk Architecture*. Athens: U of Georgia P, 1988.

Benjamin, Jessica. *Bonds of Love: Psychoanalysis, Feminism, and the Problem of Domination*. New York: Pantheon, 1988.

Benjamin, Walter. *Charles Baudelaire: A Lyric Poet in the Age of High Capitalism*. Trans. Harry Zohn. London: New Left, 1973.

Bentley, Nancy. "White Slaves: The Mulatto Hero in Antebellum Fiction." *American Literature* 65.3 (1993): 501–22.

Bercovitch, Sacvan. *The American Jeremiad*. Madison: U of Wisconsin P, 1979.

———, ed. *The Cambridge History of American Literature*. Vol. 2. New York: Cambridge UP, 1995.

Bergman, Peter M., and Mort Bergman. *The Chronological History of the Negro in America*. New York: New Amer. Lib., 1969.

Berkson, Dorothy. Introduction. *Oldtown Folks*. By Harriet Beecher Stowe. New Brunswick: Rutgers UP, 1987. ix–xxxvi.

———. "'So We All Became Mothers': Harriet Beecher Stowe, Charlotte Perkins Gilman, and the New World of Women's Culture." *Feminism, Utopia, and Narrative*. Ed. Libby Falk Jones and Sarah Webster Goodwin. Tennessee Studies in Literature 32. Knoxville: U of Tennessee P, 1990. 100–15.

Berlin, James A. Foreword. D. Downing vii–xii.

Bersani, Leo. "Representation and Its Discontents." *Allegory and Representation*. Ed. Stephen Greenblatt. Baltimore: Johns Hopkins UP, 1981. 145–62.

Berson, Misha. "Cabin Fever." *American Theatre* May 1991: 16+.

Bibb, Henry. *Narrative of the Life and Adventures of Henry Bibb, an American Slave, Written by Himself. Puttin' on Ole Massa: The Slave Narratives of Henry Bibb, William Wells Brown, and Solomon Northrup*. Ed. Gilbert Osofsky. New York: Harper, 1969. 53–171.

Birdoff, Harry. *The World's Greatest Hit*. New York: Vanni, 1947.

Bizzell, Patricia. "The Teacher's Authority: Negotiating Difference in the Classroom." D. Downing 194–201.

Blassingame, John, ed. *New Perspectives in Black Studies*. Urbana: U of Illinois P, 1971.

Bloch, Ruth H. "American Feminine Ideals in Transition: The Rise of the Moral Mother, 1785–1815." *Feminist Studies* 4.2 (1978): 101–26.

Bogle, Donald. *Toms, Coons, Mulattoes, Mammies, and Bucks*. New York: Bantam, 1974.

Boydston, Jeanne, Mary Kelley, and Anne Margolis, eds. *The Limits of Sisterhood: The Beecher Sisters on Women's Rights and Woman's Sphere*. Chapel Hill: U of North Carolina P, 1988.

Boynton, Henry W. *Annals of American Bookselling 1638–1850*. New York: Wiley, 1932.

Brawley, Benjamin. *A Social History of the American Negro: Being a History of the Negro Problem in the United States; Including a History and Study of the Republic of Liberia*. New York: Macmillan, 1921.

Brodhead, Richard H. "Sparing the Rod: Discipline and Fiction in Antebellum America." *Representations* 21 (1988): 67–96.

Brown, Gillian. *Domestic Individualism: Imagining Self in Nineteenth-Century America*. Berkeley: U of California P, 1990.

———. "Getting in the Kitchen with Dinah: Domestic Politics in *Uncle Tom's Cabin*." *American Quarterly* 36 (1984): 503–23.

Brown, William Wells. *Clotel; or, The President's Daughter*. New York: Carol, 1989.

———. *The Escape; or, A Leap for Freedom*. Boston: Wallcut, 1858.

Buell, Lawrence. "Calvinism Romanticized: Harriet Beecher Stowe, Samuel Hopkins, and *The Minister's Wooing*." *ESQ: A Journal of the American Renaissance* 24 (1978): 119–32. Rpt. in Ammons, *Critical Essays* 259–75.

———. *New England Literary Culture: From Revolution through Renaissance*. New York: Cambridge UP, 1986.

Burke, Kenneth. *A Grammar of Motives and a Rhetoric of Motives*. New York: Meridian, 1962.

———. *A Rhetoric of Motives*. Berkeley: U of California P, 1969.

Bush, Harold K., Jr. *American Declarations: Rebellion and Repentance in American Cultural History*. Urbana: U of Illinois P, 1999.

Bushnell, Horace. *Sermons*. Ed. Conrad Cherry. New York: Paulist, 1985.

Butler, Judith. *Bodies That Matter: On the Discursive Limits of "Sex."* New York: Routledge, 1993.

Bynum, Victoria E. *Unruly Women: The Politics of Social and Sexual Control in the Old South*. Chapel Hill: U of North Carolina P, 1992.

Caldwell, Charles. *Thoughts on the Original Unity of the Human Race*. New York: Bliss, 1830.

Calhoun, Craig Jackson. "The Radicalism of Tradition: Community Strength or Venerable Disguise and Borrowed Language?" *American Journal of Sociology* 88 (1983): 886–914.

Califia, Pat. "Feminism and Sadomasochism." Jackson and Scott, *Feminism* 230–38.

Campbell, Karlyn Kohrs. "Style and Content in the Rhetoric of Early Afro-American Feminists." *Quarterly Journal of Speech* 72.4 (1986): 434–45.

Caplan, Paula. *The Myth of Female Masochism*. 1985. Toronto: U of Toronto Press, 1993.

Caskey, Marie. *Chariot of Fire: Religion and the Beecher Family*. New Haven: Yale UP, 1978.

Child, Lydia Maria. *The American Frugal Housewife*. Boston: Carter and Hendee. 1830.

———. *Appeal in Favor of That Class of Americans Called Africans*. 1833. Amherst: U of Massachusetts P, 1996.

———. Introduction. Jacobs 3–4.

Clark, Clifford E., Jr. *The American Family Home, 1800–1960*. Chapel Hill: U of North Carolina P, 1986.

———. "Domestic Architecture as an Index to Social History: The Romantic Revival and the Cult of Domesticity in America, 1840–1870." *Journal of Interdisciplinary History* 7.1 (1976): 33–56.

———. *Henry Ward Beecher: Spokesman for a Middle-Class America*. Urbana: U of Illinois P, 1978.

Cleage, Albert. *Black Christian Nationalism*. Detroit: Luxor, 1987.

———. *The Black Messiah*. Trenton: Africa World, 1989.

Cleaver, Eldridge. *Soul on Ice*. New York: McGraw, 1968.

Condit, Celeste Michelle, and John Louis Lucaites. *Crafting Equality: America's Anglo-African Word*. Chicago: U of Chicago P, 1993.

Cone, James. *A Black Theology of Liberation: Twentieth Anniversary Edition with Critical Responses*. New York: Orbis, 1990.

———. *For My People: Black Theology and the Black Church*. New York: Orbis, 1984.

Cott, Nancy F. *The Bonds of Womanhood: "Woman's Sphere" in New England, 1780–1835*. New Haven: Yale UP, 1977.

———. *The Grounding of Modern Feminism*. New Haven: Yale UP, 1987.

———. "Passionlessness: An Interpretation of Victorian Sexual Ideology, 1790–1850." *Signs* 4.2 (1978): 219–36.

Croly, David, and George Wakeman. *Miscegenation: The Theory of the Blending of the Races, Applied to the American White Man and Negro*. London: Trübnen, 1864.

Cross, Barbara M., ed. *The Autobiography of Lyman Beecher*. 2 vols. Cambridge: Harvard UP, 1961.

Currier & Ives: A Catalogue Raisonné. A Comprehensive Catalogue of the Lithographs of Nathaniel Currier, James Merritt Ives, and Charles Currier, Including Ephemera Associated with the Firm, 1834–1907. 2 vols. Detroit: Gale Research, 1984.

Currier & Ives Favorites. New York: Museum of the City of New York, 1978.

Czestochowski, Joseph S. *The American Landscape Tradition: A Study and Gallery of Paintings*. New York, 1982.

Davidson, Cathy N., ed. *No More Separate Spheres*. Spec. issue of *American Literature* 70 (1998): 443–63.

———. *Revolution and the Word: The Rise of the Novel in America*. New York: Oxford UP, 1986.

Davis, Angela Y. *Women, Race, and Class*. New York: Vintage, 1981.

Davis, Charles T., and Henry Louis Gates, Jr., eds. *The Slave's Narrative*. New York: Oxford UP, 1985.

Degler, Carl N. "What Ought to Be and What Was: Women's Sexuality in the Nineteenth Century." *Women and Health in America: Historical Readings*. Ed. Judith Walzer Leavitt. Madison: U of Wisconsin P, 1984.

Delaney, Martin. *Blake; or, The Huts of America*. Boston: Beacon, 1970.

———. *The Condition, Elevation, Emigration, and Destiny of the Colored People of the United States*. 1852. New York: Arno, 1969.

De St. Jorre, John. "The Unmasking of O." *New Yorker* Aug. 1994: 42–50.

Detweiler, Philip F. "The Changing Reputation of the Declaration of Independence: The First Fifty Years." *William and Mary Quarterly* 19 (1972): 557–74.

Dickens, Charles. *The Letters of Charles Dickens.* Ed. Graham Story, Kathleen Tillotson, and Nina Burgis. Vol. 6. Oxford: Clarendon, 1988.

Doctorow, E. L. "Out of the Parlor and into the Fray." Rev. of *Harriet Beecher Stowe: A Life,* by Joan D. Hedrick. *New York Times* 13 Feb. 1994, late ed., sec. 7: 3.

Donovan, Josephine. Uncle Tom's Cabin: *Evil, Affliction, and Redemptive Love.* Boston: Twayne, 1991.

Dorsey, Peter. "De-authorizing Slavery: Realism in Stowe's *Uncle Tom's Cabin* and Brown's *Clotel.*" *ESQ: A Journal of the American Renaissance* 41.4 (1995): 256–88.

Douglas, Ann. *The Feminization of American Culture.* New York: Knopf, 1977.

Douglass, Frederick. *The Life and Writings of Frederick Douglass.* Ed. Philip Foner. Vol. 2. New York: International, 1950–75.

———. *Narrative of the Life of Frederick Douglass. The Classic Slave Narratives.* Ed. Henry Louis Gates, Jr. New York: Mentor, 1987. 243–331.

———. *Narrative of the Life of Frederick Douglass, an American Slave, Written by Himself.* Ed. Houston A. Baker, Jr. New York: Penguin, 1982.

———. "What to the Slave Is the Fourth of July?" *The Frederick Douglass Papers.* Ed. John W. Blassingame. Ser. 1, vol. 2. New Haven: Yale UP, 1982. 359–88.

Downing, Andrew Jackson. *The Architecture of Country Houses.* New York: Appleton, 1850.

———. *Cottage Residences, Rural Architecture, and Landscape Gardening.* 1842. New York: Amer. Life Found., 1967.

Downing, David B., ed. *Changing Classroom Practices: Resources for Literary and Cultural Studies.* Urbana: NCTE, 1994.

Duneier, Mitchell. *Slim's Table: Race, Respectability, and Masculinity.* Chicago: U of Chicago P, 1992.

Dyson, Michael Eric. *Reflecting Black: African-American Cultural Criticism.* Minneapolis: U of Minnesota P, 1993.

Edwards, Jonathan. *The Nature of True Virtue.* 1765. *Ethical Writings.* Ed. Paul Ramsey. New Haven: Yale UP, 1989. 537–627. Vol. 8 of *The Works of Jonathan Edwards.* Perry Miller and John Smith, gen. eds. 11 vols. 1957– .

———. *The Philosophy of Jonathan Edwards from His Private Notebooks.* Ed. Harvey G. Townsend. Eugene: U of Oregon P, 1955.

———. *Some Thoughts concerning the Revival.* 1742. *The Great Awakening.* Ed. C. C. Goen. New Haven: Yale UP, 1972. 289–530. Vol. 4 of *The Works of Jonathan Edwards.* Perry Miller and John E. Smith, gen. eds. 11 vols. 1957– .

Elbow, Peter. "What Do We Mean When We Talk about Voice in Texts?" Yancey 1–35.

Elliott, Emory, ed. *The Columbia History of the American Novel.* New York: Columbia UP, 1991.

———. ed. *The Columbia Literary History of the United States.* New York: Columbia UP, 1988.

Elliott, E. N. *Cotton Is King, and Pro-slavery Arguments: Comprising the Writings of Hammond, Harper, Christy, Stringfellow, Hodge, Bledsoe, and Cartwright, on This Important Subject*. Augusta: Pritchard, 1860.

Ellison, Ralph. *Invisible Man*. New York: Random, 1952.

Fanon, Frantz. *Black Skin, White Masks*. New York: Grove, 1967.

Faust, Drew Gilpin, ed. *The Ideology of Slavery: Proslavery Thought in the Antebellum South, 1830–1860*. Baton Rouge: Louisiana State UP, 1981.

Fern, Fanny. *Ruth Hall and Other Writings*. Ed. Joyce Warren. New Brunswick: Rutgers UP, 1986.

Fiedler, Leslie A. *Love and Death in the American Novel*. New York: Criterion, 1960.

Fields, Annie. *Life and Letters of Harriet Beecher Stowe*. Boston: Houghton, 1897.

Fiering, Norman. *Jonathan Edwards's Moral Thought and Its British Context*. Chapel Hill: U of North Carolina P, 1981.

Fisher, Philip. *Hard Facts: Setting and Form in the American Novel*. New York: Oxford UP, 1985.

Fitzhugh, George. *Cannibals All! or, Slaves without Masters*, 1857. Cambridge: Harvard UP, 1973.

———. "Southern Thought." Faust 272–99.

Fleischner, Jennifer. *Mastering Slavery: Memory, Family, and Identity in Women's Slave Narratives*. New York: New York UP, 1996.

Flexner, Eleanor, and Ellen Fitzpatrick, eds. *Century of Struggle: The Women's Rights Movement in the United States*. Cambridge: Harvard UP, 1996.

Fliegelman, Jay. *Declaring Independence: Jefferson, Natural Language, and the Culture of Performance*. Stanford: Stanford UP, 1993.

Foner, Eric, and Olivia Mahoney. *A House Divided: America in the Age of Lincoln*. New York: Norton, 1990.

Foner, Philip. *We the Other People*. Urbana: U of Illinois P, 1976.

Foreman, P. Gabrielle. "Manifest in Signs: The Politics of Sex and Representation in *Incidents in the Life of a Slave Girl*." Garfield and Zafar 76–99.

Foster, Frances Smith. *Written by Herself: Literary Production by African American Women, 1746–1892*. Bloomington: Indiana UP, 1993.

Fox-Genovese, Elizabeth. *Within the Plantation Household: Black and White Women of the Old South*. Chapel Hill: U of North Carolina P, 1988.

Franklin, John Hope. *From Slavery to Freedom: A History of African Americans*. New York: Knopf, 1994.

Fraser, Nancy. *Unruly Practices: Power, Discourse, and Gender in Contemporary Social Theory*. Minneapolis: U of Minnesota P, 1989.

Fredrickson, George M. *The Black Image in the White Mind: The Debate on Afro-American Character and Destiny, 1817–1914*. New York: Harper, 1971.

———. "Uncle Tom and the Anglo-Saxons: Romantic Racialism in the North." Frederickson, *Black Image* 97–129. Rpt. in H. Stowe, *Uncle Tom's Cabin*, ed. Ammons 429–38.

Freeman-Grenville, G. S. P. *Chronology of World History: A Calendar of Principal Events from 3000 BC to AD 1973*. London: Collings, 1975.

Freisinger, Randall R. "Voicing the Self: Toward a Pedagogy of Resistance in a Post-modern Age." Yancey 242–74.

Freud, Sigmund. "A Child Is Being Beaten." Rieff 107–32.

Fuller, Margaret. "American Literature." *Papers on Literature and Art*. New York: Fowlers, 1852. 123–59.

Furnas, J. C. *Goodbye to Uncle Tom*. New York: Sloane, 1956.

———. "Goodbye to Uncle Tom: An Excerpt." Ammons, *Essays* 105–11.

Garfield, Deborah M. "Earwitness: Female Abolitionism, Sexuality, and *Incidents in the Life of a Slave Girl*." Garfield and Zafar 100–30.

Garfield, Deborah M., and Rafia Zafar, eds. *Harriet Jacobs and* Incidents in the Life of a Slave Girl: *New Critical Essays*. Cambridge: Cambridge UP, 1996.

Garrison, William Lloyd. Preface. *The Classic Slave Narratives*. Ed. Henry Louis Gates, Jr. New York: Mentor, 1987. 245–51.

[Garrison, William Lloyd]. Review of *Uncle Tom's Cabin*. *Liberator* 22 (1852): 50.

Gaspar, David Barry, and Darlene Clark Hines, eds. *More Than Chattel: Black Women and Slavery in the Americas*. Bloomington: Indiana UP, 1996.

Gates, Henry Louis, Jr., ed. *Reading Black, Reading Feminist: A Critical Anthology*. New York: Meridian, 1990.

Genovese, Eugene D. *Roll, Jordan, Roll: The World the Slaves Made*. New York: Vintage, 1976.

Giroux, Henry A. "Is There a Place for Cultural Studies in Colleges of Education?" Giroux and Shannon 231–47.

Giroux, Henry A., and Patrick Shannon, eds. *Education and Cultural Studies: Toward a Performative Practice*. New York: Routledge, 1997.

Gittleman, Edwin. "Jefferson's Slave Narrative: The Declaration of Independence as a Literary Text." *Early American Literature* 8 (1974): 239–56.

Goetsch, Paul, and Gerd Hurm, eds. *The Fourth of July: Political Oratory and Literary Reactions, 1776–1876*. Tubingen, Ger.: Gunter Narr, 1992.

Goldsby, Jacqueline. "'I Disguised My Hand': Writing Versions of the Truth in Harriet Jacobs's *Incidents in the Life of a Slave Girl* and John Jacobs's 'A True Tale of Slavery.'" Garfield and Zafar 11–43.

Goodrich, Samuel. *Recollections of a Lifetime*. New York: Arundel, 1856.

Gorn, Elliot J. "'Gauge and Bite, Pull Hair and Scratch': The Social Significance of Fighting in the Southern Backcountry." *American Historical Review* 90 (1985): 18–43.

Gossett, Thomas F. *Race: The History of an Idea in America*. 1963. New York: Oxford UP, 1996.

———. Uncle Tom's Cabin *and American Culture*. Dallas: Southern Methodist UP, 1985.

Graff, Gerald. *Beyond the Culture Wars: How Teaching the Conflicts Can Revitalize American Education*. New York: Norton, 1992.

Grant, Jacquelyn. *White Women's Christ and Black Women's Jesus: Feminist Christology and Womanist Response*. Atlanta: Scholars, 1989.

Green, Harvey. *The Light of the Home: An Intimate View of the Lives of Women in Victorian America*. New York: Pantheon, 1983.

Green, Vivien M. "Hiram Powers's *Greek Slave*: Emblem of Freedom." *American Art Journal* 14 (1982): 31–39.

Grier, Katherine C. *Culture and Comfort: People, Parlors, and Upholstery, 1850–1930.* Rochester: Strong Museum, 1988.

Griffith, Cyril E. *The African Dream: Martin R. Delany and the Emergence of Pan-African Thought.* University Park: Pennsylvania State UP, 1975.

Gustafson, Thomas. *Representative Words: Politics, Literature, and the American Language, 1776–1865.* New York: Cambridge UP, 1992.

Hall, David D. "Introduction: The Uses of Literacy in New England, 1600–1850. *Printing and Society in Early America.* Ed. William L. Joyce, David D. Hall, Richard D. Brown, and John B. Hench. Worcester: Amer. Antiquarian Soc. 1983. 1–47.

Haller, John S., and Robin M. Haller. *The Physician and Sexuality in Victorian America.* Urbana: U of Illinois P, 1974.

Halttunen, Karen. "Gothic Imagination and Social Reform: The Haunted Houses of Lyman Beecher, Henry Ward Beecher, and Harriet Beecher Stowe." Sundquist, *New Essays* 107–33.

———. "Humanitarianism and the Pornography of Pain in Anglo-American Culture." *American Historical Review* 100 (1995): 303–35.

Hammond, James Henry. *Two Letters on Slavery in the United States, Addressed to Thomas Clarkson, Esq.* Faust 168–205. Rpt. of *Letter to an English Abolitionist.* 1845.

Handlin, David P. *The American Home: Architecture and Society, 1815–1915.* Boston: Little, 1979.

Hanly, Margaret Ann Fitzpatrick, ed. *Essential Papers on Masochism.* New York: New York UP, 1995.

Harding, Vincent. *There Is a River: The Black Struggle for Freedom in America.* Orlando: Harcourt, 1981.

Harper, Frances E. W. *A Brighter Coming Day.* Ed. Frances Smith Foster. New York: Feminist, 1990.

———. *Complete Poems of Frances E. W. Harper.* Ed. Maryemma Graham. New York: Oxford UP, 1988.

Harris, J. William. *Plain Folk and Gentry in a Slave Society: White Liberty and Black Slavery in Augusta's Hinterlands.* Middletown: Wesleyan UP, 1985.

Harrold, Stanley. *Gamaliel Bailey and Antislavery Union.* Kent: Kent State UP, 1986.

Hart, James D. *The Popular Book: A History of America's Literary Taste.* Berkeley: U of California P, 1963.

Hart, Lynda. "Doing It Anyway: Lesbian Sado-masochism and Performance." *Performance and Cultural Politics.* Ed. Elin Diamond. New York: Routledge, 1996. 48–61.

Hawthorne, Nathaniel. *The Scarlet Letter.* 1850. New York: Heritage, 1935.

Hayes, Floyd W., III, and Arlyne Lazerson, eds. *A Turbulent Voyage: Readings in African-American Studies.* San Diego: Collegiate, 1997.

Hedrick, Joan. *Harriet Beecher Stowe: A Life.* New York: Oxford UP, 1994.

———. " 'Peaceable Fruits': The Ministry of Harriet Beecher Stowe." *American Quarterly* 40 (1988): 307–32.

Henderson, Mary C. "[Tom Shows]". H. Stowe, *Uncle Tom's Cabin*, ed. Ammons 454–55.

Henretta, James A., W. Elliot Brownlee, David Brody, and Susan Ware. *America's History*. Vol. 1: to 1877. 2nd ed. New York: Worth, 1993.

Hentz, Caroline Lee. *The Planter's Northern Bride*. 1854. Chapel Hill: U of North Carolina P, 1970.

Hine, Darlene Clark, ed. *The State of Afro-American History: Past, Present, and Future*. Baton Rouge: Louisiana State UP, 1986.

Hirsch, Stephen. "Uncle Tomitudes: The Popular Reaction to *Uncle Tom's Cabin*." *Studies in the American Renaissance*. Ed. Joel Myerson. Boston: Twayne, 1978. 303–30.

Hitchcock, Peter. "The Othering of Cultural Studies." *Third Text* 25 (1993–94): 12.

Hodge, Francis. *Yankee Theatre: The Image of America on the Stage, 1825–1850*. Austin: U of Texas P, 1964.

Hollibaugh, Amber. "Desire for the Future: Radical Hope in Passion and Pleasure." Vance 401–10.

Holmes, George F. "[Rev. of *Uncle Tom's Cabin*.]" H. Stowe, *Uncle Tom's Cabin*, ed. Ammons, 467–77.

hooks, bell. *Black Looks: Race and Representation*. Boston: South End, 1992.

Howat, John K. *The Hudson River and Its Painters*. New York, 1982.

Hughes, Langston, and Milton Meltzer. *Black Magic: A Pictorial History of the African American in the Performing Arts*. 1967. New York: DeCapo, 1990.

Hull, Gloria T., Patricia Bell Scott, and Barbara Smith, eds. *All the Women Are White, All the Blacks Are Men, but Some of Us Are Brave: Black Women's Studies*. New York: Feminist, 1982.

Hurm, Gerd. "A 'Noisy Carnival': Parodies and Burlesques of Fourth of July Rhetoric." Goetsch and Hurm 239–58.

Hyman, Linda. "*The Greek Slave* by Hiram Powers: High Art as Popular Culture." *Art Journal* 35 (1976): 216–23.

Jackson, Stevi, and Sue Scott, eds. *Feminism and Sexuality: A Reader*. New York: Columbia UP, 1996.

———. "Sexual Skirmishes and Feminist Factions." Jackson and Scott, *Feminism* 1–31.

Jacobs, Harriet A. *Incidents in the Life of a Slave Girl, Written by Herself*. Ed. Jean Fagan Yellin. Cambridge: Harvard UP, 1987.

Jagger, Alison M., ed. *Living with Contradictions: Controversies in Feminist Social Ethics*. Boulder: Westview, 1994.

Jefferson, Margo. "Theatrical Art That Rises Up from Ruins." *New York Times* 6 Jan. 1998: E1+.

Jefferson, Thomas. *Notes on the State of Virginia*. 1784–85. Chapel Hill: Inst. of Early Amer. History and Culture, 1955.

———. *Writings*. Ed. Merrill D. Peterson. New York: Lib. of Amer., 1984.

Jeffreys, Sheila. *The Lesbian Heresy*. North Melbourne, Austral.: Spinifex, 1993.

Jehlen, Myra. "The Family Militant: Domesticity versus Slavery in *Uncle Tom's Cabin*." *Criticism* 31 (1989): 383–400.

Jenkins, Jennifer L. "Failed Mothers and Fallen Houses: The Crisis of Domesticity in *Uncle Tom's Cabin.*" *ESQ: A Journal of the American Renaissance* 38.2 (1992): 161–87.

Jenkins, William Sumner. *Pro-slavery Thought in the Old South.* Gloucester: Peter Smith, 1960.

Johnson, James Weldon. *The Autobiography of an Ex-Colored Man.* Ed. Henry Louis Gates, Jr. New York: Avon, 1965.

Jones, Jacqueline. *Labor of Love, Labor of Sorrow: Black Women, Work, and the Family from Slavery to the Present.* New York: Basic, 1985.

Kahane, Claire. "The Gothic Mirror." *The (M)Other Tongue: Essays in Feminist Psychoanalytic Interpretation.* Ed. Shirley Nelson Garner, Claire Kahane, and Madelon Sprengnether. Ithaca: Cornell UP, 1985. 334–51.

Karcher, Carolyn. "Rape, Murder, and Revenge in 'Slavery's Pleasant Homes': Lydia Maria Child's Antislavery Fiction and the Limits of Genre." Samuels, *Culture* 58–72.

Karenga, Maulana. *Introduction to Black Studies.* 2d ed. Los Angeles: U of Sankore P, 1993.

Kasson, Joy S. *Marble Queens and Captives: Women in Nineteenth-Century American Sculpture.* New Haven: Yale UP, 1990.

Kelley, Mary. *Private Woman, Public Stage: Literary Domesticity in Nineteenth-Century America.* New York: Oxford UP, 1984.

Kennedy, John Pendleton. *Swallow Barn; or, A Sojourn in the Old Dominion.* 1832, 1853. Ed. Lucinda H. MacKethan. Baton Rouge: Louisiana State UP, 1986.

Kimball, Gayle. *The Religious Ideas of Harriet Beecher Stowe: Her Gospel of Womanhood.* New York: Mellen, 1982.

King, John Owen, III. *The Iron of Melancholy: Structures of Spiritual Conversion in America from the Puritan Conscience to Victorian Neurosis.* Middletown: Wesleyan UP, 1983.

Kirkham, E. Bruce. *The Building of* Uncle Tom's Cabin. Knoxville: U of Tennessee P, 1977.

Knott, Robanna S. "Harriet Jacobs: The Edenton Biography." Diss. U of North Carolina, 1994.

Krafft-Ebing, Richard von. *Psychopathia Sexualis: A Medico-Forensic Study.* 1886. Trans. Harry E. Wedeck. New York: Putnam, 1965.

Kristeva, Julia. *Powers of Horror: An Essay on Abjection.* New York: Columbia UP, 1982.

Kuspit, Donald B., Linda C. Simmons, and Richard Stewart. *Painting in the South, 1564–1980.* Richmond: Virginia Museum, 1983.

Lang, Amy Schrager. "Class and the Strategies of Sympathy." Samuels, *Culture* 128–42.

Langland, Elizabeth. *Nobody's Angels: Middle-Class Women and Domestic Ideology in Victorian Culture.* Ithaca: Cornell UP, 1995.

Lauter, Paul, et al., eds. *The Heath Anthology of American Literature.* 3rd ed. 2 vols. New York: Houghton, 1998.

Lehuu, Isabelle. "Sentimental Figures: Reading *Godey's Lady's Book* in Antebellum America." Samuels, *Culture* 73–91.

LeMelle, Tilden. "The Status of Black Studies in the Second Decade: The Ideological Imperative." *The Next Decade: Theoretical and Research Issues in African Studies*. Ed. James Turner. Ithaca: Cornell Univ. Africana Studies Center, 1984. 47–61.

Lerner, Gerda. "The Myth of the 'Bad' Black Woman." *Black Women in White America: A Documentary History*. New York: Vintage, 1972. 163–71.

Leverenz, David. *Manhood and the American Renaissance*. Ithaca: Cornell UP, 1989.

Levine, Lawrence W. *Black Culture, Black Consciousness: Afro-American Folk Thought from Slavery to Freedom*. Oxford: Oxford UP, 1977.

Levine, Robert S. "*Uncle Tom's Cabin* in *Frederick Douglass' Paper*: An Analysis of Reception." *American Literature* 64 (1992): 71–93. Rpt. in H. Stowe, *Uncle Tom's Cabin*, ed. Ammons 523–42.

Liebenow, J. Gus. *Liberia: The Quest for Democracy*. Bloomington: Indiana UP, 1987.

Linden, Robin Ruth, et al. *Against Sadomasochism: A Radical Feminist Analysis*. San Francisco: Frog in the Well, 1982.

Locke, John. *Two Treatises of Government*. Ed. W. S. Carpenter. London: Dent, 1992.

Lott, Eric. *Love and Theft: Blackface Minstrelsy and the American Working Class*. New York: Oxford UP, 1993.

———. "'The Seeming Counterfeit': Racial Politics and Early Blackface Minstrelsy." *American Quarterly* 43.2 (1991) 223–54.

Lowance, Mason I., Jr., Ellen E. Westbrook, and R. C. De Prospo, eds. *The Stowe Debate: Rhetorical Strategies in* Uncle Tom's Cabin. Amherst: U of Massachusetts P, 1994.

Lundin, Roger. *The Culture of Interpretation: Christian Faith and the Postmodern World*. Grand Rapids: Eerdman's, 1993.

MacFarlane, Lisa Watt. "'If Ever I Get to Where I Can': The Competing Rhetorics of Social Reform in *Uncle Tom's Cabin*." *American Transcendental Quarterly* 4 (1990): 135–47.

MacKethan, Lucinda H. *Daughters of Time: Creating Woman's Voice in Southern Story*. Athens: U of Georgia P, 1990.

MacPherson, C. B. *The Political Theory of Possessive Individualism: Hobbes to Locke*. New York: Oxford UP, 1962.

Maier, Pauline. *American Scripture: Making the Declaration of Independence*. New York: Knopf, 1997.

Mansfield, Nick. *Masochism: The Art of Power*. Westport: Praeger, 1997.

Marcus, Marcia. *A Taste for Pain: On Masochism and Female Sexuality*. New York: St. Martin's, 1981.

Martin, Terence. *Parables of Possbility*. New York: Columbia UP, 1994.

Marx, Karl. *Capital*. Vol. 1. Ed. Friedrich Engels. Trans. Samuel Moore and Edward Aveling. New York: Mod. Lib., 1906.

Massé, Michelle. *In the Name of Love: Women, Masochism, and the Gothic*. Ithaca: Cornell UP, 1992.

Matthews, Geena. "*Just a Housewife*": The Rise and Fall of Domesticity in America. New York: Oxford UP, 1987.

May, Henry F. Introduction. *Oldtown Folks*. By Harriet Beecher Stowe. Cambridge: Harvard UP, 1966. 3–43.

McCardell, John. *The Idea of a Southern Nation: Southern Nationalists and Southern Nationalism, 1830–1860*. New York: Norton, 1979.

McCloud, Scott. *Understanding Comics: The Invisible Art*. Northampton: Kitchen Sink, 1993.

Melville, Herman. *Moby-Dick*. Evanston: Northwestern UP, 1988.

———. *Moby Dick; or, The Whale*. 1851. New York: Barnes, 1994.

Montgomery, Jill, and Ann C. Greif, eds. *Masochism: The Treatment of Self-Inflicted Suffering*. Madison: Intl. UP, 1989.

Moody, Richard. *America Takes the Stage: Romanticism in American Drama and Theatre*. 1955. New York: Kraus, 1969.

Morgan, Edmund S. *American Slavery, American Freedom: The Ordeal of Colonial Virginia*. New York: Norton, 1975.

———. *Visible Saints: The History of a Puritan Idea*. New York: New York UP, 1963.

Morrison, Toni. *Beloved*. New York: Plume, 1987.

———. *The Bluest Eye*. 1970. New York: Penguin, 1985.

———. Interview with Bill Moyers. *A Writer's Work*. PBS. 1990.

———. *Playing in the Dark: Whiteness and the Literary Imagination*. New York: Vintage, 1993.

———. "Unspeakable Things Unspoken: The Afro-American Presence in American Literature." *Within the Circle: An Anthology of African American Literary Criticism from the Harlem Renaissance to the Present*. Ed. Angelyn Mitchell. Durham: Duke UP, 1994. 368–98.

Moses, Wilson Jeremiah. *Black Messiahs and Uncle Toms: Social and Literary Manipulations of a Religious Myth*. Rev. ed. University Park: Pennsylvania State UP, 1993.

Mullen, Harryette. "Runaway Tongue: Resistant Orality in *Uncle Tom's Cabin, Our Nig, Incidents in the Life of a Slave Girl*, and *Beloved*." Samuels, *Culture* 244–64.

Museum of the City of New York. *Currier and Ives Favorites*. Introduction and notes by A. K. Baragwanath. New York: Crown.

National Era 1–14 (1847–60). Rpt. in *The Black Experience in America: Negro Periodicals in the United States, 1840–1860*. Vols. 5–6. New York: Negro UP, 1969.

Nichols, Thomas Low. *Forty Years of American Life*. London, 1864.

Nissenbaum, Stephen. "New England as Region and Nation." *All Over the Map: Rethinking American Regions*. Ed. Edward L. Ayers, Patricia Nelson Limerick, Stephen Nissenbaum, and Peter S. Onuf. Baltimore: Johns Hopkins UP, 1996. 38–61.

Noble, Marianne. "The Ecstasies of Sentimental Wounding in *Uncle Tom's Cabin*." *Yale Journal of Criticism* 10.2 (1997): 295–320.

Nord, David P. *The Evangelical Origins of Mass Media in America, 1815–1835*. *Journalism Monographs* 88. 1984.

———. "Religious Reading and Readers in Antebellum America." *Journal of the Early Republic* 15.2 (1995): 241–72.

Oakes, James. *Slavery and Freedom: An Interpretation of the Old South.* New York: Vintage, 1990.

O'Connell, Catharine E. "'The Magic of the Real Presence of Distress': Sentimentality and Competing Rhetorics of Authority." Lowance, Westbrook, and De Prospo 13–36.

Olney, James. "'I Was Born': Slave Narratives, Their Status as Autobiography and as Literature." Davis and Gates 148–75.

Orwell, George. "Charles Dickens." *Dickens, Dali, and Others: Studies in Popular Culture.* New York: Reynal, 1946. 1–75.

Painter, Nell Irvin. *Sojourner Truth: A Life, a Symbol.* New York: Norton, 1996.

Parrington, Vernon Louis. "Harriet Beecher Stowe: A Daughter of Puritanism." *Main Currents in American Thought.* Vol. 2. New York: Harcourt, 1958. Rpt. in Ammons, *Critical Essays* 213–18.

Peterson, Carla L. *"Doers of the Word": African-American Women Speakers and Writers in the North (1830–1880).* New York: Oxford UP, 1995.

Pieterse, Jan Nederveen. *White on Black: Images of Africa and Blacks in Western Popular Culture.* New Haven: Yale UP, 1992.

Porter, Carolyn. "Are We Being Historical Yet?" *South Atlantic Quarterly* 87 (1988): 743–86.

Potter, David M. *The Impending Crisis, 1848–1861.* Ed. Don E. Fehrenbacher. New York: Harper, 1976.

Price, Kenneth M., and Susan Belasco Smith, eds. *Periodical Literature in Nineteenth-Century America.* Charlottesville: UP of Virginia, 1995.

Priest, Josiah. *Bible Defence of Slavery and Origin, Fortunes, and History of the Negro Race.* Glascow: Brown, 1982.

Prince, Mary. *The History of Mary Prince.* Ed. Henry Louis Gates, Jr. New York: Mentor, 1987.

The Pro-slavery Argument as Maintained by the Most Distinguished Writers of the Southern States: Containing Several Essays, on the Subject, of Chancellor Harper, Governor Hammond, Dr. Simms, and Professor Dew. Charleston: Walker, 1852.

Rader-Konofalski, Wendy. "Radicalism and Traditionalism in Harriet Beecher Stowe's *Uncle Tom's Cabin*." *Radikalismus in Literatur und Gesellschaft des 19.Jarhunderts.* Ed. Gregory Claeys and Liselotte Glage. Frankfurt: Lang, 1987. 148–82.

Railton, Stephen. *Authorship and Audience: Literary Performance in the American Renaissance.* Princeton: Princeton UP, 1991.

Rampersad, Arnold. *The Art and Imagination of W. E. B. Du Bois.* Cambridge: Harvard UP, 1976.

Rans, Geoffrey. *Cooper's Leather-Stocking Novels: A Secular Reading.* Chapel Hill: U of North Carolina P, 1991.

Review of *Uncle Tom's Cabin.* Unsigned. *National Anti-slavery Standard* 6 May 1852: 1.

Reynolds, David S. *Beneath the American Renaissance: The Subversive Imagination in the Age of Emerson and Melville.* New York: Knopf, 1988.

Reynolds, Larry J. *European Revolutions and the American Literary Renaissance*. New Haven: Yale UP, 1988.

Reynolds, Larry J., and Susan Belasco Smith, eds. *"These Sad but Glorious Days": Dispatches from Europe, 1846–1850, by Margaret Fuller*. New Haven: Yale UP, 1991.

Rich, B. Ruby. Feminism and Sexuality in the 1980s." *Feminist Studies* 12.3 (1986): 525–61.

Richardson, Nathaniel R. *Liberia's Past and Present*. London: Diplomatic, 1959.

Rieff, Philip, ed. *Sexuality and the Psychology of Love*. New York: Collier, 1963.

Ripley, C. Peter, ed. *The Black Abolitionist Papers*. Vol. 3: *The United States, 1830–1846*. Vol. 4: *The United States, 1847–1858*. Vol. 5: *The United States, 1859–1865*. Chapel Hill: U of North Carolina P, 1991–92.

Riss, Arthur. "Racial Essentialism and Family Values in *Uncle Tom's Cabin*." *American Quarterly* 46.4 (1994): 513–44.

Robbins, Sarah. "Gendering the History of the Antislavery Narrative: Juxtaposing *Uncle Tom's Cabin* with *Benito Cereno, Beloved*, and *Middle Passage*." *American Quarterly* 49 (1997): 531–73.

Roberts, Diane. *The Myth of Aunt Jemima: Representations of Race and Region*. New York: Routledge, 1994.

Robinson, Armstead L., et al., eds. *Black Studies in the University: A Symposium*. New Haven: Yale UP, 1969.

Romero, Lora. "Bio-political Resistance in Domestic Ideology and *Uncle Tom's Cabin*." *American Literary History* 1 (1989): 719–34.

Romines, Ann. *The Home Plot: Women, Writing, and Domestic Ritual*. Amherst: U of Massachusetts P, 1992.

Roppolo, Joseph P. "Harriet Beecher Stowe and New Orleans: A Study in Hate." *New England Quarterly* 30 (1957): 346–62.

Rose, Mike. *Lives on the Boundary*. New York: Penguin, 1989.

Rugoff, Milton. *The Beechers: An American Family in the Nineteenth Century*. New York: Harper, 1981.

Samuels, Shirley, ed. *The Culture of Sentiment: Race, Gender, and Sentimentality in Nineteenth-Century America*. New York: Oxford UP, 1992.

———. "The Identity of Slavery." Samuels, *Culture* 157–71.

Sanchez-Eppler, Karen. "Bodily Bonds: The Intersecting Rhetorics of Feminism and Abolition." *Representations* 24 (1988): 28–59. Rpt. in Samuels, *Culture* 92–114.

Sand, George. Rev. of *Uncle Tom's Cabin*. H. Stowe, *Uncle Tom's Cabin*, ed. Ammons, 459–63.

Sarson, Steven. "Harriet Beecher Stowe and American Slavery." *New Companion* 7 (1989): 33–45.

Sellers, Charles. *The Market Revolution: Jacksonian America 1815–1846*. New York: Oxford UP, 1991.

Shick, Tom W. *Behold the Promised Land: A History of Afro-American Settler Society in Nineteenth-Century Liberia*. Baltimore: Johns Hopkins UP, 1977.

Singer, Linda. "Bodies—Pleasures—Powers." Jackson and Scott, *Feminism* 263–75.

Sitton, Fred. "The Indian Play in American Drama, 1750–1900." Diss. Northwestern U, 1962.

Six Women's Slave Narratives. Introd. William L. Andrews. Schomburg Library of Nineteenth-Century Black Women Writers. New York: Oxford UP, 1988.

Sklar, Kathryn Kish. *Catharine Beecher: A Study in American Domesticity.* New York: Norton, 1976.

Smith, James Wesley. *Sojourners in Search of Freedom: The Settlement of Liberia by Black Americans.* New York: UP of America, 1987.

Smith, Samuel Stanhope. *Essay on the Causes of the Variety of Complexion and Figure in the Human Species.* 1787. Ed. Winthrop D. Jordan. Cambridge: Harvard UP, 1965.

Smith, Susan Belasco. "Serialization and the Nature of *Uncle Tom's Cabin.*" *Periodical Literature in Nineteenth-Century America.* Price and Smith 69–89.

Smith, Susan Belasco, and Kenneth M. Price. "Introduction: Periodical Literature in Social and Historical Context." Price and Smith 3–16.

Snead, James. *White Screens, Black Images.* Ed. Colin MacCabe and Cornel West. New York: Routledge, 1994.

Spillers, Hortense J. "Changing the Letter: The Yokes, the Jokes of Discourse, or, Mrs. Stowe, Mr. Reed." *Slavery and the Literary Imagination.* Ed. Deborah McDowell and Arnold Rampersad. Baltimore: Johns Hopkins UP, 1989. 26–61. Rpt. in H. Stowe, *Uncle Tom's Cabin,* ed. Ammons 542–68.

———. "Mama's Baby, Papa's Maybe: An American Grammar Book." *Diacritics* 17.2 (1987): 65–81.

Spiritual Narratives. Introd. Susan Houchins. Schomburg Library of Nineteenth-Century Black Women Writers. New York: Oxford UP, 1988.

Stepto, Robert B. "Sharing the Thunder: The Literary Exchanges of Harriet Beecher Stowe, Henry Bibb, and Frederick Douglass." Sundquist, *New Essays* 135–53.

Stewart, James Brewer. *Holy Warriors: The Abolitionists and American Slavery.* New York: Hill, 1976.

Stewart, Robert. *The Illustrated Almanac of Historical Facts from the Dawn of the Christian Era to the New World Order.* New York: Prentice, 1992.

Stoddard, Roger E. "Morphology and the Book from an American Perspective." *Printing History* 9.1 (1987): 2–14.

Stowe, Charles Edward. *Life of Harriet Beecher Stowe, Compiled from Her Letters and Journals.* 1889. Detroit: Gale Research, 1967.

Stowe, Charles Edward, and Lyman Beecher Stowe. *Harriet Beecher Stowe: The Story of Her Life.* Boston: Houghton, 1911.

Stowe, Harriet Beecher. *The Chimney Corner.* Boston: Ticknor, 1868.

———. *Dred: A Tale of the Great Dismal Swamp.* 1856. 2 vols. New York: AMS, 1970.

———. *House and Home Papers.* Boston: Ticknor, 1865.

———. *Household Papers and Stories.* New York: AMS, 1967. Vol. 8 of the Riverside edition of *The Writings of Harriet Beecher Stowe.*

———. *A Key to* Uncle Tom's Cabin. Boston: Jewett, 1853.

———. *A Key to* Uncle Tom's Cabin. 1853. New York: Arno, 1968.

———. Letter to Gamaliel Bailey. 9 March 1851. Garrison Collection, Boston Public Library.

———. *Men of Our Times; or, Leading Patriots of the Day*. Hartford: Hartford, 1868.

Stringfellow, Thornton. *A Brief Examination of Scripture Testimony on the Institution of Slavery*. 1850. Faust 136–67.

Sundiata, I. K. *Black Scandal: America and the Liberian Labor Crisis, 1929–1936*. Philadelphia: Inst. for the Study of Human Issues, 1980.

Sundquist, Eric. Introduction. Sundquist, *New Essays* 1–44.

———, ed. *New Essays on* Uncle Tom's Cabin. Cambridge: Cambridge UP, 1986.

———. *To Wake the Nations: Race and the Making of American Literature*. Cambridge: Belknap, 1993.

Takaki, Ronald. *A Different Mirror: A History of Multicultural America*. Boston: Little, 1993.

Tebbel, John. *A History of Book Publishing in the United States*. Vol. 1. New York: Bowker, 1972. 4 vols.

Thompson, Lawrence. "The Printing and Publishing Activities of the American Tract Society from 1825–1850." *Papers of the Bibliographic Society of America* 45 (1941): 81–114.

Thompson, Vincent Bakpetu. *The Making of the African Diaspora in the Americas, 1441–1900*. New York: Longman, 1987.

Thoreau, Henry David. "Civil Disobedience." *The Portable Thoreau*. Ed. Carl Bode. New York: Viking, 1947. 109–37.

———. *Journal 4: 1851–1852*. Ed. Leonard N. Neufeldt and Nancy Craig Simmons. Princeton: Princeton UP, 1992.

———. *Resistance to Civil Government*. 1849. New York: Twayne, 1967.

———. *Walden; or, Life in the Woods*. 1854. Boston: Beacon, 1997.

———. *Walden*. Ed. J. Lyndon Shanley. Princeton: Princeton UP, 1971.

Toll, Robert. *Blacking Up: The Minstrel Show in Nineteenth-Century America*. New York: Oxford UP, 1974.

Tompkins, Jane P. Afterword. Warner 584–608.

———. *Sensational Designs: The Cultural Work of American Fiction, 1790–1860*. New York: Oxford UP, 1985.

———. "Sentimental Power: *Uncle Tom's Cabin* and the Politics of Literary History." Tompkins, *Sensational Designs* 122–46. Rpt. in H. Stowe, *Uncle Tom's Cabin*, ed. Ammons 501–22.

Tracy, Susan. *In the Master's Eye*. Boston: U of Massachusetts P, 1994.

Travers, Len. *Celebrating the Fourth: Independence Day and the Rites of Nationalism in the Early Republic*. Amherst: U of Massachusetts P, 1997.

Turner, Patricia A. *Ceramic Uncles and Celluloid Mammies: Black Images and Their Influence on Culture*. New York: Anchor, 1994.

Twain, Mark. *The Adventures of Huckleberry Finn*. 1885. New York: Random, 1996.

Valade, Roger M., III. *The Essential Black Literature Guide*. Detroit: Visible Ink, 1996.

Vance, Carole S., ed. *Pleasure and Danger: Exploring Female Sexuality*. New York: Pandora, 1984.

Van Ermen, Eduard. *The United States in Old Maps and Prints*. Wilmington: Atomium, 1990.

Van Why, Joseph S., and Earl French, eds. *Nook Farm*. Hartford: Stowe-Day Foundation, 1975.

Vaux, Calvert. *Villas and Cottages*. New York, 1857.

Veeser, H. Aram. *The New Historicism*. New York: Routledge, 1989.

Wagenknecht, Edward. *Cavalcade of the American Novel: From the Birth of the Nation to the Middle of the Twentieth Century*. New York: Holt, 1952.

———. *Harriet Beecher Stowe: The Known and the Unknown*. New York: Oxford UP, 1965.

Walker, David. *Appeal to the Coloured Citizens of the World*. 1829. New York: Hill, 1965.

Ward, Geoffrey C., Ric Burns, and Ken Burns. *The Civil War: An Illustrated History*. New York: Knopf, 1990.

Ward, John William. Afterword. H. Stowe. *Uncle Tom's Cabin*, Signet-NAL ed. 478–94.

Warner, Susan. *The Wide, Wide World*. 1850. New York: Feminist, 1987.

Warren, Joyce W., ed. *The (Other) American Traditions: Nineteenth-Century Women Writers*. New Brunswick: Rutgers UP, 1993.

Waters, Ronald G. *The Antislavery Appeal: American Abolitionism after 1830*. Baltimore: Johns Hopkins UP, 1976.

Weinberg, Thomas, and G. W. Levi Kamel. *SandM: Studies in Sadomasochism*. Buffalo: Prometheus, 1983.

Welter, Barbara. "The Cult of True Womanhood, 1820–1860." *American Quarterly* 18 (1966): 151–74.

Welter, Rush. *The Mind of America, 1820–1860*. New York: Columbia UP, 1975.

West, Cornel. *Prophecy Deliverance! An Afro-American Revolutionary Christianity*. Philadelphia: Westminster, 1982.

———. *Prophetic Thought in Postmodern Times*. Monroe: Common Courage, 1993. Vol. 1 of *Beyond Eurocentrism and Multiculturalism*.

Wexler, Laura. "Tender Violence: Literary Eavesdropping, Domestic Fiction, and Educational Reform." Samuels, *Culture* 9–38.

[Whitman, Walt]. "Walt Whitman and His Poems." *United States Review* 5 (Sept. 1855): 206.

Wiegman, Robyn. "Visual Modernity." *American Anatomies: Theorizing Race and Gender*. Durham: Duke UP, 1995. 21–42.

Williams, Adriana. *Covarrubias*. Austin: U of Texas P, 1994.

Williams, Raymond. *Communications*. New York: Barnes, 1967.

Wills, Garry. *Lincoln at Gettysburg: The Words That Remade America*. New York: Simon, 1992.

Wilmeth, Don B., ed. *Staging the Nation: Plays from the American Theater, 1787–1909*. Boston: Bedford, 1998.

Wilson, Edmund. *Patriotic Gore: Studies in the Literature of the American Civil War*. New York: Oxford UP, 1962.

Wilson, Forrest. *Crusader in Crinoline: The Life of Harriet Beecher Stowe*. Philadelphia: Lippincott, 1941.

Wilson, Harriet E. *Our Nig; or, Sketches from the Life of a Free Black*. Ed. Henry Louis Gates, Jr. New York: Vintage, 1983.

Wilson, William J. [Ethiop]. "[Rev. of *Uncle Tom's Cabin*.]" H. Stowe, *Uncle Tom's Cabin*, ed. Ammons 466–67.

Winks, Robin W. "The Making of a Slave Narrative: Josiah Henson and Uncle Tom, a Case Study." Davis and Gates 112–46.

Winthrop, John. "A Model of Charity." *The Puritans*. Ed. Perry Miller and Thomas H. Johnson. New York: American Book, 1938. 195–99.

Wright, Gwendolyn. *Building the Dream: A Social History of Housing in America*. New York: Pantheon, 1981.

Wright, Richard. *Uncle Tom's Children*. 1938. New York: Harper, 1993.

Wyatt-Brown, Bertram. "The Mask of Obedience: Male Slave Psychology in the Old South." *American Historical Review* 93 (1988). 1228–52.

Yancey, Kathleen Blake, ed. *Voices on Voice: Perspectives, Definitions, Inquiry*. Urbana: NCTE, 1994.

Yarbrough, Richard. "Strategies of Black Characterization in *Uncle Tom's Cabin* and the Early Afro-American Novel." Sundquist, *New Essays* 45–84.

Yarbrough, Stephen R., and John C. Adams. *Delightful Conviction: Jonathan Edwards and the Rhetoric of Conversion*. Great American Orators 20. Westport: Greenwood, 1993.

Yellin, Jean Fagan. "Doing It Herself: *Uncle Tom's Cabin* and Woman's Role in the Slavery Crisis." Sundquist, *New Essays* 85–105.

———. *The Intricate Knot: Black Figures in American Literature, 1776–1863*. New York: New York UP, 1972.

———. Introduction. Jacobs xiii–xxxiv.

———. "Through Her Brother's Eyes: Incidents and 'A True Tale.'" Garfield and Zafar 44–56.

Zanardi, Claudia, ed. *Essential Papers on the Psychology of Women*. New York: New York UP, 1990.

Zboray, Ronald J. *A Fictive People: Antebellum Economic Development and the American Reading Public*. New York: Oxford UP, 1993.

INDEX

Modern Language Association of America
Approaches to Teaching World Literature
Joseph Gibaldi, series editor

Achebe's Things Fall Apart. Ed. Bernth Lindfors. 1991.
Arthurian Tradition. Ed. Maureen Fries and Jeanie Watson. 1992.
Atwood's The Handmaid's Tale *and Other Works*. Ed. Sharon R. Wilson,
    Thomas B. Friedman, and Shannon Hengen. 1996.
Austen's Pride and Prejudice. Ed. Marcia McClintock Folsom. 1993.
Baudelaire's Flowers of Evil. Ed. Laurence M. Porter. 2000.
Beckett's Waiting for Godot. Ed. June Schlueter and Enoch Brater. 1991.
Beowulf. Ed. Jess B. Bessinger, Jr., and Robert F. Yeager. 1984.
Blake's Songs of Innocence and of Experience. Ed. Robert F. Gleckner and
    Mark L. Greenberg. 1989.
British Women Poets of the Romantic Period. Ed. Stephen C. Behrendt and
    Harriet Kramer Linkin. 1997.
Brontë's Jane Eyre. Ed. Diane Long Hoeveler and Beth Lau. 1993.
Byron's Poetry. Ed. Frederick W. Shilstone. 1991.
Camus's The Plague. Ed. Steven G. Kellman. 1985.
Cather's My Ántonia. Ed. Susan J. Rosowski. 1989.
Cervantes' Don Quixote. Ed. Richard Bjornson. 1984.
Chaucer's Canterbury Tales. Ed. Joseph Gibaldi. 1980.
Chopin's The Awakening. Ed. Bernard Koloski. 1988.
Coleridge's Poetry and Prose. Ed. Richard E. Matlak. 1991.
Dante's Divine Comedy. Ed. Carole Slade. 1982.
Dickens' David Copperfield. Ed. Richard J. Dunn. 1984.
Dickinson's Poetry. Ed. Robin Riley Fast and Christine Mack Gordon. 1989.
Narrative of the Life of Frederick Douglass. Ed. James C. Hall. 1999.
Eliot's Middlemarch. Ed. Kathleen Blake. 1990.
Eliot's Poetry and Plays. Ed. Jewel Spears Brooker. 1988.
Ellison's Invisible Man. Ed. Susan Resneck Parr and Pancho Savery. 1989.
Faulkner's The Sound and the Fury. Ed. Stephen Hahn and Arthur F. Kinney. 1996.
Flaubert's Madame Bovary. Ed. Laurence M. Porter and Eugene F. Gray. 1995.
García Márquez's One Hundred Years of Solitude. Ed. María Elena de Valdés and
    Mario J. Valdés. 1990.
Goethe's Faust. Ed. Douglas J. McMillan. 1987.
Hebrew Bible as Literature in Translation. Ed. Barry N. Olshen and
    Yael S. Feldman. 1989.
Homer's Iliad *and* Odyssey. Ed. Kostas Myrsiades. 1987.
Ibsen's A Doll House. Ed. Yvonne Shafer. 1985.
Works of Samuel Johnson. Ed. David R. Anderson and Gwin J. Kolb. 1993.
Joyce's Ulysses. Ed. Kathleen McCormick and Erwin R. Steinberg. 1993.
Kafka's Short Fiction. Ed. Richard T. Gray. 1995.
Keats's Poetry. Ed. Walter H. Evert and Jack W. Rhodes. 1991.
Kingston's The Woman Warrior. Ed. Shirley Geok-lin Lim. 1991.

Lafayette's The Princess of Clèves. Ed. Faith E. Beasley and Katharine Ann
   Jensen. 1998.
Lessing's The Golden Notebook. Ed. Carey Kaplan and Ellen Cronan Rose. 1989.
Mann's Death in Venice *and Other Short Fiction*. Ed. Jeffrey B. Berlin. 1992.
Medieval English Drama. Ed. Richard K. Emmerson. 1990.
Melville's Moby-Dick. Ed. Martin Bickman. 1985.
Metaphysical Poets. Ed. Sidney Gottlieb. 1990.
Miller's Death of a Salesman. Ed. Matthew C. Roudané. 1995.
Milton's Paradise Lost. Ed. Galbraith M. Crump. 1986.
Molière's Tartuffe *and Other Plays*. Ed. James F. Gaines and
   Michael S. Koppisch. 1995.
Momaday's The Way to Rainy Mountain. Ed. Kenneth M. Roemer. 1988.
Montaigne's Essays. Ed. Patrick Henry. 1994.
Novels of Toni Morrison. Ed. Nellie Y. McKay and Kathryn Earle. 1997.
Murasaki Shikibu's The Tale of Genji. Ed. Edward Kamens. 1993.
Pope's Poetry. Ed. Wallace Jackson and R. Paul Yoder. 1993.
Shakespeare's King Lear. Ed. Robert H. Ray. 1986.
Shakespeare's The Tempest *and Other Late Romances*. Ed. Maurice Hunt. 1992.
Shelley's Frankenstein. Ed. Stephen C. Behrendt. 1990.
Shelley's Poetry. Ed. Spencer Hall. 1990.
Sir Gawain and the Green Knight. Ed. Miriam Youngerman Miller and
   Jane Chance. 1986.
Spenser's Faerie Queene. Ed. David Lee Miller and Alexander Dunlop. 1994.
Stendhal's The Red and the Black. Ed. Dean de la Motte and Stirling Haig. 1999.
Sterne's Tristram Shandy. Ed. Melvyn New. 1989.
Stowe's Uncle Tom's Cabin. Ed. Elizabeth Ammons and Susan Belasco. 2000.
Swift's Gulliver's Travels. Ed. Edward J. Rielly. 1988.
Thoreau's Walden *and Other Works*. Ed. Richard J. Schneider. 1996.
Voltaire's Candide. Ed. Renée Waldinger. 1987.
Whitman's Leaves of Grass. Ed. Donald D. Kummings. 1990.
Wordsworth's Poetry. Ed. Spencer Hall, with Jonathan Ramsey. 1986.
Wright's Native Son. Ed. James A. Miller. 1997.